PERFORMER TRAINING AND TECHNOLOGY

Performer Training and Technology employs philosophical approaches to technology, including postphenomenology and Heidegger's thinking, to examine the way technology manifests, influences and becomes used in performer training discourse and practice.

The book offers in-depth discussions of present and past performer training practices through a lens that has never been applied before; considers the employment of key digital artefacts; and develops a series of analytical tools that can be useful in scholarly and practical explorations. An array of intriguing subjects are covered including the role of electric lights in Stanislavsky's work on concentration; the use of handheld tools, such as sticks in Zarrilli's psychophysical training and Meyerhold's Biomechanics; the emergence of new forms of training in relation to motion capture technology; and the way the mobile phone complicates notions and practices of attention in learning and training contexts.

This book is of vital relevance to performer training scholars and practitioners; theatre, performance, and dance scholars and students; and especially those interested in philosophies of technology.

Maria Kapsali is a Lecturer in Physical Performance in the School of Performance and Cultural Industries at the University of Leeds.

Perspectives on Performer Training

Series Editors: Maria Kapsali and Rebecca Loukes

Perspectives on Performer Training explores vital issues in twenty-first century global performer training. The series foregrounds training practices that are either emerging and/or have escaped scholarly attention and reconsiders well-known approaches in order to create new understanding. The books dissolve boundaries between scholarship, professional practice and teaching and will appeal to an international audience of practitioners, researchers and students. As such, the series employs both theoretical and practical perspectives, provides analyses of key training exercises for use in the studio, and makes available previously unpublished interviews and archival material. The series aims to push the limits of existing canons, indeed, to question processes of canonisation per se; examine processes of knowledge transmission; and subject formation. The series assumes that histories and practices of performer training can offer insights and understanding beyond the walls of the studio and the books offer contributions not only to the fields of theatre, dance and performance but to urgent interdisciplinary conversations around key themes, such as technology, health and well-being, the creative industries and globalisation.

Performer Training and Technology
Preparing Our Selves
Maria Kapsali

www.routledge.com/Perspectives-on-Performer-Training/book-series/PoPT

PERFORMER TRAINING AND TECHNOLOGY

Preparing Our Selves

Maria Kapsali

LONDON AND NEW YORK

First published 2021
by Routledge
2 Park Square, Milton Park, Abingdon, Oxon OX14 4RN

and by Routledge
52 Vanderbilt Avenue, New York, NY 10017

Routledge is an imprint of the Taylor & Francis Group, an informa business

© 2021 Maria Kapsali

British Library Cataloguing-in-Publication Data
A catalogue record for this book is available from the British Library

Library of Congress Cataloging-in-Publication Data
A catalog record has been requested for this book

ISBN: 978-1-138-67780-7 (hbk)
ISBN: 978-1-138-67781-4 (pbk)
ISBN: 978-1-315-55932-2 (ebk)

Typeset in Bembo
by Wearset Ltd, Boldon, Tyne and Wear

To my grandfather, Athanasios Eleftheriadis (1923–2019), a talented car mechanic and a brilliant storyteller.

CONTENTS

List of figures   *ix*

Preface   *x*

Acknowledgements   *xiii*

1   Introduction   1

    What is performer training? – an expanded field 8

    What is technology? 11

    Performer training and the digital 14

    Methodology and themes 20

    Outline of the book 23

2   Between technique and technology: the actor's instrument
and the actor's paradox   30

    Introduction 30

    Part I 36

    Part II 46

    Part III 50

    Conclusion: how does performer training become technological? 53

3   Beyond technique: critiquing technology and actor training
in the 1960s   60

    Introduction 60

    American avant-garde theatre in the 1960s 63

    Critiquing technology: Martin Heidegger and Herbert Marcuse 68

    Techne: artworks and aesthetic sensibility 72

Training for liberation: avant-garde theatre and training practice 75
The Open Theatre 77
Conclusion: the promise of avant-garde actor training 84

4   Using and making tools   89
    Introduction 89
    Intra- and extra-organic tools 94
    I–Technology–World relationships in performer training 98
    Conclusion 111

5   Training the *homo cellularis*: attention and the mobile phone in
    performer training   120
    Introduction 120
    Training attention 128
    Attention beyond distraction 132
    Feel/Hear/See/Do: towards a practice of polyattentiveness 135
    Conclusion: performer training as a practice of immunity? 142

6   Training to be captured   147
    Introduction 147
    'Training for' motion capture 153
    'Training with' motion capture 163
    'Training for' – 'Training with': a dialectic 170
    Conclusion 177

    Conclusion: tools for preparation   182

    Index   *190*

FIGURES

2.1 Machines de Théatre, Planche XXII, Reproduced from the
    National Library of Malta   41
6.1 Motion Capture recording of Biomechanics, UCLAN   148
6.2 Shapes in Motion Workshop, 'Primate Performance' taught by
    Sarah Perry   159
6.3 Patrick Wiabel's avatar and Marcel Marceau's avatar performing
    the 'At the Bar' adagio   165
6.4 'Falling Upwards', screenshot from Capturing Stillness Project   167
6.5 Flamenco dancer working with HoloLens in Amsterdam,
    Holland   168
6.6 Presence – Absence Axis   171
6.7 Tradition – Innovation Axis   173
6.8 Heteronomy – Autonomy Axis   176

PREFACE

I started writing this book when my daughter entered primary school education. At the time, I noted the parallels between her attempt to master the newly encountered symbols of the alphabet and my effort to navigate philosophical examinations of technology. Later, another parallel emerged: in starting school my daughter was becoming engaged in the constitution of the 'alphabetical self' (Rotman 2008). By learning to use the technologies of books, pens and paper, and by becoming able to capture into writing sensations, thoughts and feelings a gap between her and the world was opening up. Such a gap would enable her to gain a distance from and reflect on her world but also, as philosopher David Abram (1997) argues, cause her to cease experiencing it in its breathing, animating, expressive fullness. Here, arguably, was technology in all its efficacy: structuring a subject and defining her relationship to reality. Eventually, the barely legible scribblings my daughter brought home from school exemplified the key insight this book rests on: that the emergence of new forms of subjectivity as well as the ability to use any technology (be it a pen, the alphabet or a keyboard) are interconnected and require training.

The making of this book is also closely intertwined with the place in which it has been written. This is a place where, in the late nineteenth century, the industrial elite of Victorian Britain relocated from the city centre in search of better living conditions. Up and down, I walk a road interspersed with mansions speaking of a time of unprecedented wealth. Technology, back then, had brought (some) people closer to a better life, where death could be kept at bay by advances in medicine and hygiene, and living standards could be improved by machines – at least for those who owned them. Some of these grand houses now serve as dwelling and working spaces; some are left to the elements. At the same time, the previously abandoned city centre is vibrating with the buzz of another revolution, this time a digital one. In this instance, 'alphabetical selves' give way to 'dispersed selves' in configurations, which, still being underway, cannot be adequately conceptualised and captured. The buzz is for sure far more subdued. There are no grand houses and no mythic fortunes this time, at least not here in Leeds. Yet, a whiff of the same promise lingers in the air (which is dangerously polluted even in the once respectable suburb): just within our grasp, but not quite, is a better life that technology will make possible. And this time, the promise is that the benefits will reach the many. The topography of my physical perambulations subtly influenced the content of my mental ones. The declining grandeur of the deserted mansions exerted a charm, which slowly turned into the conviction that the current (post)digital moment – the city down there teeming with excitement for the latest immersive technology – needs to be placed within a larger idea of technology. Not only because industrial technologies are still a big part of our lives. But also because, like the road I tread every day that links future (digital) innovation with past (industrial) achievement, technology, as Dominic Smith (2018) notes, is still understood as a way to 'somewhere': a fuller life, a better future, a fairer system, cleaner air.

Finally, this book was written during a period of increasing political and economic uncertainty, often tempered by appeals to adequate preparation. In 2019, as a European Citizen living in the UK, I was advised by the UK Government – through a £100 million advertising campaign – to 'get ready' in case of the country leaving the European Custom Union without a withdrawal agreement (GOV UK 2019, www.gov.uk/get-ready-brexit-check). During the same year and across the political spectrum, training emerged as a key strategy mobilised by Extinction Rebellion in their endeavour to secure legislation towards combating the climate crisis. Dedicating a separate tab to 'trainings' on their website, the movement stated that 'we take preparation for rebellion seriously. Training is key to the preparation of our thoughts and actions' (Extinction Rebellion 2020, https://rebellion.earth/act-now/trainings/). A year later, preparation, this time with regards to the early purchase of protective and testing equipment, marked the line between life and death, as national health care systems and their workers were fighting the Covid-19 pandemic.

Despite the obvious differences between these events, and regardless of future developments, preparation emerges as a key mechanism for dealing with contemporary challenges. Against their severity, performer training may appear not only small, but irrelevant. Yet, at its core there is a commitment to the belief that persons and the world are not fixed but constituted through an ongoing process in which we participate and can intervene: how we prepare, and how we prepare our selves, can make a difference. This book draws on my experience of a series of encounters with performer training practice, spanning 25 years and variously aiming: to learn, to unlearn; to make a self, to forget the self; to be alone, to be with others; to do more, to do nothing at all. Although different in their rationale, all these endeavours, sometimes expressing it explicitly, sometimes insinuating it just beneath the surface, made the promise that training, like technology, can effect change at an individual, inter-personal, and, increasingly lately, ecological level. At the heart of this book is the desire to articulate how the practices and discourses that comprise the means of preparation in the field of performer training reveal, construct and are conditioned by the subjectivities that emerge within a technologised lifeworld. Arguably, such a project becomes particularly urgent during a time that demands nothing less than a radical thinking of the way we live and act in the world.

References

Abram, D. 1997. *The Spell of the Sensuous*. New York: Vintage Books.

Extinction Rebellion. 2020. Trainings. https://rebellion.earth/act-now/trainings/ [accessed 1 May 2020]

GOV UK. 2019. Check how to get ready for new rules in 2021. www.gov.uk/get-ready-brexit-check [accessed 1 May 2020]

Rotman, B. 2008. *Becoming Beside Ourselves*. Durham: Duke University Press.

Smith, D. 2018. *Exceptional Technologies*. London: Bloomsbury.

ACKNOWLEDGEMENTS

This book developed out of several interactions with a great many people; long discussions over chapter drafts, email correspondence on specific questions, hasty chats in corridors and on pavements, winding walks in the woods, giddy explanations over drinks, interviews on Skype, updates over the phone, sleepy accounts of progress at bedtime. My sense is that these interactions not only made the book better, by offering me the opportunity to clarify my vision, take into consideration things I would not have thought, be corrected, explain again and again 'what the book is about', until finally I could understand myself. They also exemplify that even so-called single-authored books are powered by collective encounters and support. We think and understand with others.

Specific others that should be mentioned here: my colleagues at the School of Performance and Cultural Industries, for providing a collegial and intellectually stimulating environment and generously supporting this project; the members of the Performer Training, Preparation and Pedagogy Research Group at the University of Leeds, for bearing with long drafts and giving me sound advice; Scott Palmer for sharing his knowledge on light; Haili Ma for guiding me through definitions of the creative industries; and Jonathan Pitches, who has been an untiring mentor and who followed the progress of this project with unwavering interest. Colleagues from other institutions who uncomplainingly read draft after draft and made incisive comments: Dorinda Hulton, who offered invaluable guidance on the Open Theatre; Graham Ley, who has been advising me from the beginning of the project until the very end with an admirable combination of kindness and rigour; and Robert Rosenberger who generously shared his expertise on philosophy of technology. Rose Whyman, who invited me to share parts of the book at a Research Seminar in the Department of Drama and Theatre Arts at the University of Birmingham; Stefan Aquilina who offered excellent advice on Stanislavsky; Vicki Ann Cremona, who taught me to be patient with primary sources; Paul Allain and Frank

Camilleri, who published and gave me precious feedback on a journal article that was later developed into a chapter for this book. A very big thank you goes to the researchers and practitioners who shared their work so generously: Jeanine Thompson, Vita Berezina-Blackburn, Alex Oliszewski, Sarah Whatley, Ruth Gibson, Rosa Cisneros, Marisa Zanotti, Steph Kehoe, Sarah Perry, Terence Mann, Asha Jennings-Grant, and the team at the Mocap Vaults. Huge thanks also go to Rebecca Loukes, who created the space for this book to exist and whose support, guidance and generosity extends way beyond this project. I am very thankful to Ben Piggott and the team at Routledge who have supported both the series and the book from their early conception. I am also deeply grateful to the community of parents at Spring Bank Primary for creating such a supportive and nurturing environment for kids and adults alike. Special thanks to Nir for asking lightly and listening deeply, to Vanja for being solidly there, and to Sarah for sharing her world. Finally, special thanks to Yanis for his computer wizardry and patience, to my parents for believing in this project, to Francesco for the home cooking and the dish washing, and to Nefeli for making each day magical.

1

INTRODUCTION

This book examines the intersections between performer training and technology. Its immediate task is to understand how technology has influenced performer training discourse and practice and how different artefacts have been or can be used in the learning process. This book also sets out to examine how performer training and technology are co-shaped by their possible interactions and how the space 'between' them can be(come) a productive site of praxis. It is assumed that such praxis may not only involve the use of existing technological artefacts within a predefined performer training context, but also catalyse a reconsideration, negotiation and reformulation of what we think performer training and technology respectively are. Central to such praxis is the idea of preparation, regarded here both as a defining process of what training is expected to achieve as well as a sense of individual and collective responsibility towards developing appropriate forms of response to a series of interlinked and mounting crises.

In a certain respect, this book deals with a nascent area of study. The use of technology in performer training practice has not yet produced, or at least not been credited for producing, the well-tested and authoritative methods twentieth-century performer training history can rightfully boast about. Accounts on this area have only started appearing recently (Allain et al. 2019; Camilleri 2019; Crossley 2012; Crossley 2019; Delbridge 2015; Evans 2019; Klich 2012; Oliver 2012; Pitches 2014; Wake 2018), even though on the ground there is considerable experimentation, especially with digital devices. In fact, apart from a handful of cases (Camilleri 2019; Margolies 2016) that explicitly focus on the materiality of performer training, or on intermedial performance (Havens 2010; Scott and Barton 2019), there has been a tendency amongst performer training scholarship to overlook technology, especially pre-digital technologies, in favour of other aspects of training practice. As Frank Camilleri (2019) argues, twentieth-century discourse on performer training has been dominated by a multifaceted interest in the trainee's psychophysicality, often at the expense of the material, including the technological, aspects of the practice. As a result, and as I will discuss in more detail in Chapter 2, theatre technology is often associated with the technical and technological infrastructure of performance, whereas questions of the performer's process and preparation are placed within the remit of technique and thus demarcated from questions of technology.

The gap between these two areas is lessening. In the field of theatre and performance there has been a proliferation of titles that deal either with historic (Reilly 2013) or contemporary technologies (Bay-Cheng et al. 2010; Bay-Cheng et al. 2015; Broadhurst and Machon 2011; Dixon 2007). The emphasis in the majority of these volumes is placed on the influence and/or use of various technologies in processes of performance-making, the way they complicate the ontology of the performing event as well as the way they affect the experience of the audience. As such, concerns with the performer's process during performance has been so far secondary, whereas a consideration of the preparatory phase of such process has been marginal. Studies that do consider the performer's training often refer to the concept of the 'intermedial performer' (Havens 2010; Scott and Barton 2019). The term signals a state of symbiosis and mutual receptivity between the performer's embodied process and the operation of different technologies during the creation of live events. Studies, often with reference to the authors' own artistic practice (Kozel 2007; Havens 2010; Scott and Barton 2019), have begun examining the various interactions that develop between bodyminds and machines, providing sophisticated articulations of how performers and technologies may be understood independently as well as in conjunction with one another. What these accounts do not offer, however, is an examination of the pedagogies, histories and assumptions of performer training practice that arguably underpin current experimentation.

One of the intentions of this book is to demonstrate that although digital technologies raise a range of questions and possibilities, the presence of technology in performer training is not a new thing but has for a long time been underlying the way the performer's work and preparation has been understood and developed. The aim of this book is to capture and respond to some of the issues foregrounded in working with digital technologies, but also to position contemporary encounters with digital artefacts within a larger critical framework. As such, this book aspires to open a new avenue of enquiry, a new way of looking at and doing performer training, but possibly also a new way of looking at and 'doing' technology. Specifically, it prioritises an attempt to articulate possible ways in which the relationship between performer training and technology can be thought about, over an exhaustive mapping of the experimentation that is taking place on the ground.

In this respect, this book seeks to complement previous studies that interrogated the historical and scientific developments (Pitches 2006; Whyman 2008) as well as the ideological discourses (Evans 2009; Margolis and Renaud 2010; Murray 2015; Keefe and Murray 2005; Zarrilli 2002) that underpin either specific aspects of performer training or performer training as a human activity (Matthews 2011; Spatz 2015). As these volumes show, whether explicitly or not, performer training scholarship, if not practice, has adopted a reflexive stance and developed a critical awareness of its constituent parts: the terminologies, discourses, exercises and methods of transmission that make up distinct pedagogies. Exemplary of such stance is Simon Murray's call to 'identify and foreground a politics of actor training, where positions and claims of neutrality, disinterest or ignorance are untenable' (2015: 57). Murray's proposal points to the possibility of performer training creating a place where 'we can play, imagine, become unruly, collaborate and experiment with prefigurative behaviours and relations which resist the encroachments of economic and cultural commodification' (2015: 57). Echoing Murray, Ben Spatz similarly asks 'if the politics of actor training' may extend beyond the preparation of 'young actors for the stage, but intersect directly with other kinds of embodied pedagogies by revealing and foreclosing possible avenues of everyday practice' (2015: 7). Training, then, becomes reconstituted as a praxis of resistance and a site where different relationships with the everyday can be rehearsed. It is in this configuration that a common ground with technology begins to emerge.

Expressing a concern for the intensifying presence of technology in contemporary societies, scholars (for example Crary 2013; Stiegler 2010a; Stiegler 2010b; Wendland et al. 2019) argue that technology needs to be examined not only in terms of the functionalities and effects of isolated artefacts, but also as a consolidation of a way of being in a world that increasingly makes environmental processes, human actions, biological cycles and psychic landscapes legible only in terms of use and optimisation. Jonathan Crary, for example, contends that whereas 'markets and global infrastructure for continuous work and consumption have been in place for some time, [...] now a human subject is in the making to coincide with these more intensively' (2013: 2–3). What Crary and other scholars emphasise is that technology, especially in the context of global capitalism, is no longer limited to making things (consumer products, machines, equipment, infrastructure) but is insidiously underpinning the way humans are constituted as subjects and how they operate in the world. What is more, the penetration of digital technologies in several aspects of daily life entails that we now live in a technological environment that we can neither fully conceive of nor control, since technology operates in ways that transcend human modes of perception. Aislinn O'Donnell, for example, notes that

> the surplus of information produced by algorithm-based exchange-flows of data and information exceeds any human capacity for assimilation or comprehension. It verges on an experience of the sublime, paralysed, but without the moment of redemption or any sense of the power of one's faculties.
>
> (2016: 33)

In response, scholars highlight the need to develop alternative relations to technology. Some assign this task to education (Thomson 2019; Wrathall 2019), whilst others (for example Dreyfus 2002; Lemmens 2017) emphasise the importance of developing forms of practice, including artistic practice, that transcend the kinds of use stipulated by external agendas, which often serve hegemonic, yet invisible, corporate interests. A key idea that emerges repeatedly and cuts across accounts of technology (Hansen 2015; Marcuse 1969; Wrathall 2019) as well as artistic practice that involves technology (Kozel 2007; Whatley 2015) is the need for the development of a new sensibility. According to Mark Wrathall sensibility is 'a condition in which we come to grasp the *sense* that governs our activities – we are aware, in other words, why it makes sense to do something or refrain from doing something' (2019: 31 emphasis original). Some scholars (Dreyfus 2002) argue that the development of such a disposition can better emerge from practices that do not involve technology, whilst others suggest that such sensibility can only be possible through interactions with technologies. Mark Hansen, for example, contests that the 'loss of agential human powers [that has resulted from media technologies] can only be recompensed by the expanded sensory contact with "worldly sensibility" that twenty-first century media make possible' (2015: 5).[1] As I will explain in more detail, this debate can be traced also in the field of performance and performer training, with some practitioners (for example Alfreds 2013; Hunter, in Loverdou 2014) arguing that performance should consciously resist the spread of technology, whilst others (for example Garoian and Gaudelius 2001; Kozel 2007) suggest that it can offer a productive space to explore our relationship with it.[2] Despite this contention, a key point of agreement is that sensibility has an intrinsic embodied dimension and, as Wrathall observes, alternative relations to technology cannot be limited to the teaching of 'decontextualised theories'; they are premised on the development of 'bodily skills' (2019: 34). Wrathall, in fact, speaks of a kind of 'training' that 'could be accomplished through an apprenticeship in skilful behaviour' (2019: 34).

We see, therefore, that there is a crucial point where performer training and technology meet: from one end, thinkers of contemporary culture call for a new disposition, a new sensibility that can bring forward new modes of operation and ways of being in the world. From the other end, scholars of performer training appreciate that training can catalyse a critical redefinition of selfhood and repositioning of the subject in the world. It is precisely the seam between these two positions that this book seeks to mine. Specifically in relation to technology, this book aims to test what I call the 'promise' of performer training: can performer training, in its double function as an education in embodiment as well as a form of education that has a significant embodied dimension, be(come) a privileged site for exploring how relationships to technology are constituted? Even more ambitiously, can it offer the space/tools/opportunities for rehearsing alternative ways of approaching technology that could engender the 'new sensibility' that is envisioned by scholars of both technology and performance? Under what conditions can such promise be fulfilled?

The idea that an alternative relationship to technology – and the many forms this might take – is both needed and in need of preparation is not new. It is encountered, for example, in Martin Heidegger's seminal essay 'The Question Concerning Technology', to be discussed in Chapter 3, which intended to put forward a way of thinking about technology that will 'prepare a free relationship to it' (1977: 3).

Indeed, Wrathall observes that Heidegger's later work has been devoted to 'developing a curriculum for training us to see through the never ending whirl of technological optionalisation' (2019: 29). Yet, such 'curriculum' is exclusively in written form, which, presumably leads Wrathall to call for the inclusion of 'bodily skills' (2019: 36). A crucial point, still to receive attention, then, concerns the *process* of preparation, especially if we agree that such process is by necessity an embodied one.

A well-known example in philosophical literature on technology illustrates the issue. In one of his essays, Heidegger bemoans the use of the typewriter, arguing that its materiality disrupts the fluidity of handwriting and homogenises the uniqueness not only of written characters but thinking. In his critique of Heidegger's understanding of technology, Don Ihde (2010) points out that Heidegger's argument derives from an inability to use the specific technology in a competent manner: Heidegger cannot typewrite and, unsurprisingly, he finds that the equipment gets in the way of the task expected to be accomplished. Ihde further notes that before any technology can be used skilfully and smoothly, 'there has to be a learning and accommodation/resistance process' (2010: 124).

Moreover, in a related study that considers cultural variations in the design and use of bow and arrow, Ihde acknowledges that 'one can see that the simple machine paired with skilled embodiment practices now produces a new *tool trajectory*' (2012: 184, emphasis original). Here again, Ihde, echoes a wider thesis that different relationships to technology are premised on the development of new practices, and explicitly recognises the importance of embodied skill in effecting changes in the material artefact and taking its use in a new direction. What is, however, not considered in depth is the process through which such skill becomes acquired. Yet, as performer training amply demonstrates, learning how to use equipment, or indeed developing a new kind of practice, does not follow a fixed trajectory leading to a predetermined result. It is, as Rebecca Loukes observes in relation to her work with sticks – to be discussed in more detail in Chapter 4 – 'not a given; it is something that is "cultivated"' (Zarrilli et al. 2013: 244). And such cultivation is complex, processual, intersubjective, historically and culturally contingent, and produces different forms of experience, knowledge and expertise. Form this point of view, and as Murray attests, 'skill and competence acquisition […] are generative rather than fixed structures' (2015: 54). Since the use of technology relies on a fluid process of learning, then training is by default central to the idea that relationships to technology need not be fixed; they can be tested, reconsidered, and constituted anew. Wrathall's assertion, therefore, signals a welcome appreciation of the fact that training can be a place where relationships with technology are not simply established but *negotiated*, precisely because – I would add – training covers the space between inept and adept performance.

Nonetheless, against the thesis that an alternative relationship to technology can be trained or effected through training, stands a more pessimistic view that holds that any such effort is, at best, naïve, at worst, complicit with hegemonic interests. Since technology – the argument goes – now shapes nothing less than the very sensorium of human beings, regardless of whether a specific artefact is used or not, any attempt to occupy a position outside of this matrix is untenable. David Berry, for example, notes that,

> As our reliance on these technical systems grows, the technical groups responsible for these systems grow in importance – such that their rationalities, expressed through particular logics, embedded in the interface and the code become *internalised* within the user as a particular habitus, or way of doing appropriate to certain activities.
>
> (2014: 38, emphasis added)

Echoing Berry, Crary examines a range of cultural habits that have been naturalised in Western societies, including, for example, the proliferation of screens in domestic and public spaces. He diagnoses a 'systemic colonization of individual experience' by networked technologies (2013: 52), which makes other ways of life either marginalised (2013: 50) or, worse still, unimaginable. Such assessment of the present moment may be dismissed as pessimistic or reductive. It could be retorted, for example, that attributing such an influence to technology fails to properly acknowledge the very aspects of human activity that escape it. Nonetheless, even if this counter-argument is upheld, an important question still remains: considering that performer training is a cultural activity that takes place in the midst of the relentless 24/7 world Crary adumbrates, how could it offer the space for alternative possibilities? In other words, what is so special about performer training that sets it apart? Indeed, on what grounds might one even *propose* that performer training can be set apart?

Central to the book's ambition to test whether the learning and creative processes involved in performer training may offer the space for negotiating relationships with technology, is the contention that performer training is technological in and of itself. As intimated already, the book follows the premise that performer training does not simply involve skill acquisition that will be achieved by an already formed subject; rather it constitutes subjects by effecting profound changes in the trainee's embodiment and selfhood. Reviewing a range of different approaches to performer training, Ian Watson observes that although training appears to prioritise the performer's professionalisation, with a range of methods focusing on the mastery of a certain craft, 'the craft portends to a wider world, a broader spectrum of experience, learning and education' (2015: 15). Following this line of thought, this book seeks to shed light on arguably the most banal yet foundational aspect of performer training: that training turns the trainee into an instrument.

This operation can have both empowering and disempowering results. On the one hand, training expands the means of expression available to the trainee, in the process opening up potential subject positions and enhancing one's sense of creative and artistic agency (Evans 2009: 143–75; Murray 2015). On the other hand, training also institutes docility and compliance, preparing the trainee to fit within, and accept, established economic and professional structures (Evans 2009: 122–4;

Murray 2015). It bears noting that these two perspectives are not mutually exclusive but invoke a dialectic between discipline and unruliness (Evans 2009), embodiment and inscription that is played out on the trainee's body and possibly throughout one's career.

The aim of the book is to capture the different attitudes towards ideas of mastery but also demonstrate that training, like technology, is master-ful: it can both discipline the subject in a series of normative positions (for example, in terms of body ideals and identity politics) but also enable the transgression of existing norms through facilitating mastery in terms of creativity, expression and collaboration. Although this tension has been acknowledged and discussed within studies of performer training (Evans 2009; Murray 2015), my intention is to contribute to existing scholarship by demonstrating how the performer-as-instrument trope is inextricably connected with understandings of technology. Following Gunkel and Taylor's distinction between instruments and instrumentality (2014: 163), the aim of this book is to examine both the use of technological *instruments* in performer training and consider the wider process of *instrumentalisation* that training is. With regards to the first, the book endeavours to cover a range of instruments directly employed in performer training practice, as well as different ways in which these instruments may be used. With regards to the second, the book explores how different performer training pedagogies, regardless of whether they employ technological equipment, set in motion the development of an instrument of expression.

The contention of this book, then, is that performer training may serve as a suitable praxis for probing relationships with technology, because training, whether it uses tools or not, effects a process of instrumentalisation at the most intimate level of the trainee's bodymind. To put it simply: if performer training can allow us to negotiate our relationship to technology, this is not because it is alien to it but because it is very much like it. As such, the remit of this book extends beyond the examination of technological equipment in performer training. By exploring performer training through philosophical approaches to technology, an additional aim is to juxtapose two defining aspects of performer training practice: the process of preparation that renders the trainee into an instrument of expression in relation to the promise of training to develop new ways of being in the world. As I will argue, the deeply embodied, intersubjective and artefactual nature of both of these processes makes this exploration relevant to both performer training and technology.

The rest of the introduction offers an overview of current approaches to the study of performer training and technology, including digital culture. First, I discuss the way performer training and technology have developed as separate fields of study and, second, I explore current approaches towards technology within the performer training field and digital training specifically. Third, I outline the methodology according to which this book is intending to set up and exploit the series of 'and's' that stands between the two terms.

What is performer training? – an expanded field

It is worth starting an overview with an essay that similarly tried to take stock of the field nearly 30 years ago. In response to what seemed in 1995 as an overwhelming proliferation of training courses, Clive Barker tried to create order by positioning actor training in relation to the theatre it was supposed to serve. Entitled 'What training – for What Theatre?' Barker's essay gives the impression of a snowball effect, since, according to his account, approaches to actor training proliferated throughout the twentieth century at an increasing speed. This, eventually, left 'young people entering the theatre today [i.e. 1995] [...] faced with a bewildering profusion of possible choices' (Barker 1995: 100). The choices that Barker recognised involved a variety of academic and non-academic courses; a diverse range of approaches, often themselves an eclectic mixture of several techniques; and an equally varied set of destinations to which such training(s) could eventually lead.

Today's landscape features similar characteristics, and if anything, the destination of training seems to have diversified to such an extent that belies any attempt to accurately predict, or indeed reach consensus on, what a career path might look like. Reflecting on a panel on actor training organised in 2004, Lissa Tyler Renaud muses on some of the possible understandings of the word 'actor':

> One person meant the artist who knew dramatic literature; one meant the person off the street who knew how to handle a close-up in a dog food commercial. One meant the actor who was on quest; one meant the 'talent' who was hoping for a television series. Some thought an actor should specialise in one medium; some thought an actor could only make a living if he [sic] could work in all media. Some thought the trained actor would be working around the world; some imagined him never leaving the recording booth.
>
> (Margolis and Renaud 2010: 80)

As Renaud's account demonstrates, apart from manifesting in several ways, the actor's professional identity is embroiled in larger discourses, such as popular culture, globalisation, mediatisation and self-actualisation. Moreover, conceptualisations and practices of acting as an art form have also undergone significant change. Paul Allain and Jen Harvie's definition of 'acting' identifies two categories. One is character-based acting, where the actor has to create and represent a character usually within an aesthetic of psychological realism. The other is 'postmodern acting', which challenges the ideas of a 'unified subject' and treats the actor as a scenographic element of a larger *mise-en-scène* and/or consists of task-based rather than character-led activities (Allain and Harvie 2014: 147–8). In a similar vein, Phillip Zarrilli draws a distinction between 'the actor-as-interpreter' and the 'actor-as-maker' (Zarrilli et al. 2013: 7). Although these categories might blur in actual practice, they signal a shift in what the actor does or is expected to be able to do. Indeed, Zarrilli's generic terms could be broken down into additional sub-categories, such as the 'actor-musician', the 'actor-singer', the 'actor-puppeteer', and, with direct reference to intermedial performance, the 'activating performer-technician' (Scott and Barton 2019: 68). The implications for training are evident. Whereas training for the 'conventional' actor-as-interpreter would focus on the composite process of creating a character primarily through interpreting and delivering a given text, the proliferation of new performance genres and dramaturgies points to an inexhaustible set of skills an actor might need; for example, writing new text, working with puppetry, devising and operating technological devices whilst performing.

Dance training features similar developments. The distinction between character-based and postmodern acting, noted by Allain and Harvie, echoes with the division between 'traditional' and 'post-modern' or 'post-Judson' dance training. According to Melanie Bales and Rebecca Nettl-Fiol, the latter is characterised by 'the use of alternative movement practices in dance technique or *as* dance technique, with various ones in and out of favour […]; ballet as an adjunct technique for most modern dancers; and the eclectic, self-styled approach to training' (2008: ix, emphasis original). As such, 'dancers become their own guides in putting together their training packages' (Bales and Nettl-Fiol 2008: x). As Joshua Monten's (2008) auto-biographical account demonstrates in the same volume, trainees are often taxed with the difficult task of negotiating a range of – often – incompatible corporeal demands and ideological positions underpinning distinct techniques.

Furthermore, and similar to acting, the eclecticism of dance training has a knock-on effect on the artist's professional identity. Monten points out that when training includes several approaches and influences, the performer may be idealised as a 'crossover dancer' being 'capable of any technique' (Tharp 1992: 54 cited in Monten 2008: 62). The performer may also be denigrated to a 'hired body' which 'homogenises all styles and vocabularies beneath sleek, impenetrable surface' (Foster Leigh 1997: 255 cited in Monten 2008: 63). A more balanced view is offered by Veronica Dittman who sees training as part of a constant process of self-fashioning, whereby dancers 'create their own curriculum in the service of a unique dance identity of their own design' (2008: 22). This process, Dittman attests, gives rise to 'slash artists': 'dancer/choreographer/teacher, dancer/lighting designer, dancer/computer programmer/graphic designer, dancer/writer/masseuse' (2008: 24). What is more, the increasing hybridisation of performing arts genres blurs the boundaries between dancers and actors.

In the light of the diversity of current provision, in this book performer training is understood as an expanded practice in the following three senses: professionally, chronologically and socially. Chiming with the way theatrical performance is now seen as part of an 'expanded field', which includes participatory, intermedial, digital, verbatim and site-specific practices amongst a range of other cultural activities that have a strong performative or theatrical element (Lavender 2016), training is also positioned as an expanded field expected to serve, as noted above, not only a variety of performance genres, but also to engender artists who straddle conceptual, professional and disciplinary boundaries. Training, also, expands in a chronological sense since it is likely to extend beyond the completion of a formal curriculum or degree programme and constitutes an ongoing process of accumulation of skills and exposure to different approaches. As Ian Watson observes, training may take place 'on the job', as well as through ad hoc workshops, and as such may accumulate over a series of artistic encounters across an entire career (2015: 11–12). What is more, training is bound to exert an influence beyond the immediate goal that it is expected to serve. As Watson observes, 'one may well have a singular purpose for studying [a particular regime], but the embodied learning involved can have a lifetime of implications' (2015: 13). In other words, even if a training programme reaches a conclusion, its effects may be carried forward through, for example, the trainee's independent practice and/or a working ethos that guides an entire career.

From this point of view, it is not surprising that in recent titles, performer training has been placed side-by-side with social practices that also have a strong embodied dimension but that focus on the formation of identity rather than the development of artistic skill. For example, performer training has been examined in relation to monastic discipline (Matthews 2011), as well as theories and practices of gender performativity (Spatz 2015). As these studies demonstrate, there is often a slippage or cross-fertilisation between regimes of self-development that are situated outside the performing arts and become appropriated as a means of preparation for performance. An example of this is the range of somatic disciplines, now incorporated in performer training curricula, that had originally developed for, and are still offered to, the general public. Reversely, there is a migration of performance training techniques into other forms of professional or personal development. Examples include the use of masks in leadership training (Peisley 2016), as well as the appropriation of performer training practices for the development of environmental awareness (Coe and Goodwin 2019). In these last developments, we see that performer training becomes de-coupled from the performing arts and instead acquires an autonomy as a form of cultural practice that can move across and between fields, including professional and amateur, artistic and non-artistic, individual and collective. From a current perspective, then, it seems that Barker's question 'What Training – for What Theatre?' not only invites even more possible answers; it has also been rendered superfluous.

Although the current book centres on instances of performer training that are situated within the performing arts, or even more generally the creative industries, it retains, in line with the aforementioned studies, an anthropological interest in training, i.e. an appreciation that performer training is in dialogue with and may well extend into and morph with other fields of human activity.[3] In light of this picture, this book uses the term 'performer training' to denote both the plethora and diversity of practices that an aspiring or established performance artist may engage in at any point in their career. At the same time, though, the analysis will be mindful of the many differences in approach, style, genre, history and pedagogy that comprise the wider 'performer training' ecology. Similarly, throughout the book I will favour the term 'performer' as a more generic denomination that can accommodate the variety of training backgrounds artists may become involved with, as well as the hybrid professional identities that transcend boundaries between different genres. I will, however, preserve the terms 'actor' and 'dancer' whenever I draw on discussions that feature them.

What is technology?

Similar to the range of activities and approaches encompassed within the generic denomination 'performer training', technology is an equally polyvalent term. An amalgamation of two Greek words – *techne* and *logos* – technology can be broadly understood as the logic of making. As Carl Mitcham and Adam Briggle point out, the term encountered in German, French and other European languages is 'technics', which denotes the 'general study of technique', whereas 'technology' in European languages other than English refers more narrowly to the 'logical analysis of technics' (2012: 42). In English, then, technology

> can be approached in terms of physical artefacts, processes or techniques, and social implications. In the initial case, technology is thought as a distinctive kind of physical object (something other than nature); in the second as a distinctive type of human action (often emphasizing functional efficiency); in the third as a distinctive social order either objectively (mass production) or subjectively (consumer society).
>
> (Mitcham and Briggle 2012: 40)

The term technology, in other words, encompasses artefacts; the ways in which these artefacts are used and made; as well as the social, cultural and economic conditions that shape and are shaped by such use. Such multiplicity entails that technology can be studied from several disciplinary perspectives, including anthropology, philosophy, history and social sciences, as well as more recent branches of knowledge, such as media and communication studies and digital humanities. The study of technology has also coalesced into a discrete sub-field of philosophy.

Tracing a history of the field of philosophy of technology, Don Ihde points out that science and philosophy evolved in tandem and, during classical antiquity, 'science', as a form of observation of natural phenomena, was under the purview of philosophy, branded as 'natural philosophy' (1993: 5). Developments in arts and crafts, on the other hand, developed separately and were considered inferior to philosophy: 'no matter how excellent the product, craft/arts skills must take second or third place to the purely contemplative or ideal related theory of the philosopher' (Ihde 1993: 26). What Ihde traces, in other words, is a preference of philosophy to prioritise the theoretical side of science, whilst overlooking 'the instrumental and technological side of actual scientific practice' (1993: 29). Things change radically from the late nineteenth century onwards, as philosophers begin to appreciate that '*experiments entail technologies or instruments against which and in relation to which the phenomenon is compared*' (Ihde 1993: 6, emphasis original). Philosophers, in other words, came to the realisation that 'science itself is also *technologically embodied*. Without instruments and laboratories, there was no science' (Ihde 2009: 7, emphasis original).

Ihde gives the frequently cited example of the theory of thermodynamics, pointing out that this followed the steam engine: 'science, in effect, derived its understanding of thermodynamics *from observations and experiments upon technology* rather than from "Nature"' (2009: 41, emphasis original). A foundational premise to the emergence of philosophy of technology is, therefore, an understanding of technology as a way of approaching nature that precedes science.

Accordingly, examinations of technology are underpinned by two fundamental questions. The first concerns the relation between society and technological development. On the one hand, a determinist thesis argues that technology is an autonomous force that advances independently of social systems and values (Ihde 1993: 48–9; Feenberg 1995: 4–5). On the other hand, a social constructivist perspective retorts that technological artefacts and their use are not predetermined; it is societies that decide on matters of design, production and use, and it is people and their actions that shape technology. Although this perspective does not automatically ensure an emancipatory or democratic use of technology, it still permits the possibility of change.

Another parameter around which debates on technology are positioned involves the issuing of normative judgements on technological artefacts specifically as well as technology in general. Is technology a 'good' or a 'bad' thing? Can the benefits of one particular technology in one particular context outweigh its negative impact in another? According to which criteria should these evaluations be made? Although this is an ongoing theme, it is of interest here that contemporary scholars identify three main attitudes towards technology, manifesting in discrete periods of Western history. As Steven Dorrestijn explains, 'the first phase of philosophical thinking about technology' stretches from the Enlightenment into the twentieth century. This period is tied with the remarkable rate of scientific, technological and social change of the eighteenth century as well as the ensuing Industrial Revolution. During the Enlightenment, technology, still understood in conjunction with science and technical crafts, is inextricably woven with ideas of human progress, including economic flourishing, social justice and political emancipation. According to Dorrestijn, it was assumed that 'scarcity and unequal distribution of technology were the only hindrances to the full benefit of the wonders of technology' (2017: 313).

The second period, dating from and following the two world wars, is also concerned with questions of access, but it is also marked by a critical, and in some cases 'pessimistic and dystopian' view (Dorrestijn 2017: 315). Technology, in this case, becomes associated both with the social problems resulting from the rapid industrialisation of Western countries and the environmental and humanitarian havoc wreaked by the powerful weapons used in the two world wars. Technology can thus no longer be seen (solely) as a means for perfecting the human condition, and it is rather understood as an end in itself that enslaves human beings, and becomes 'an obstacle to a proper human way of life' (Dorrestijn 2017: 315). Rather than prioritising the positive effects of technology and engaging with questions of improvement, this second wave is concerned with the adverse effects of technology, and accordingly with the ways in which these effects can be limited or alleviated. It is during this second wave, and in response to a deeply felt sense of destruction, that a deterministic understanding of technology emerges across a range of different thinkers. As Ihde explains, in these accounts technology is understood to 'have become autonomous and no longer under human control, aimed towards a *totalisation* of its form' (Ihde 1993: 33, emphasis original).

The third phase, roughly positioned from the 1970s onwards, can be seen as a response to the penetration of technological artefacts in daily life, as well as the close symbiosis between technological devices and the human body. This third phase is marked by an emphasis on the interdependence and hybridisation between humans and technology. It is stressed that technology is not something extrinsic to humans that can be clearly and definitively distinguished from 'nature'. Rather, technology is part of the human lifeworld, since it is the very medium through which this world is experienced and acted upon. Accordingly, the belief that technology is a relatively recent development specific to Western modernity becomes debunked: '*there are no human cultures which are pre-technological*' stresses Ihde, since, 'all humans have a material culture with complexly patterned praxes involving artefacts' (1993: 49, emphasis original).

The analysis, then, shifts from a preoccupation with technology as an autonomous force and takes an 'empirical turn' (Dorrestijn 2017: 316). According to an empirical approach, there is no such thing as capitalised 'Technology' encapsulating an independent and/or uncontrollable force. There are only instances of human–technology interaction contingent upon the properties and affordances of the artefact, the dispositions of the user, and the characteristics of the culture–nature in which user and artefact are located. An empirical turn, then, insists that technologies need to be examined in their specific social/political/geographical manifestations and points out that technology and society, devices and persons are always implicated in their co-constitution. This third wave, then, is neither negative nor positive towards technology, but '*ambivalent*' (Dorrestijn 2017: 317, emphasis original).

Alongside scholarship that deals with technology, there is also a proliferation of studies that focus specifically on the digital. Characterised as 'an ever multiplying and mostly impossible to pin down referent' (Blake 2014: 11), the 'digital' is extensively used in scholarly discourse, as well as everyday parlance, both as a noun and an adjective to define a set of keywords, such as culture, age, education and, indeed, training. The digital, then, denotes not only the acculturation of specific technologies but also particular ways of engaging with the world. As Charlie Gere observes, 'to some extent our culture is becoming so thoroughly digital that the term *digital culture* risks becoming tautological' (2008: 7, emphasis original). In a similar vein, Berry argues that 'we are entering a post-digital world in which the digital has become completely bound up with and constitutive of everyday life and the so-called digital economy' (2014: 2). The digital therefore marks a distinct area of study examined both through the application of the second and third philosophical approach to technology outlined above, as well as through other lenses such as critical and feminist theory. It also splits into separate academic sub-fields, such as digital media and internet studies.

Within the range of perspectives from which the digital is studied, some contemporary thinkers, as noted already, express increasing disquiet with regards to both the diffusion of digital devices and networks into daily life as well as the storage, circulation and manipulation of data and the inability of existing legal or political frameworks to control such flows. Yet, information technologies and ubiquitous computing are also explored as sites of novel experiences of embodiment, as well as a powerful means for resistance and emancipation. There is, for example, a significant body of work of artists, activists and scientists studying the interconnections between human and machine, rehearsing strategies of critique as well as attempts at alternative presents and futures (Kozel 2007; Garoian and Gaudelius 2001; Zulinska 2002).

Central to these attempts is the notion of the posthuman, an appreciation that 'many humans now, and increasingly will, live with chemically, surgically, technologically modified bodies and/or in close conjunction (networked) with machines and other organic forms' (Nayar 2014: 3). In addition to spelling a change in human ontology, the posthuman also denotes a critical stance that seeks to dethrone the (white, male) autonomous human subject that has been assumed at the centre of discourse. The human subject then is understood 'as an assemblage, co-evolving with other forms of life, enmeshed with the environment and technology' (Nayar 2014: 4). Correspondingly, in a posthuman subjectivity 'distributed cognition replaces autonomous will; embodiment replaces a body seen as a support system for the mind; and a dynamic partnership between human and intelligent machines replaces the liberal humanist subject's manifest destiny to dominate and control nature' (Hayles 1999: 288). In other words, the coupling of machine and human need not be solely a cause for concern; it can be a site of political regeneration. Indeed, according to Katherine Hayles the penetration of digital technologies in daily life entail that a number of 'interventions' are possible, including: 'making new media [...]; adapting present media to subversive ends [...]; using digital media to reenvision academic practices, environments, and strategies [...] (2012: 83). The digital, then, is studied not only in terms of the way it manifests through systems, devices and culture but also in terms of the changes it effects on human ontology. As the next section demonstrates, the differing approaches to digital culture adumbrated thus far also permeate the field of performer training. What is more, the penetration of the digital and the concomitant notions of the posthuman/posthumanism raise fundamental questions about both theatre and education. If the world and its inhabitants have undergone such radical change, how should people be educated?

Performer training and the digital

One way in which the relationship between performer training and the digital has been approached is in terms of the changes that take place in professional environments. Concluding his study on movement training for actors in 2009, Mark Evans brought attention to the pervasive technologisation of professional settings and asked: 'How does a performer prepare for a performance that may take place against a "blue screen", be re-modelled and digitally transplanted onto another "actor" and then further "enhanced" through editing?' (2009: 180). In a similar vein in November 2014, Robin Nelson issued a call for interest, entitled 'The Intermedial Actor Prepares', premised on the need to 'address the perceived gap in the provision of performer training Europe-wide particularly for those who trained a decade or more ago, before new media impacted on live performance' (Nelson 2014: np). There is a sense, in other words, that existing training systems may no longer be adequate or suitable to address the technologisation of the performing arts industry and equip performers with the appropriate or necessary skills to engage with the changing landscape. The use of digital technologies, then, is envisaged as a means to address emerging needs.

In addition to the use of digital technologies in the film and performing arts industry, an emerging sub-category of performer training is concerned with the development of skills specific to the creation of intermedial performance. Drawing on several examples of contemporary performance as well as their own practice, Jo Scott and Bruce Barton argue that intermedial work is premised on a symbiosis between performer and technology. Chiming with earlier accounts on the use of technology in performance, such as Susan Kozel's seminal *Closer* (2007), Scott and Barton point out that technologies are no longer 'merely tools' (2019: 78) which might compete with the performer for status and attention. They rather propose that the performer's 'presence' and 'agency' are constituted in relation to the behaviour and performance of technological devices through a range of 'actions, interactions, and relationships' involving both human and technological counterparts (Scott and Barton 2019: 63). Their account draws two important conclusions for performer training. One is that 'training as a performer in this context is not about attaining "mastery" or a comprehensive set of stable attributes, but rather involves developing heightened awareness and a skills-based responsiveness to a rapidly evolving set of dynamics' (Scott and Barton 2019: 65–6). Their second conclusion is that the skills they have identified as necessary for 'work[ing] with and through technology [...] are not necessarily part of current actor and performer training' (Scott and Barton 2019: 87). Scott and Barton argue, therefore, that intermedial performance not only requires a set of competencies, which are not addressed by existing curricula and pedagogies, it also brings forth embodied and technical realities that require fresh conceptualisations of key aspects of the performer's work.

Finally, a third way in which the relationship between performer training and the digital can be cast, is in terms of the wider changes effected by the diffusion of digital culture. This pertains both to the training space as well as the trainees' development before they even begin training. According to Katherine Hayles, 'children who grow up in information-intensive environments will literally have brains wired differently than children who grow up in other kinds of cultures and situations' (2012: 100). Although it is still a moot point whether digital technologies cause epigenetic change, it is evident that cultural habits at home, in the classroom and, indeed, in the theatre space are changing. For example, Caroline Wake (2018), in her overview of the use of digital resources in performing arts learning environments, brings attention to the way the once notional 'empty space' of the training studio has been populated by devices owned by trainees, technological infrastructure provided by institutions, and habits ensuing from the use of digital artefacts. Similarly, in their introduction to the special issue 'Digital Training' of the *Theatre Dance and Performance Training Journal*, the editors pose a series of open-ended questions:

> What tools and platforms can be brought to bear on the experience of training; how might they enhance training processes and, by extension, teaching, rehearsing and even performing? How do screens and devices influence the time, place and space of training? For example, what is their effect on the trainee's attention or the student's ability to be self-reflexive, or their capacity for notation? Does the trainer's role change in such an environment and, if so, how?
>
> (Allain et al. 2019: 165)

The place of training within digital culture raises therefore two critical questions. One is whether the pedagogies, assumptions and ways of working that comprise performer training practice are appropriate for the new generation of students – regardless of whether technologies are involved in professional contexts. The other is whether digital technologies, those branded as 'learning technologies' as well as those that have been acculturated within everyday contexts, could be harnessed for training purposes.

Accordingly, performer trainers and theatre educators demonstrate an awareness of the changing landscape of artistic practice and daily life as well as a desire to employ technology in order to address pedagogical issues they encounter in their teaching. Possibly the most common use of technology in performer training involves the use of online spaces designed to support modes of blended learning. Provided by institutions, online depositories have been incorporated across anglophone higher education in the last decade. In this instance, the uptake of the technology follows an institutional agenda, and educators are primarily tasked with selecting and organising the content to be deposited in these spaces. Blended learning has also offered additional possibilities, for example through providing blog spaces that extend classroom-based interaction and discussion.

In addition to institutionally managed spaces, there is also a proliferation of commercial platforms supported by publishing enterprises and designed to act independently of face-to-face transmission (Allain et al. 2019; Pitches 2019). Massive Open Online Courses (MOOCs), such as Jonathan Pitches' 'Introduction to Physical Actor Training'; subscription-based repositories, such as Digital Theatre+ and the Routledge Performance Archive; as well as outputs of research projects, such as 'Motion Bank' and 'Physical Actor Training: An Online A–Z', constitute rich and carefully curated depositories of training material. In this manner, they effect a considerable change in the ecology of training by remediating performer training knowledge, which is fundamentally embodied and expected, at least until recently, to be transmitted through face-to-face interactions. Indeed, engagement with these resources suggests that learning can take place in radically different modalities. The delivery of the material and its reception are distanced both geographically and temporally, mediated through an electronic interface, and can operate independently of an institutionally based curriculum.[4] Herein lies, according to Pitches, the emergence of 'digital training': 'the appropriation of [digital] technologies by a tutor/leader/expert/ambassador/role-model to document and/or transmit some level of embodied experience and knowledge' (2014: 4).

Another manifestation of digital training involves the use of technologies in studio practice. In this case, training centres around the choice of a particular piece of hardware, which can be widely available, owned by the trainees and/or provided by the institution, and is used or becomes repurposed for pedagogical ends. A common example is the use of recording equipment, such as Flip and Go-Pro cameras, as a means to enhance the students' ability to reflect on their learning and creative process (Bannon and Kirk 2014; Burtt 2014). Another variation involves the use of computers and cameras towards the development of compositional and dramaturgical skills for intermedial performance (Crossley 2012; Oliver 2012; Scott and Barton 2019). In addition to hardware use, there are also instances of appropriation of online platforms as tools for teaching key aspects of theatre studies. Sarah Crews and Christina Papagiannouli (2019) have worked with social media platforms in order to teach the work of canonical practitioners, whereas a project between the University of Coventry and the University of Tampere used telepresence technologies with the aim to pair two geographically remote groups towards the creation of a performance of a Shakespearean text (Gorman et al. 2019).

A less common occurrence involves the design of bespoke software aiming to address specific interests or pedagogic purposes. An example of this, to be discussed in more detail in Chapter 5, is a mobile phone application developed by Marisa Zanotti and bgroup in 2012 for the teaching of choreography (Zanotti 2014). Another project is the Double Skin/Double Mind installation developed in 2006 by Emio Greco and Peter Scholten in collaboration with dance notators, technologists, researchers, a cognitive scientist and a media designer. DS/DM is a 'virtual version' of a workshop that Greco and Scholten have been using in their teaching since 1996, and aims to familiarise the participants with Greco's movement language as well as enhance the participants' body awareness and prompt them 'to discover new interpretations of their dancing body' (Bermudez et al. 2011: 1). Finally, there are developments of forms of training that aim to serve the needs of a specific technology. The most salient example, to be discussed extensively in Chapter 6, is the development of training for motion capture.

In tandem with the range of experimentation noted above, there are also attempts to institute new forms of pedagogy that respond to key aspects of digital culture and performance. For example, Rosemary Klich recognises in the notion of the posthuman a potential for rethinking how learning takes place. She calls for a post-human pedagogy specific to the performing arts, which 'dismisses notions of objective and accepted knowledge and promotes a methodology of learning that places students within a network involving human, non-human, animal, technological, material and organic elements' (Klich 2012: 168). Echoing Klich, but with a more focused interest on performer training, Camilleri asks the field to acknowledge that 'the "world" [is] no longer limited to the organic and natural but extended to a post-natural technological environment' (2019: xvi). He points out that twentieth-century performer training has been dominated by a psychophysical paradigm that prioritised the performer's presence and the development of the performer's bodymind. He thus proposes the term 'postpsychophysical' (Camilleri 2019), which seeks to complement a dominant discourse of psychophysicality with an appreciation of the role of materiality, including technology, in the shaping of the human condition in general and performer training in particular.

As we see then, there is a rich production of practice that features both experiments with the opportunities offered by digital equipment as well as explorations of the way technology may affect learning spaces and curricula. Nonetheless, these developments should also be viewed in relation to the range of practices that do not involve digital technologies. Crossley, for example, notes that students, prior to entering higher education in the UK, often receive tuition in 'psycho-physical or physical methodologies' (2012: 178). Accordingly, they might 'select performing arts programmes at university because of the promise of the viscerality and the co-present experience with fellow actors and an audience' (Crossley 2012: 178). A pedagogical approach aligned with the posthuman that dislodges the performer from the centre of the *mise-en-scene* might appear to them not only unfamiliar, but deeply unsettling.

In addition to the tensions noted by Crossley, Caroline Wake observes that 'some staff and students come to the performing arts precisely to escape the digital technologies and practices that saturate contemporary life and are thus unwilling to reintroduce them into classroom, rehearsal, and performance spaces' (2018: 63). Performing arts training and practice, in other words, are expected to provide repose from technological encroachment. This argument is repeated by renowned theatre makers associated with psychophysical practices. In his widely popular book on techniques of theatre storytelling, Mike Alfreds goes as far as to equate the use of technology with junk food and accordingly positions theatre storytelling as a form of detox (2013: 33–4). A similar position is repeated by Kathryn Hunter, who in an interview on her collaboration with Peter Brook in *The Valley of Astonishment*, argues that 'there will be a time when people will […] have grown bored with the isolation that technology has brought on to our lives. […] In the future, theatre will be even more popular, because people need it' (Hunter in Loverdou 2014: 3, my translation).

The sharp dichotomy between 'live' theatre and mediated forms of performance and communication has also been cast in terms of a contest between the live actor and the technological device. Kristen Linklater concludes her seminal volume

Freeing the Natural Voice (1976) by noting that 'today's actors, if they are to compete for audiences with the technological powers of film, electronically souped-up music and television, must generate within themselves an electric presence that transcends technological excitement' (Linklater 1976: 210, quoted in Evans 2015: xxix). Nearly 40 years and many iPhone releases later, John Richardson makes a similar point in relation to the viewing habits of teenage audiences:

> the 'criterion' – whether a play is good enough to keep people off their devices – is an important element of theatre experience. The performers on stage are working against the audience members' temptation to check their devices at all times, their power diminished.
>
> (2014: 377)

We see therefore that in these instances the performing arts and attendant forms of training are positioned in an explicitly antagonistic relation to technology, whether this is part of the audience's cultural landscape or their very belongings.

Yet, as it has been widely noted, the performing arts have never been entirely free of technology. As mentioned already, scholars point to the proliferation of intermedial work as well as new practices in recorded media, such as films and video games, which necessitate a renewal of the performer's preparation as well as a reconsideration of the centrality of the human in creative contexts. Camilleri further brings attention to the range of technological advancements that facilitated training. He points out that technology offered the time and material conditions, as well as the 'sophisticated knowledge', that 'led to the articulation of concepts and practices like "psychophysicality" and "bodymind" in the final decades of the [twentieth] century' (Camilleri 2019: 54). Camilleri's study is a very welcome addition to the field and I share his observation that the dominance of the psychophysical, expressed in tropes such as the 'empty space' and the 'neutral body', encouraged a form of myopia that overlooked the role that technology played in constituting psychophysicality. I also share with Camilleri the aim to position technology at the centre of the enquiry and recognise the often unassuming, yet structuring, presence of technological artefacts within psychophysical practices.

However, one aspect that is significantly downplayed in Camilleri's study is that a technologised world might not be an optimal world, or even a good one. As Berry reminds us, the posthuman subject, can also be 'extremely conservative, passive and consumerist' (2014: 11). Similarly, Rosi Braidotti notes that posthuman entanglements of flesh and machine are not always politically progressive, but often serve market imperatives and can cause their 'own forms of inhumanity' (2013: 3). From this point of view, it could be argued then that, although the tendency of performer training practitioners and scholars to overlook or outright antagonise the technological might appear strangely impervious to the evident use of technology in performance, it might also serve as a form of resistance; an effort to escape – however romantically or pointlessly – the stranglehold of, often compulsory, technological advancement. Instead of dismissing these positions as erroneous or short-sighted, the aspiration of this book is to contain them within a larger frame-work that can include differing understandings of technology, as well as various examples of practice.

Methodology and themes

In view of the range of attitudes towards and understandings of technology pre-sented above, the aim of this book is to develop a methodological framework broad and 'nimble' enough to accommodate a range of relationships between performer training and technology. The material is structured along four axes. The first axis includes specific practices and/or aspects of performer training; the second axis consists of specific approaches to, or analytical methods of, philosophy of techno-logy; the third axis involves a set of critical concepts or nodal points that are rel-evant to both performer training and technology; the fourth axis contains specific technological artefacts that may be involved in the conceptualisation and/or devel-opment of performer training practice. These four axes are positioned in the fol-lowing relationship: performer training (axis 1) is examined through the lens of philosophy of technology (axis 2) and in relation to nodal points (axis 3) that cut across both domains as well as with reference to specific technological artefacts (axis 4). By braiding these four threads, the methodology aspires to set in motion a dynamic inter-relationship between the two fields that is inclusive of a range of artefacts as well as different forms of use and also sensitive to the performer's process of instrumentalisation.

In order to ensure diversity, the analysis includes a considerable range of pedago-gies, including canonical and emergent, local and transnational, privately led and institutionally supported. In order to maintain consistency, key approaches are revisited from one chapter to the next through different lenses. Still, many training regimes as well as emerging training practices are not included in the discussion. Moreover, all examples derive from Western settings and mainly anglophone sources, and as a consequence non-Western practices are not examined. However, as noted already, this book does not aim to offer an exhaustive account of per-former training practices that involve technology. Nor does it intend to offer a recipe according to which technology should be used or thought. Rather the selec-tion of the material has been guided by two chief priorities.

One is to capture, articulate and contextualise a set of different relationships between performer training and technology and acknowledge that these relation-ships may manifest but are not exhausted in: conceptual affinities; instances of use; cases of repurposing; and even practices of critique. Crucially, it is imperative to recognise that several, and even contradictory, attitudes may inhere within the same body of work. An example from a practice discussed in further detail in Chapter 3 illustrates this point. As I will discuss, a foundational aspect of the Open Theatre was a desire to resist the pervasive technological rationality that character-ised North American society in the 1960s. In the writings of Joseph Chaikin, the group's founder and artistic director, the television is often singled out as exemplary of the homogenising, alienating and flattening effect of technological rationality. Yet, the television also served the Open Theatre as a primary source for some of their most important innovations in both form and content. Here then, we are faced with an explicitly critical position towards technology, which finds its expression in a theatre language that focuses on the actor's presence *and* draws on the content and form of a dominant technological device. Such a body of work demonstrates a complex stance that cannot be simply termed anti-technological.

The second and interrelated task driving this book is the development of an ability to recognise technology when it is present and accordingly account for it. This might sound self-evident but is in fact quite complicated. To begin with, the practice of performer training is replete with objects. Yet, the history and function of these objects *as* technological artefacts has rarely been acknowledged, let alone subjected to serious consideration. The aim therefore is to examine the way these objects are employed in training, not in terms of the mechanics of specific exercises, but rather with an eye towards the wider attitudes towards materiality, knowledge production and aesthetic formation that underpin and become engendered by their use. What is more, one of the premises of this book is that technology, whether actualised through a particular device or existing as a potentiality, underpins the way human subjects understand and act in the world. From this point of view, it is of little consequence whether an artefact is there or not. Rather, the key question is *which* artefact we choose to focus on. Chapters 2 and 3 discuss instances of performer training that, strictly speaking, featured no technological artefact, yet were considerably informed by technologies that were popular at the time. Chapter 4 examines the use of material, often handheld, objects. Chapters 5 and 6 consider the presence and use of two digital technologies, which for very different reasons and in very different ways, exert considerable influence on performer training practice. Equally, this book is also concerned with processes of instrumentalisation and examines how different understandings of the 'performer's instrument' or the 'performer as instrument' relate to understandings of technology.

The spectrum covered by the five chapters that follow aims to illustrate the many ways in which technology as well as its influence may manifest. It also aims to bypass a methodological problem that can emerge in an analysis that is fixated on the inclusion or exclusion of artefacts. As noted already, the Open Theatre, at least as existing sources attest, never used electric or electronic devices in their training; yet, their innovations on the actor's technique were inspired by a popular medium. An analytical approach guided by the presence of technological artefacts would arguably miss their contribution. Similar problems emerge in relation to a more recent development. As I will discuss in the last chapter, introductory workshops that claim to prepare performers to work with motion capture feature no such technology. Yet, they are explicitly positioned as a means of professionalisation tailored to the needs of the motion capture industry. These examples of practice reveal, then, that what may count as an appropriate case study for examining the relationship between performer training and technology cannot be deduced simply on the basis of the presence or absence of a technological artefact.

Accordingly, the selection of different perspectives on technology employed in each chapter aims to cover the diverse ways in which technology manifests in the performer training sphere. The different approaches selected also foreground the shifts and turns in the normative judgements that underpin different evaluations. As such, the chapters employ as lenses, respectively, a positive (Chapter 2), a critical (Chapter 3) and an empirical (Chapters 4, 5, 6) approach to the study of technology with the view to examine developments in performer training that are contemporaneous with these philosophical approaches. The aim is to test the explanatory power of philosophical approaches to technology against a field that features a range of attitudes towards technology, a plethora of different kinds of instruments, as well as an enduring understanding of the performer as an instrument.

The range of philosophical approaches to technology presented in this book is by no means exhaustive. Many thinkers have been omitted, whereas others, in order to be able to present their work in depth, have been prioritised. Heidegger's work on technology features quite strongly, not only because his thinking proved so seminal in the field but also because, as I will discuss in more detail in Chapter 6, his work on technology has been revisited by contemporary scholars and practitioners of performance. What is more, the pessimistic tone that marks Heidegger's analysis, although it has been dismissed as overly negative and reductive, rings alarmingly true in relation to recent developments in neoliberal economies and the creative industries in particular. As I will argue in Chapter 4, Heidegger's analysis enables us to see the connections between the development of the performer's instrument, which the practice of performer training is expected to serve, and the marketisation of the performer's self that is advocated as a pragmatic response to economic pressures.

Another approach to philosophy of technology favoured in this study is the school of postphenomenology, and especially the work of its founder, Don Ihde. Although postphenomenology is not the only approach within current 'empirical' examinations of technology, its tools and theories are employed in the analysis of contemporary performer training practice because of the emphasis it places on the user's embodied process and context. As such, postphenomenology can both account for the trainee's relationship with her tools but also foreground the contribution that in-depth embodied practices, such as the ones fostered through performer training, can make in our dealings with technology. As we shall see in Chapters 4, 5 and 6 the function of equipment in performer training practice is underpinned by manifold relationships, which can both adhere to but also trouble established agendas. As these chapters will discuss, performer training can helpfully extend the analytical frameworks of postphenomenology in order to account for the processual, intersubjective and expressive character that may underpin relationships between users, technologies and the world.

By highlighting the different ways in which performer training and technology are intertwined in precise moments and contexts, the aspiration of this book is to foreground what might matter, what might be worth our concern, and what might prepare us, to use Heidegger's term, to respond appropriately to our present moment. The aim is not to offer an ethical or pragmatic evaluation for or against the use of technology in performer training. Rather the aim is to kick start an approach towards performer training that acknowledges its deep affinities with technology and thus catalyses the (re)consideration of past, present or future encounters with technology. For this reason, the book concludes with a set of analytical tools that will hopefully prove useful to future examinations. The nexus, i.e. the series of 'and's' that joins the two terms in the book's title, suggests that here is a rich philosophical and praxical territory, the mapping and examination of which may extend beyond the confines of this book. The hope is that the specific themes explored here will spark further examination of the subject.

Outline of the book

Chapter 2 examines the establishment of the enduring trope of the actor's instrument. It positions the emergence of this understanding during the period of intense technologisation that took place in the late eighteenth century. It then traces the establishment of actor training and the actor as instrument trope, during the nineteenth and early twentieth century, in tandem with an emphasis on mastery of both organic and inorganic matter. The nodal point here is the idea of technique and specifically its conceptualisation in terms of efficiency and repeatability, whereas the key artefacts are automata and theatre lights. As I will argue, through a close reading of Dennis Diderot's *The Paradox of Acting*, advancements in the performance of machines and performing automata during the late eighteenth century established a set of standards, which became transposed to the work of human actors. With reference to writings that followed Diderot's text, I will argue that the competencies and attributes of machines continued to influence conceptualisations of acting and actor training practice into the nineteenth and beginning of the twentieth century. The chapter also explores the way the actor's instrument relates to understandings of and developments in the use of theatre instruments, particularly theatre lights. Although theatre lights have been exhaustively examined in relation to scenography and theatre technology (Baugh 2005; Palmer 2013), the chapter concludes with a discussion of the way this key aspect of theatre technology has had a direct application in Konstantin Stanislavsky's actor training pedagogy.

Chapter 3 continues with the consideration of the actor's instrument and examines how this common metaphor was subjected to critique by experimental theatre practitioners in the United States in the 1960s. The chapter demonstrates that this critique resonated with, and in some cases directly drew from, the so-called 'classical' philosophy of technology, which presented a disparaging stance towards technology. The chapter focuses on the way, during the 1960s, the performer-as-instrument trope was challenged, at least within avant-garde circles, and how training became concerned not so much with the production of a controlled performance but with the development of a human subject that transcends instrumentality. The nodal point remains the notion of technique, but is juxtaposed with the notion of techne, a philosophical concept that is etymologically cognate with both technique and technology and has been identified by philosophers of technology as a possible response to technological dominance. The key artefact is the television, which at the time constituted both a prime medium through which an ideology of technological rationality was communicated, as well as a resource for theatrical innovation. This chapter, therefore, will present the first case study of the promise of training to serve as a site of resistance and accordingly it will review the way this promise fared in relation to the work of the Open Theatre.

Chapter 4 considers twentieth-century and contemporary practice through the lens of postphenomenology, a key philosophical approach of the 'empirical turn'. The nodal point here is processes of tool making and using, as these manifest across a range of pedagogies. By expanding the standard postphenomenological understanding of 'tool', the chapter argues that the tools that are made in and through performer training include both material objects, that are out 'there' in the world, as well as organic resources that are intimately tied with the performer's physio- and psycho-logical processes. Complementing the previous two chapters, which analyse the performer-as-instrument trope in relation to approaches to technology, Chapter 4 argues that, because a definitive aim of performer training is to render psychophysical resources into tools of expression, the very process of training is technological at an intimate and embodied level. The chapter concludes with a juxtaposition between the kind of expressive instrumentalisation engendered though performer training practice and the professional instrumentalisation that is expected in the field of the creative industries. On the one hand it demonstrates that the promise of performer training to develop a responsive attitude to the world is cultivated through the trainee's relationship to tools and material objects. On the other hand, it also points out that a form of compulsory entrepreneurialism with which performer training is increasingly expected to align can also be seen as another manifestation of technological rationality.

Chapters 5 and 6 examine contemporary practice in relation to digital culture and technologies. Chapter 5 examines the use of mobile phones in performer training and complements the postphenomenological methodological framework set up in the previous chapter with the concept of *pharmakon*, as developed in the work of Bernard Stiegler. The nodal point here is the question of attention, as a faculty that is both foundational of performer training pedagogy as well as central to current debates on the effects of digital technologies. The aim of the chapter is to explore the 'promise' of performer training to offer a space for negotiating relationships with technology, and specifically the regimes of attention that emerge within information-saturated environments. The chapter will argue that performer training can enable the harnessing of the mobile phone for pedagogical ends, but this necessitates a reconsideration of the operative assumptions of what attention is. In other words, the chapter will argue that the promise of training is premised both on appropriating the technological artefact for pedagogical purposes as well as on rethinking fundamental aspects of performer training practice.

Chapter 6 deals with motion capture and examines a range of training practices that have emerged in response to this technology. It proposes a mapping of these practices in terms of 'training for' and 'training with' with the view to institute a dialectic between different forms of contemporary practice. The former includes instances of practice that aim to prepare performers for professional environments that utilise motion capture technology, creating thus new employment opportunities. The latter uses this technology directly in the curricula of training programmes, with the intention to enhance the delivery of existing pedagogies, creating the possibility of new forms of knowledge production. The nodal point are questions of presence, tradition and autonomy. In addition to drawing on scholarship on motion capture, the chapter also employs the concept of 'gestalt switch', a bi-focal approach that appreciates both the dangers inherent in as well as opportunities offered by technology. Accordingly, the chapter argues that the promise of training can be traced in practices of 'training with', which presuppose that a gestalt switch in the way technology is viewed and practised can be effected through cultivation at a somatic and individual level. It also argues, however, that these experiments, and consequently the fulfilment of the training's promise, are dependent on institutional support, which has its own agendas.

The book concludes by presenting five analytical tools, developed from the examination of the case studies that featured in the preceding chapters. It presents the way these tools were mobilised in this study and also points towards the way these tools might be useful in future studies of performer training and technology, as well as in wider considerations of embodied practices of preparation. The book therefore concludes by projecting forwards to the future of performer training as well as towards emerging approaches that utilise performer training practice beyond the professionalisation of the performer. The book finishes with the invitation, hopefully to be picked up by others, that the preparatory mechanisms of performer training practice may foster the development of an embodied ethos that on the one hand lessens detrimental, or outright destructive, practices and, on the other, fosters affirmative attitudes of co-habitation and co-existence.

Notes

1 Hansen proposes 'worldly sensibility' as a term that denotes 'a domain of sensibility that exceeds what humans can process as "sensations"' (2016: 39). In this respect, it is both autonomous of 'human experience' and offers the 'potential to "renew the sensuous" basis of experience' (Hansen 2016: 33).

2 Attitudes that respectively resist and embrace technology, and theatre technology in particular, are by no means a recent phenomenon. In relation to developments in lighting technology during the eighteenth and nineteenth century, Scott Palmer notes that actors at the Comédie-Française 'consistently delayed the implementation of technological improvements' (2013: 55). By contrast, and as we shall see in Chapter 2, Henry Irving at the Lyceum Theatre in London invested heavily in infrastructure for the safe use of lighting gas and worked with live electrical current in his celebrated role in *The Corsican Brothers* (Palmer 2013).

3 As Galloway and Dunlop (2007) demonstrate in an extensive literature review, the terms cultural and creative industries are contested. They include several sectors and are defined according to a range of key elements. I use the term creative industries throughout this book, following the definition offered by the Department for Digital, Culture,

Media and Sports in 2001, according to which the creative industries include: advertising and marketing; architecture; arts and antiques markets; crafts; design; film, TV, video, radio and photography; IT, software and computer services; museums, galleries and libraries; music, performing and visual arts; and publishing (DCMS 2001). The range of professional and economic activities encompassed in this definition is particularly telling for the employment of performing artists. As I have argued, performing artists are no longer solely employed in the theatre and film sector, but may work in several others, including, advertising, museums and galleries, and increasingly video games. Furthermore, their work may be part of 'industrially produced commercial entertainment', which is the 'classical' definition of the cultural industries (Galloway and Dunlop 2007: 18) but can also take place in low-tech artisan environments.

4 In the case of MOOCs, a degree of remote interaction amongst the educators and the participants is possible during times when the educational platform is 'live'. However, even in these cases, interactions take place across different time zones and may be characterised by a temporal lag between the posting of individual comments.

References

Alfreds, M. 2013. *Then What Happens?* London: Nick Hern Books.

Allain, P., Bennett-Worth, L. S., Camilleri, F. and McLaughlin, J. 2019. 'Editorial', *Theatre Dance and Performance Training Journal*, Special Issue Digital Training, 10 (2), pp. 165–8.

Allain, P. and Harvie, J. 2014. *The Routledge Companion to Theatre and Performance*. London: Routledge.

Bales, M. and Nettl-Fiol, R. (eds) 2008. *The Body Eclectic: Evolving Practices in Dance Training*. Urbana and Chicago: University of Illinois Press.

Bannon, F. and Kirk, C. 2014. 'Deepening Discipline: Digital Reflection and Choreography', *Research in Dance Education*, 15 (3), pp. 289–302. doi.org/10.1080/14647893.201 4.910185.

Barker, C. 1995. 'What Training – for What Theatre?' *New Theatre Quarterly*, Vol. 11 (42), pp. 99–108.

Baugh, C. 2005. *Theatre Performance and Technology: The Development of Scenography in the Twentieth Century*. Hampshire: Palgrave.

Bay-Cheng, S., Kattenbelt, C., Lavender, A. and Nelson, R. (eds) 2010. *Mapping Intermediality in Performance*. Amsterdam: Amsterdam University Press.

Bay-Cheng, S., Parker-Starbuck, J. and Saltz, D. Z. 2015. *Performance and Media*. Ann Arbor: University of Michigan Press.

Bermudez, B., de Lahunta, S., Hoogenboom, M., Ziegler, C., Bevilacqua, F., Fdili Alaoui, S. and Meneses Gutierrez, B. 2011. 'The Double Skin/Double Mind Interactive Installation', *Journal of Artistic Research, Research Catalogue*, www.researchcatalogue.net/view/?weave=1585 [accessed 27 March 2015].

Berry, M. D. 2014. *Critical Theory and the Digital*. New York: Bloomsbury.

Blake, B. 2014. *Theatre and the Digital*. Hampshire: Palgrave Macmillan.

Braidotti, R. 2013. *The Posthuman*. Cambridge: Polity.

Broadhurst, S. and Machon, J. 2011. *Performance and Technology*. Hampshire: Palgrave Macmillan.

Burtt, J. 2014. 'Outline of Talk on Video Feedback', Conference Paper, *TaPRA Performer Training Working Group*, Royal Holloway, University of London.

Camilleri, F. 2019. *Performer Training Reconfigured: Post-Psychophysical Perspectives for the Twenty-First Century*. London: Bloomsbury.

Coe, K. and Goodwin, T. 2019. *Kinship, Spring 2019*. https://kinshipworkshop.info/ [accessed 23 April 2020].

Crary, J. 2013. *24/7 Late Capitalism and the End of Sleep*. London: Verso.

Crews, S. and Papagiannouli, C. 2019. 'InstaStan – FaceBrook – Brecht+: a performer training methodology for the age of the internet', *Theatre Dance and Performance Training Journal*, Special Issue Digital Training, 10 (2), pp. 187–204. doi.org/10.1080/19443927. 2019.1613260.

Crossley, M. 2019 (ed.). *Intermedial Theatre*. London: Springer.

Crossley, M. 2012. 'From LeCompte to Lepage: Student performer engagement with intermedial practice', *International Journal of Performance Arts and Digital Media*, 8 (2), pp. 171–88. doi: 10.1386/padm.8.2.171_1.

DCMS. 2001. *Creative Industries Mapping Document*, DCMS, London.

Delbridge, M. 2015. *Motion Capture in Performance: An Introduction*. Hampshire: Palgrave, Pivot.

Dittman, V. 2008. 'A New York Dancer'. In: *The Body Eclectic: Evolving Practices in Dance Training*, edited by Melanie Bales and Rebecca Nettl-Fiol. Urbana and Chicago: University of Illinois Press, pp. 22–7.

Dixon, S. 2007. *Digital Performance: A History of New Media in Theatre, Dance, Performance Art, and Installation*. Cambridge, MA: MIT.

Dorrestijn, S. 2017. 'The Care of our Hybrid Selves: Ethics in Times of Technical Mediation', *Foundations of Science*, 22 (2), pp. 311–21. doi: 10.1007/s10699-015-9440-0.

Dreyfus, H. 2002. 'Heidegger on gaining a free relation to technology'. In: *Heidegger Reexamined: art, poetry, and technology*, edited by Hubert Dreyfus and Mark Wrathall. London: Routledge, pp. 163–74.

Evans, M. 2019. *Performance, Movement and the Body*. Hampshire: Palgrave Macmillan.

Evans, M. 2015. 'Introduction'. In: *The Actor Training Reader*, edited by Mark Evans. London: Routledge, pp. xix–xxxi.

Evans, M. 2009. *Movement Training for the Modern Actor*. London: Routledge.

Feenberg, A. 1995. 'Subversive Rationalisation: Technology, Power and Democracy'. In: *Technology and the Politics of Knowledge*, edited by Andrew Feenberg and Alastair Hannay. Bloomington: Indiana University Press, pp. 3–22.

Galloway, S. and Dunlop, S. 2007. 'A Critique of Definitions of the Cultural and Creative Industries in Public Policy', *International Journal of Cultural Policy*, 13 (1), pp. 17–31. doi: 10.1080/10286630701201657.

Garoian, R. C. and Gaudelius, M. Y. 2001. 'Cyborg Pedagogy: Performing Resistance in the Digital Age', *Studies in Art Education*, 42 (4), pp. 333–47. doi/abs/10.1080/0039354 1.2001.11651708.

Gere, C. 2008. *Digital Culture* (2nd edition). London: Reaktion Books.

Gorman, T., Syrja, T. and Kanninen M. 2019. 'There is a world everywhere: rehearsing and training through immersive telepresence', *Theatre Dance and Performance Training Journal*, Special Issue Digital Training, 10 (2), pp. 208–26. doi.org/10.1080/19443927.2019.161049.

Gunkel, J. D. and Taylor, A. P. 2014. *Heidegger and the Media*. Cambridge: Polity.

Hansen, B. N. M. 2016. 'Topology of Sensibility'. In: *Ubiquitous Computing, Complexity and Culture*, edited by Ulrik Ekman, Jay David Bolter, Lily Diaz-Kommonen, Morten Søndergaard and Maria Engberg (eds). New York: Routledge, pp. 33–47.

Hansen, B. N. M. 2015. *Feed-Forward: On the Future of Twenty-First-Century Media*. Chicago: The University of Chicago Press.

Havens, H. 2010. 'The Intermedial Performer Prepares'. In: *Mapping Intermediality in Performance*, edited by Sarah Bay-Cheng, Chiel Kattenbelt, Andy Lavender and Robin Nelson. Amsterdam: Amsterdam University Press, pp. 230–6.

Hayles, K. 2012. *How We Think: Digital Media and Contemporary Technogenesis*. Chicago: University of Chicago Press.

Hayles, K. 1999. *How We Became Posthuman*. Chicago: University of Chicago Press.

Heidegger, M. 1977. 'The Question Concerning Technology'. In: *The Question Concerning Technology and Other Essays*, translated by William Lovitt. New York: Harper, pp. 3–35.

Ihde, D. 2012. *Experimental Phenomenology: Multistabilities* (2nd edition). Albany: SUNY Press.

Ihde, D. 2010. *Heidegger's Technologies: Postphenomenological perspectives*. New York: Fordham University Press.

Ihde, D. 2009. *Postphenomenology and Technoscience: The Peking Lectures*, Albany: State University of New York.

Ihde, D. 1993. *Philosophy of Technology: An introduction*. New York: Paragon House.

Keefe, J. and Murray, S. (eds) 2005. *Physical Theatres: A Critical Reader*. London: Routledge.

Klich, R. 2012. 'The "unfinished" subject: Pedagogy and performance in the company of copies, robots, mutants and cyborgs', *International Journal of Performance Arts and Digital Media*, 8 (2), 155–70. doi: 10.1386/padm.8.2.155_1.

Kozel, S. 2007. *Closer: Performance, Technologies, Phenomenology*. Cambridge, MA: MIT.

Lavender, A. 2016. *Performance in the Twenty-First Century: Theatres of Engagement*, London: Routledge.

Lemmens, P. 2017. 'Thinking through Media: Stieglerian remarks on a possible postphenomenology of media'. In: *Postphenomenology and Media: Essays on Human-Media-World Relations*, edited by Yoni Van Den Eede, Stacey O'Neal Irwin and Galit Wellner. Lanham: Lexington, pp. 185–206.

Loverdou, M. 2014. Interview with Kathryn Hunter, *To Vima*, 24 April 2014 (translation mine).

Marcuse, H. 1969. *An Essay on Liberation*. Boston: Beacon Press.

Margolies, E. 2016. *Props*. London: Palgrave Macmillan International Higher Education.

Margolis, E. and Renaud, T. L. (eds) 2010. *The Politics of American Actor Training*. New York, London: Routledge.

Matthews, J. 2011. *Training for Performance*. London: Methuen Drama.

Mitcham, C. and Briggle, A. 2012. 'Theorizing Technology'. In: *The Good Life in a Technological Age*, edited by Philip Brey, Adam Briggle and Edward Spence. New York: Routledge, pp. 35–51.

Monten, J. 2008. 'Something Old, Something New, Something Borrowed'. In: *The Body Eclectic: Evolving Practices in Dance Training*, edited by Melanie Bales and Rebecca Nettl-Fiol. Urbana and Chicago: University of Illinois Press, pp. 52–67.

Murray, S. 2015. 'Keywords in performer training', *Theatre, Dance and Performance Training*, Vol. 6 (1), pp. 46–58.

Nayar, K. P. 2014. *Posthumanism*. Cambridge: Polity Press.

Nelson, R. 2014. *The Intermedial Performer Prepares*, Call for Interest, Central School of Speech and Drama, posted online www.intermediality.org/content/robin-nelson-intermedial-performer-prepares [accessed 26 March 2015].

O'Donnell, A. 2016. 'Experimental Philosophy and Experimental Pedagogy'. In: *Arts, Pedagogy and Cultural Resistance: New Materialisms*, edited by Anna Hickey-Moody and Tara Page, London and New York: Rowman and Littlefield, pp. 21–40.

Oliver, M. 2012. 'Me-but-not-me: Teaching the digital double', *International Journal of Performance Arts and Digital Media*, 8 (2), pp. 189–204. doi: 10.1386/padm.8.2.189_1.

Palmer, S. 2013. *Light*. Hampshire: Palgrave Macmillan.

Peisley, A. 2016. 'Masks for leadership development in a business school', *Theatre Dance and Performance Training Blog*, http://theatredanceperformancetraining.org/2016/05/masks-for-leadership-development-in-a-business-school/ [accessed 19 November 2019].

Pitches, J. 2019. 'Simultaneity and asynchronicity in performer training: a case study of Massive Open Online Courses as training tools'. In: *Time and Performer Training*, edited by Mark Evans, Konstantinos Thomaidis and Libby Worth. London: Routledge, pp. 181–93.

Pitches, J. 2014. *From Vertical to Horizontal: The Future of Russian Actor Training in a Digital Age*, Conference paper, Russian Theatre Research Network UK.

Pitches, J. 2006. *Science and the Stanislavsky Tradition of Acting*. Oxon and New York: Routledge.

Reilly, K. (ed.) 2013. *Theatre, Performance and Analogue Technology: Historical Interfaces and Intermedialities*. Hampshire: Palgrave.

Richardson, J. 2014. 'Powerful Devices: how teens' smartphones disrupt power in the theatre, classroom and beyond', *Learning, Media and Technology*, 39 (3), pp. 368–85. doi. org/10.1080/17439884.2013.867867.

Scott, J. and Barton, B. 2019. 'The Performer in Intermedial Theatre'. In: *Intermedial Theatre*, edited by Mark Crossley. London: Springer.

Spatz, B. 2015. *What a Body Can Do*. Oxon: Routledge.

Stiegler, B. 2010a. *For a New Critique of Political Economy*, translated by Daniel Ross. Cambridge: Polity.

Stiegler, B. 2010b. *Taking Care of Youth and the Generations*, translated by Stephen Barker. Stanford: Stanford University Press.

Thomson, I. 2019. 'Technology, ontotheology, education', In: *Heidegger on Technology*, edited by Aaron James Wendland, Christopher Merwin and Charles Hadjioannou. London: Routledge, pp. 174–93.

Wake, C. 2018. 'Two decades of digital pedagogies in the performing arts: a comparative survey of theatre, performance, and dance', *International Journal of Performance Arts and Digital Media*, 14 (1), 52–69. doi: 10.1080/14794713.2018.1464097.

Watson, I. 2015. 'Introduction to Part II: The Purpose of Actor Training'. In: *The Actor Training Reader*, edited by Mark Evans. London: Routledge, pp. 9–19.

Wendland, J., Merwin, C. and Hadjioannou, C. (eds) 2019. *Heidegger on Technology*. London: Routledge.

Whatley, S. 2015. 'Motion Capture and the Dancer'. In: *Attending to Movement*, edited by Sarah Whatley, Natalie Garrett Brown and Kirsty Alexander. Axminster: Triarchy Press, pp. 193–204.

Whyman, R. 2008. *The Stanislavsky System of Acting: Legacy and Influence in Modern Performance*. Cambridge: Cambridge University Press.

Wrathall, M. 2019. 'The task of thinking in a technological age'. In: *Heidegger on Technology*, edited by Aaron James Wendland, Christopher Merwin, and Christos Hadjioannou. London: Routledge, pp. 13–38.

Zanotti, M. 2014. App for Screen Dance, Conference Paper, *TaPRA Performer Training Working Group*, Royal Holloway, University of London.

Zarrilli, P. 2002. *Acting (re)considered: A Theoretical and Practical Guide* (2nd edition). London and New York: Routledge.

Zarrilli, P., Daboo, J. and Loukes, R. 2013. *Acting: Psychophysical Phenomenon and Process*. Hampshire: Palgrave Macmillan.

Zulinska, J. (ed.) 2002. *The Cyborg Experiments: The Extensions of the Body in the Media Age*. London, New York: Continuum.

2

BETWEEN TECHNIQUE AND TECHNOLOGY

The actor's instrument and the actor's paradox

Introduction

This chapter and the next aim to advance the foundational argument of this book: that performer training may be understood as a technological activity in and of itself regardless of whether a technological device is in use or not. Both chapters engage with questions of technique and the close relationship, both etymologically and semantically, between technique and technology. Specifically, both chapters deal with the most common trope in acting theory and practice: that the actor is an instrument of expression. Unlike other arts, where there is a clear ontological demarcation between artists and materials, in acting – the argument goes – the artist and the material of her art are one and the same. As Coquelin pithily put it: 'one part of him [sic] is the performer, the instrumentalist; another, the instrument to be played on' (Coquelin et al. 1932: 31). Accordingly, Nathan Stucky and Jessica Tomell-Presto note that, in relation to performer training, 'the first approach within the representative literature is a recurring metaphor that describes how the actor should view the training of the body; the body is compared to an instrument' (2004: 110). A closer look at the primary sources Stucky and Tomell-Presto cite further reveals that trainers often have in mind not just the body, but a wider notion of expressivity or indeed the actor's entire self. For example, in the writings of Konstantin Stanislavsky, the actor's expressivity is positioned as a musical instrument, which needs to be 'tuned' and kept in 'good condition' (2008a: 131). In other examples, the instrument according to which the actor is understood is a machine (2008a: 580).

Although an understanding of the actor as an instrument appears to be both common and common-sense, it is also, as both chapters aim to show, polyvalent as well as ideologically and historically contingent. This chapter examines the establishment of the actor's instrument, as an idea as well as a practice, from the eighteenth until the early twentieth century, and the concomitant development of actor training as a space devoted to the refinement of such an instrument. It also investigates the way the *actor's* instrument developed in relation to *theatre* instruments; that is, materials and devices that were created and/or used for the stage. Specifically, this chapter will focus on theatre lights, a key element of theatrical experience that has undergone significant development from the late eighteenth century and has a seminal impact on the aesthetics and reception of the theatrical event.[1]

The chapter begins with *The Paradox of Acting*, an eighteenth-century essay by French philosopher Dennis Diderot (1713–84), translated and published in English in 1883. It then engages with two key contexts of late-nineteenth/early-twentieth-century theatrical practice: an Anglophone context and a Russian context. For the Anglophone tradition, I will draw on the writings of actor and theatre manager Henry Irving (1838–1905), including his preface to the English translation of Diderot's text in 1883 (the translation I will be using throughout the chapter); the essay 'The Actor and the Über-Marionette' (1908) by Edward Gordon Craig (1872–1966), as well as his book *Henry Irving* (1930); and *The Art of the Actor* (1932), an essay by French actor Constant Coquelin (1841–1909), which, in its English translation, included an introduction by Elsie Fogerty (1865–1945) and a reprinted interview by Dame Madge Kendal (1848–1935).[2] For the Russian context I will concentrate on the work of Konstantin Stanislavsky (1863–1938), and will draw on his autobiographical account *My Life in Art* (2008b) as well as his seminal *An Actor's Work* (2008a), a fictional diary of a young student actor called Kostya who participates in an actor training course led by the actor and master Tortsov.

Diderot's text has been singled out as a starting point not only because of its significant impact on acting discourse from the eighteenth century onwards, but because, as I will argue, the text also provides a unique meeting point between technique and technology. On the one hand, and as it has been acknowledged, the *Paradox* is the first modern text to suggest that acting, like any other craft, needs to be controlled and mastered by technique. On the other hand, the text emerged in a period of intense technologisation, to which Diderot, especially in his role as chief editor of the *Encyclopaedia*, made a great intellectual contribution. Although this aspect of Diderot's work is well-known, the connections between the actor's technical accomplishment, for which Diderot is arguing in the *Paradox*, and the technologisation of other crafts and industries during the eighteenth century have not been adequately examined. The first task of this chapter then is to demonstrate that an understanding of the actor's work, as presented in the *Paradox*, evolved in tandem with developments in, and an appreciation of, the performance of machines.

The second task of this chapter is to explore the relationship between theatre technology and acting technique. As mentioned in the Introduction, training/ acting and technology are often positioned in an antagonistic relationship. Christopher Baugh, for example, observes that 'theatre histories have frequently presented the actor as being continually challenged and possibly threatened by technology and its associated spectacle' (2005: 6). Accordingly, performer training scholarship prioritises the work of the performer and is often prone to overlook the influence of technology on training, especially in relation to regimes that predate digital technologies. As a result, until the recent interest in intermedial and digital performance, the study of technology within theatre studies has been limited to 'theatre technology' and dealt with developments in theatre architecture, design and lighting. Developments in acting, on the other hand, tend to be placed under the banner of technique. Specifically in relation to the eighteenth century, Pannill Camp draws a distinction between:

> Certain practices connected to the body [that can be recognised] as technological – say David Garrick's wire-actuated 'fright wig' for the role of Hamlet, which the actor used to make his hair stand on end when the Danish prince saw his father's ghost […] and performance 'techniques', such as the musical way actors spoke the twelve-syllable lines of Alexandrine verse common to French tragedies […].
>
> (2017: 181–2)

Camp argues that such distinction may allow us to 'draw a bright line between these uses of tools and performance "techniques"' (2017: 182). Whilst such a line may be useful, it positions in advance, and rather prematurely, the actor's technique in a realm separate from technology. Yet, as we shall see, the two are closely interlinked. The first thing worth noting is that both Diderot, as well as the nineteenth- and twentieth-century innovators singled out here, dealt with acting technique and theatre technology: Diderot wrote a treatise on acting, but also oversaw an extended entry on theatre buildings and machinery in the *Encyclopaedia*; Henry Irving, who prefaced the English translation of the *Paradox*, undertook important innovations in theatre lighting at the Lyceum Theatre and was the most celebrated actor of his generation; Gordon Craig, who worked with Irving and closely read the *Paradox*, advanced new conceptions for both stage design, lights and acting; Stanislavsky, who collaborated with Craig and was familiar both with the *Paradox* and with Irving's work, developed one of the most enduring and comprehensive systems of acting but also got his hands dirty with all aspects of theatre production, including lights.

   Second, as is well established in studies of theatre history, from the eighteenth century onwards, advancements in technology were readily adopted in theatre buildings, whilst the stage often served as a means to experiment with and popularise the latest technologies. Indeed, 'new' technologies had a direct impact on all aspects of the theatrical enterprise and often drove its constituent parts. For example, as Sophie Nield notes, the stage machinery available to nineteenth-century theatre led to the call that 'an author should so construct his plot, that flats and set scenes might alternate the one the other' (Mayhew 1840: 250 cited in Nield 2017: 207). Similarly, Stanislavsky, after he captures, through an accidental lighting state, the atmosphere of the symbolist play *Hannele* (staged in 1896), proceeds in the following manner:

Eureka! I had found it! All I had to do was find where the light had come from [...]. I called for the lighting man and wrote everything down with him: the strength of light, the lamp, I used a special mark to indicate where the ray of light fell. I now had to find the acting to match the lighting effect. That was not difficult since it dictated all the rest.

(2008b: 140)

The work of the aforementioned practitioners demonstrates therefore that the 'bright line' evoked by Camp is a lot dimmer, at least during late nineteenth- and early twentieth-century performance practice, both in ideological and practical terms. As a result, even if such a line may serve heuristic purposes, it can also lead to a kind of myopia: preventing analysis from identifying the material substrate that underpins the development of the actor's technique as well as the ways in which technological influences can extend well beyond stage design and props. Worthy of note here is that during the nineteenth century, not only was technology an important part of theatrical experimentation and spectacle, which could 'dictate', as Stanislavsky puts it, other aspects of the theatrical act. As Christopher Baugh argues, the theatre itself became understood as a '*machine*, as a physical construct that theatrically locates and enables the public art of performance' (2005: 45, emphasis original). Baugh argues that such understanding emerges with the wave of modernism, which advocated that the materiality of the stage should be approached in and of itself as a locus of meaning-making rather than as a means for the creation of illusion.

Despite the evident break that distinguished the so-called 'new movement of the theatre' from the preceding naturalism, there is a remarkable continuity in terms of the relationship between acting technique and theatre technology. The continuity is this: from Diderot's *Paradox* until the early twentieth century, both material (stage properties and mechanisms) and organic resources (the actors' body and mind) are understood as instruments to be mastered and perfected. However – and this is the interesting bit – there is a significant discrepancy in the way inorganic and organic matter were respectively understood. On the one hand, from the eighteenth century onwards, material reality will be regarded as fully malleable, controllable and predictable – indeed, as I will demonstrate, the *Encyclopaedia* will present this vision over 20 years in both written and pictorial mode. On the other hand, the actor's psychophysiology is considered to be resistant, volatile and unreliable and thus threatens, or at least is inconsistent with, spectacles and practices of control. Unless, of course, it is trained. The overall contention of this chapter then is that training is technological because it emerges as a response to the conviction that organic and inorganic materialities can and should be mastered through technique. This chapter will demonstrate the way this conviction emerges in the eighteenth century in response to the increasing capacities and enhanced performance of machines, including performing automata, and then operates as an underpinning principle that guides the systematisation of actor training practice during the late nineteenth and early twentieth century. As I will argue, the tension between controllable inorganic matter and volatile organic one emerges in the *Paradox*; is operative in both the acting and stage management practices of Henry Irving; underpins Fogerty's rationale for the institution of a drama school in the UK; explicitly appears in Craig's provocation that actors should be substituted by an Übermarionette; and is evident in one of Stanislavsky's most well-known concepts.

Of note here is the contextual and very influential analysis by Joseph Roach (2007 [1984]) which examines historical understandings of the actor's work in the eighteenth, nineteenth and twentieth centuries in relation to contemporaneous scientific theories. Roach identifies the *Paradox* as a pivotal text in acting discourse, both because of its ongoing influence as well as the way it combined mechanistic with vitalist understandings of the body. By following the emergence and establishment in science of a mechanistic and a vitalist model of the body respectively, Roach traces these two currents in Diderot's work and then into nineteenth- and twentieth-century theatre history and practice. 'At the root the question came down to this', explains Roach: 'Is the actor's bodily instrument to be interpreted as a spontaneously vital organism whose innate powers of feeling must somehow naturally predominate? Or is it best understood as a biological machine [...]?' (2007: 161).

Roach convincingly demonstrates that this question was indeed an important trope in exegeses of biological processes in general and the art of acting in particular. However, Roach's emphasis on science as an ideological and textual substrate of acting theory and practice occludes the important role of technology. A conceptualisation of the body and/or the actor as a machine can emerge only when machines are actually made and enter the public sphere, so that they can be observed, described, and, as I will discuss, admired. Indeed, Roach does refer to machines, performing automata especially, but he does not bestow them with the explanatory power he assigns to scientific theory. Roach's analysis, in other words, prioritises science over technology. As I explained in the Introduction, such preference has been constitutive of philosophical enquiry but has been challenged by the emergence of philosophy of technology. In line with the overall aim of this book, my intention in this chapter is to advance technology as a key frame of reference and demonstrate the remarkable connections between (acting) technique and (theatre) technology that appear as a result.

Such an approach may be particularly helpful in two respects. First, an examination of the way technology informed the conceptualisation of acting can sensitize us to the ways in which technology may infiltrate and shape immaterial practices. This can serve as a first step towards correcting a tendency to separate technique from materiality and in the process to miss the presence of technological artefacts altogether. As I will discuss in further detail, fundamental notions and exercises in Stanislavsky's work on attention and concentration, itself a foundational part of the System, are delivered through an impressive technological feat of theatrical lights. Roach discusses this aspect of Stanislavsky's work in relation to scientific theories of the time (2007: 208) and does not mention the operation of lights at all. More recent analyses trace Stanislavsky's understanding of attention to a nineteenth-century book on yoga (Carnicke 2008; White 2014). However, at the very introduction of the section in question, we are informed that 'electrical cables with light bulbs were placed at various points on the set walls' (Stanislavsky 2008a: 90). These are promptly put to use and during the description of the exercises, over 17 pages, theatrical lights are switched on and off over a hundred times. Yet, lights are entirely absent in most analyses. As I will argue, this instance of Stanislavsky's work not only exemplifies the close dialogue between acting technique and theatre technology. More fundamentally, it demonstrates that technology has a structuring effect by offering a material reality and a standard of performance against which the actor's work becomes understood and measured.

Second, once we move past the tendency to see technology as a by-product of science, and/or to fail to see technology at all, we gain a better understanding of the tension that underpins the notion of technique throughout the twentieth century. In his introduction to 13 essays of canonical performer trainers grouped under the heading 'Technique' in the *Routledge Actor Training Reader*, Jonathan Pitches notes that whilst 'good technique' is understood as an important element of acting, 'the term is nevertheless haunted by a concern that proficient technicality is only the first step towards the goal' (2015: 55). Pitches then toys with a possible way of classifying the 13 essays that captures the ambivalence with which technique is often met: 'training organics' and 'training mechanics' (2015: 61). The former, according to Pitches, exemplifies an approach that favours ongoing cultivation, which may need to become individualised and may carry ecological undertones. 'Training mechanics', on the other hand, illustrates an approach that focuses on efficacy and the production of predetermined results. Similarly, in his earlier study *Science and the Stanislavsky Tradition of Acting* (2006), Pitches examines Russian lineages of actor training through two competing scientific paradigms: the Newtonian one, which views nature as a machine controlled by laws; and the Romantic one, which approaches nature as an organic process.

Whilst I am not disputing the influence of scientific theories, as advocated by Pitches and Roach respectively, a re-examination of the work of canonical practitioners intends to tell a different story. Instead of attributing the tension that underpins notions of technique, as well as the idea of the actor as instrument, to different scientific paradigms, my intention is to locate this tension in the very process of industrialisation. The ultimate aim of this chapter is to demonstrate that the actor's instrument emerges and consolidates within a theatrical as well as social environment that increasingly operates through machines and as a machine: it is both heavily mechanised and tightly controlled. The key argument of this chapter then is that the emergence of a perceived need for actor training, as well as its consolidation in discrete regimes, such as Stanislavsky's System, was part and parcel of a wider approach towards material reality – whether this was the actor's flesh or theatre props and technologies – that was geared towards mastery and control. In other words, my contention is that the very notion of technique becomes mapped on the ability of the machine. The chapter also contends, however, that once the training of the actor's instrument is set in motion, the impossibility of the actor ever becoming a machine is also revealed: *pace* Diderot, the chapter argues that the actor's paradox lies precisely in the expectation that technique, acquired through training, will render the actor as good as a machine and yet different from it.

The material in this chapter is organised in three parts: the first part examines *The Paradox of Acting* in relation to eighteenth-century technology and Diderot's role as chief editor of the *Encyclopaedia*. It will also review the notion of automation underlining the *Paradox* in relation to eighteenth-century automata. The second part will trace how the trope of the actor's instrument reappears and/or evolves in nineteenth- and early twentieth-century theatre and actor training practice. The third part presents a case study, where theatre technology and acting pedagogy are combined towards a vocabulary and a method aimed to train a key aspect of the actor's instrument. In a remarkable synthesis between organic and technological resources, Stanislavsky employs theatre lights to train the actor's concentration and develops two hallmarks of his System: the circles of attention and the state of public solitude. Through a close reading of the exercises described in *An Actor's Work*, the third section of the chapter concludes with demonstrating that the affinities between technique and technology operate simultaneously at a discursive and practical level: in Stanislavsky's fictive actor training course, the actor's instrument both develops through technology and substantiates the actor's paradox.

Part I

Diderot's change of mind and the Encyclopaedia

The *Paradox of Acting* appeared first in 1770 but Diderot worked on and expanded this earlier version over 14 years, until his death in 1784. Although the text circulated during Diderot's life, it was published posthumously in 1830. Apart from the philosophical, social and technological developments that were taking place at the time, the text was written during a period of intense theatre activity fuelled by a recognition of the theatre as a civic institution. This was concomitant with an increase in the number of theatre buildings and theatre companies in Europe and the colonies, as well as an increase in treatises on acting in either English or French (Payne 2017). Indeed, the *Paradox* is presented as a response to an earlier essay, which argued about the importance of emotions in acting, and is framed as a dialogue between two interlocutors.[3] The First, who is given considerably more 'air time', argues that actors should not feel the emotions of the character they are playing. Rather than emotional engagement with the role, the effect of their acting should be the product of a measured and well-prepared performance. The Second, on the other hand, claims – arguably quite anaemically – that acting derives from 'sensibility' and the actor's ability to experience the character's emotions.

It bears noting that the ideas put forward in the *Paradox* cannot be seen as representative of Diderot's entire *oeuvre*. As several scholars note (Goodden 2011; Roach 2007: 117), when it comes to major philosophical questions of his day, such as the relation between body and mind, a materialist versus a vitalist understanding of animate organisms and an appreciation of craft, Diderot did not settle for one position over another. Similarly, it can be observed that the *Paradox* sits rather obliquely with Diderot's theatre criticism and the two plays he wrote earlier in his career. In an article that examines Diderot's overall contribution to theatre theory, Graham Ley detects in the *Paradox* an 'air of detachment which proves to be long past any aspirations to direct intervention in the theatre' (1995: 342). Nonetheless, the *Paradox* will prove crucial in establishing the need for an acting technique and in this sense, according to Ley, it is 'profoundly modern' (1995: 352).

The text presents two key tenets: first, that the actor should not play herself, but initially conceive and then recreate an ideal model of the role. Drawing on his ongoing exchanges with the plastic arts, Diderot explained acting in terms of the dominant paradigm of production in painting and sculpture. According to this, the artist first envisions an ideal model and then painstakingly achieves its material expression in his chosen medium.[4] Diderot, in other words, stipulates a progression from mental conception to material execution, which in the case of theatre takes place during the rehearsal period, and becomes finally communicated to an audience in performance. As such, the actor, during performance, should not fall prey to spontaneous or emotional outbursts but calmly oversee the reconstruction of this preconceived ideal model by 'the conforming of action, diction, face, voice, movement, and gesture, to an ideal type' (Diderot 1883: 22). Not only it is unthinkable for the First that the actor's emotional engagement during the performance may in turn shape, refine or finetune this ideal model, but he is adamant that any aberration from it would result in a significantly inferior product.

In this respect, the text's central argument appears in agreement with a tendency common in the eighteenth century to place sensibility below reason. It bears noting, however, that unlike some of his contemporaries, Diderot considered sensibility a defining element of human nature and acknowledged in sensibility both a moral and a creative dimension (Roach 2007: 121–2). Similarly, Marvin Carlson notes that in his earlier writings Diderot advocated that artists are characterised by an ability to 'feel deeply' (Diderot *Oeuvres* 3: 143 quoted in Carlson 1993: 161). Indeed, in the *Paradox*, the First speaker – Diderot's mouthpiece – refers to his own experience of emotional outbursts in public, also typical of Diderot himself (Diderot 1883: 40–1). The First, however, uses these examples to describe a 'man reduced at one moment to flat stupidity by sensibility, and the next rising to sublimity by the self-possession following the stifling of his sensibility' (Diderot 1883: 42).[5] In its repudiation of sensibility, the *Paradox* marks, therefore, a significant shift in Diderot's thinking.

Diderot's change of mind has been attributed to two key factors. The first was Diderot's contact with British actor David Garrick (1717–79), whose ability to exhibit a rapid succession of emotions at will became a sensation in the Parisian salons during Garrick's visit in Paris in 1764–5 (Roach 2007: 122; Carlson 1993: 161). Indeed, the *Paradox* refers to Garrick's prowess as an example of the importance of technique over sensibility (Diderot 1883: 38). The second factor was Diderot's close exchanges with artisans and artists, primarily as part of his overall endeavour with the *Encyclopaedia*. The *Encyclopédie, ou dictionnaire raisonné des sciences, des arts et des métiers* (from now on

Encyclopaedia) consisted of 17 volumes of articles and 11 volumes of illustrations that appeared over a period of 20 years (1751–72) and 'exhaustively described in words and pictures how practical things get done and proposed ways to improve them' (Sennett 2008: 90).[6]

In his effort to develop and commission material for the *Encyclopaedia*, Diderot became immersed in the crafts practised by his contemporaries, by visiting workshops, consulting with craftsmen, observing and even operating trade tools and machinery (Goodden 2011: 59; Sennett 2008: 96). According to Roach these experiences 'prompted him to reassess the role of technique in the creative process' (2007: 122) and 'challenged him repeatedly to reflect on the role of technical and mechanical processes in shaping creative energies to attain premeditated effects' (2007: 125). According to Diderot's entry in the *Encyclopaedia*, *métier*, i.e. craft, 'designates any profession that requires the use of labour, and which is limited to a certain number of mechanical operations that contribute to the same product, and which the worker repeated endlessly' (Goodden 2011: 60). Goodden further explains that the word '*mécanique*' (mechanical) denotes one of the following: 'either that a procedure required little conscious input or attention from the human worker, or that it was automated, automatic' (2011: 60). As I will argue, the *Paradox* can be seen as an extension of the *Encyclopaedia* in that it deals with acting as another version of the 'mechanical arts' and has clear echoes of automation.

To begin with, it would be instructive to consider a recurring motif that underlies the First's argument that actors should not feel the emotions they portray. In support of his thesis, the First gives examples where the actors in question are apparently able to hold entire conversations, either with their acting partners or with audience members (that were sitting on the stage or in the auditorium), whilst performing a role in front of an audience (Diderot 1883: 32–5, 37, 98).[7] In the first example, two actors – husband and wife in real life – are whispering insults to one another, whilst playing a passionate scene between two lovers during a performance that proved exceptionally successful with audiences (Diderot 1883: 32–4). In another, an actress is going through a tragic moment which, according to the First, reduced audiences to tears, whilst cajoling and making arrangements to meet her lover, who is seated on the stage (Diderot 1883: 37). An additional example mentions an actor who corrects a misplaced object on stage, whilst going through a scene (Diderot 1883: 47–8). In all these instances, the First emphasises the incongruity between the scene the actors are playing and the conversation they are holding on the side, and thus makes a case about the lack of the actor's emotional involvement in dramatically charged moments. These examples also demonstrate, however, an absence of *any* kind of involvement. They do not simply show that the actor does not feel the role's emotions; rather they represent acting as a purely mechanical task, in the sense of the word as it appeared in the *Encyclopaedia*: it is automated to such an extent that requires 'little conscious effort' and thus the actor can successfully accomplish it whilst doing something else.[8]

Important similarities can also be traced between the content of the *Paradox* and the plates of the *Encyclopaedia*. Amounting to 2,569 engravings, the plates constituted a significant element of the whole project and, as Stephen Werner (1993) notes, a major aspect of Diderot's editorship, who was in charge of commissioning and over-seeing their realisation. They not only served as complements to the written entries; they were fundamental to the ideological project the *Encyclopaedia* was committed to. Two key points of convergence between the plates and the *Paradox* are of interest here: one is the iconographic depiction of craftsmen in the *Encyclopaedia* and the written description of the actors' work in the *Paradox*; the other is the depiction of theatre machinery in the *Encyclopaedia* and the overall conception of the actor's per-formance advanced in the *Paradox*.

William Sewell compares the plates in the *Encyclopaedia* to depictions of labour and craft respectively in the sixteenth, seventeenth as well as nineteenth centuries. According to Sewell, there are four aspects of the plates in the *Encyclopaedia* that mark a radical departure from both preceding and succeeding depictions of craft (1986: 268–70). First, in the *Encyclopaedia* an image of human activity occupies the top one-third of the plate, whereas the other two-thirds are dedicated to the depic-tion of the machines and tools used in any one particular production process. The machines are thus literally foregrounded, whereas artisans and their labour recede in the upper top of the picture. Second, the spaces where the activity is held are depicted as clean, ordered and spacious and, as such, bear little resemblance to the actual workshops of the time. Third, the plates do not give a sense of the whole but rather show individual aspects of the process as independent parts. Thus, the plates communicate a 'fracturing of the flow of production' (Sewell 1986: 270). Fourth, the craftsmen are depicted in a generic way. Human faces are often obscured or unintelligible and, even when they are visible, lack specific characteristics and expressions; as a result, the position and expressionless faces of the craftsmen fore-close any communication between them.

Sewell interprets these characteristics in relation to the overall aim of the *Ency-clopaedia*. This was not only to celebrate the crafts as a fundamental part of human flourishing, but also to advance improvements in their practice by making public the techniques involved in the production process and by explaining them through science.[9] The aim of the plates, then, as well as the aim of the *Encyclopaedia* as a whole, was to open up the crafts to the gaze of the enlightened scholar. Indeed, as its subtitle suggests, the *Encyclopaedia* was dedicated to a 'society of men of letters'. In other words, and as Cynthia Koepp notes, the *Encyclopaedia* was not intended for the craftsmen it depicted (1986: 256). If anything, its price was prohibitive. The *Encyclopaedia* rather targeted the enlightened bourgeoisie. The plates of the *Encyclo-paedia* then convey a world of labour that, according to Sewell, is 'cold, analytical and deadly serious' (1986: 277), whereas, the human workers are depicted as 'docile automatons [sic] who carry out their scientifically determined tasks with the effi-ciency – and the joylessness – of machines' (1986: 277).[10]

It could be argued that the written descriptions in the *Paradox* convey a compar-able image, albeit on the theatre stage. Similarly to the bare and sterile environ-ments depicted in the plates of the *Encyclopaedia*, the *Paradox* evokes nothing of the lively conditions found in Parisian theatre auditoria and the many people that contributed to the realisation of the scenic event, such as 'stagehands, dressers, […] ticket takers, dancers, musicians, prompters, […] and even candle snuffers' (Payne 2017: 156).[11] Moreover, the discussion of the actor's process often denotes a lack of social interaction: the actor, following the poet's text, develops the inner model alone, and when she enacts it on stage, her focus is on this expression (when she is not having off-script conversations!). If we consider that the central theme of the *Paradox* is the way the actor may evoke emotions in the spectator, it is quite striking that the relation between the actor and her audience is not acknowledged. In fact, the actor's process of enacting the role and the audience's process of experiencing the emotions produced by such enactment are depicted as two parallel events, which, although they have a cause and effect relationship, do not intersect in any way. No reference, for example, is made to the ways an actor may adjust her per-formance depending on the audience's reaction, or indeed to the actor's ability to communicate and be co-present with the spectators. It is telling in this respect that the examples of direct interaction between actor and audience described in the *Paradox* refer to instances of interruption. The First gives the examples of two different actors, who in the middle of their respective tragic scene, 'come out' of the role, ask the audience to be quiet and then continue without a hitch (Diderot 1883: 46–7). This is presented by the First as another example of the benefits of being able to act without sensibility.

What I wish to highlight then, is that by refuting sensibility, it would seem that the First not only wants to put an end to the actor's emotional involvement, he also wants to stop the reciprocity of feeling between actors and audience. Indeed, Ley observes that, during the eighteenth-century, '*sensibilité*' was also a theatrical idiom denoting 'that communion of feeling, generated between performer and audience' (1995: 439). As Ley notes, the acting process described in the *Paradox* introduces a rift into the theatrical experience between actors that observe and spectators that feel, 'thus separating practitioner from audience and practice from reception' (1995: 350). After a successful performance, argues the First, 'the actor is tired, you are unhappy; he has had exertion without feeling you feeling without exertion' (Diderot 1883: 16–7). The *Paradox*, therefore, not only argues that actors should not become emotionally involved with their roles, it also stipulates that the actors should remain unaffected by the emotional response of their audience. Similar to the craftsmen in the plates of the *Encyclopaedia*, the actor is expected to keep their 'heart under control' and act from a cool head (Diderot 1883: 28). And similar to other goods, the production of emotion is positioned as a result of mechanisation. In the same way, that the *Encyclopaedia* 'expropriated' (Koepp 1986: 257; Schaffer 1999: 164) craftsmen of their virtuosity for the sake of the efficient production of goods, the actor is expropriated of affect for the sake of the efficient production of emotion. The actor, like any other craftsman, becomes a machine.[12] And such a machine is conceived and placed within and alongside the other machines that produce the theatrical event.

The plates on theatre in the *Encyclopaedia* appeared in 1772, two years after the *Paradox* first circulated.[13] The entry consists of 31 plates on theatre buildings and 49 plates on theatre machines. The first are architectural plans whereas the second depict machinery, such as levers, pulleys and traps used for scene changes and the production of special effects.[14] The pages of the latter often feature a synthesis between a drawing of the machinery, and its constituent parts, which occupy the majority of the page, and a smaller and less detailed sketch of the scenic picture and/or effect the machinery would make possible. For example, in the page reproduced here (Figure 2.1), detailed drawing of the machinery covers most of the page, whereas the scenic effects the machinery was expected to produce are depicted on the top right and top left corner respectively. The top left sketch shows the visual effect, i.e. the descent of Phaeton, whereas the top right sketch shows the two devices used to create the sound effect, i.e. thunder. In this manner, the exposition of the mechanical process is positioned in relation to the depiction of the final result, establishing thus a relationship between the workings of the machine and its effects and revealing, as was the case with plates on other crafts, the inner workings of theatre.

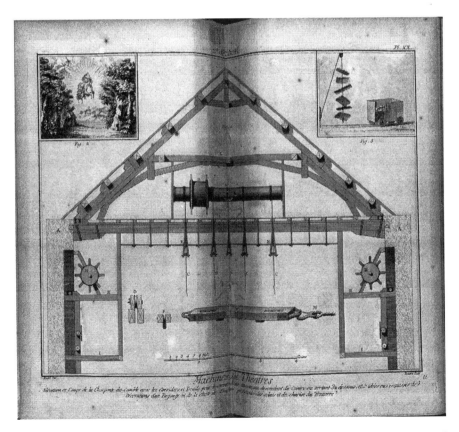

FIGURE 2.1 Machines de Théatre, Planche XXII, Reproduced from the National Library of Malta

As such, these images do not only evidence Diderot's interest in and knowledge of theatre machinery. As Werner argues, the plates are underpinned by a mode of analysis that characterises Diderot's entire *oeuvre*: 'the mode can be called "behind the scenes". Its interest lies in peering behind curtains, stripping disguises, opening up […] forbidden or secret places' (1993: 74–5). As the arrangement of the figures on the page establish a cause-and-effect relationship between sophisticated machinery and theatrical spectacle, the plates demystify the latter and demonstrate that the production of scenic effect is the result of well-designed machines. Accordingly, I would argue that the *Paradox* can be seen as the rhetorical counterpart of the wider attitude that Werner calls 'behind the scenes'. By revealing the process which the actor is supposed to undertake and positioning her within this larger theatre-machine, the *Paradox* demystifies the production of affect and insists that it can only be achieved through design and careful calculation. Just like the sound of thunder produced through the exquisite theatrical machinery depicted in the *Encyclopaedia*, tragic emotion is produced by the actor through executing a prior design with the exactitude and reliability of a '*machine de théatre*'.

The issue that Diderot encounters, however, is that unlike the machines depicted in the *Encyclopaedia*, his conception of the human body includes both mechanic and vital qualities. As Aram Vartanian explains, according to vitalism, animate beings 'exist because of an essential property or force in nature, a *principe vital*' (1981: 402). Mechanical interpretations, on the other hand, stipulated that the human body functions according to a set of rules that could be determined and explained. The tension between these two positions remains a constant trope in eighteenth-century scientific and philosophical investigations. As Vartanian argues, it is also a constant thread in Diderot's work and has posed for him 'a paradox': 'How can the organism be a mechanical assemblage of parts, and, at the same time, something that is born, grows, feels pleasure and pain, reproduces, adapts to its environment – none of which is done by an ordinary machine?' (1981: 382).

It could be argued that, if the actor's *Paradox* is seen in relation to the philosophical paradox Diderot grappled with throughout his work, then the former may have also served Diderot as a way to attempt a potential solution to the latter. The 'solution' that Diderot proposes is that the vital elements of the actor's body should come under the control of the mechanical ones, since 'the development of a machine so complex as the human body cannot be regular' (Diderot 1883: 51). Technique, assumed Diderot, would enable the actor to keep the vital elements in check and develop artistic excellence. We could say then that the expression and experience of emotion, central to debates and understandings of acting, offer Diderot an opportunity to rehearse a philosophical position that extends well beyond the actor's performance. In the actor, Diderot finds a perfect instantiation of the philosophical paradox: a breathing, living human being that must convey emotion on demand. The *Encyclopaedia* paved the way for rationalising the craftsman's messy process by stamping out the 'irregularity' that prevented the effective management of the trades and the efficient production of goods (Koepp 1986: 257). The *Paradox* puts forward the rationalisation of acting by positioning technique as a way to control irregularities and by aligning the actor's work with the operation of theatrical machinery. Diderot's argument for acting as a mechanical process can be understood further if we turn to another key aspect of eighteenth-century culture, the automata.

The actor as automaton

As stated already, the contention of this chapter is that Diderot's understanding of acting as a mechanical activity needs to be seen not only as a product of eighteenth-century scientific theorisation, but also as a response to technological advances. As Schaffer attests, 'according to a French dictionary of 1727, the word "machine" referred "in general to automata, and all those things which move by themselves whether by art or naturally"' (1999: 139–40). Machines, in other words, were defined by automation and correspondingly automation was seen as a defining characteristic of machines. In addition to the development of various instruments that related to crafts, there was also a range of automata that represented humans and animals. Such automata date back to the first century AD, particularly the inventions of Heron of Alexandria, and continued to provide a source of court and public entertainment throughout the Baroque period (see Reilly 2011).

During the eighteenth century, automata attracted scientific and popular attention, because they both featured significant technological innovation and exemplified the worldview of a clockwork universe, and thus the social order favoured by the European monarchs prior to the French Revolution.[15] Diderot was well aware of these inventions. The *Encyclopaedia* features an entry on 'automaton' penned by Diderot's co-editor, d'Alembert, as well as an entry on 'Androïde', co-written by Diderot and d'Alembert: 'an automaton in the figure of a human, which by means of certain well-arranged springs, etc. acts and performs other functions outwardly similar to those of a man' (in Landes 2011: 50). The *Encyclopaedia* also included entries by Jacques Vaucanson (1709–82), the inventor of three of the most celebrated automata of the mid-eighteenth century: the flute player, the drummer and the defecating duck.

Despite their commercial success, a number of scholars note that automata were not simply curiosities for entertainment purposes.[16] In a frequently cited observation on Vaucanson's duck, Jessica Riskin points out that 'automata were philosophical experiments, attempts to discern which aspects of living creatures could be reproduced in machinery, and to what degree, and what such reproductions might reveal about their natural subjects' (2003: 601). Automata, according to Reilly, engendered 'onto-epistemic mimesis', a process whereby 'mimesis or representation directly shapes ideas about reality through ways of being (ontology), or ways of knowing (epistemology)' (2011: 7). As such, the function and design of an automaton was approached not only as a possible explanation of the mechanics of a range of movements but also as a blueprint of an entire organism: 'if an animal really was just like an automaton, then how different was a human being from an automaton? These questions produced a new way of knowing, which, by extension produces a new sense of being' (Reilly 2011: 83). The creation of automata, therefore, set up a cyclical process whereby the technological artefact, evidently created by humans, was used as a way of knowing the human organism.

This epistemic function of automata was accentuated further by technological developments. As Riskin explains, earlier automata represented the actions of humans. A player of an instrument, for example, executed a series of gestures that imitated music playing, whereas the melody was produced by a music box hidden inside or below the artefact. Vaucanson's chief innovation, on the other hand, was that his automata not only imitated a set of actions, they *executed* them for real (Reilly 2011: 85; Riskin 2003). For example, the movements of the instrument players created actual music and the food consumed by the Duck was mechanically ingested.[17] Riskin notes a shift in emphasis from representation to simulation and accordingly observes that the aim now was 'to test the limits between synthetic and natural life' (2003: 606). The performance of automata also raised questions of whether 'artistic creativity could be automated' (Riskin 2003: 631) and served as a benchmark for evaluating the quality of human performance, with the latter often coming second. Reilly observes that a preference for the performance of automata over the performance of humans was premised on a preference for 'stamina' over 'affect' (2011: 85). In his *Encyclopaedia* entry, 'Automaton', d'Alembert argues that 'this [Vaucanson's] automaton is superior to all our real tambourine players who cannot move their tongues swiftly enough to sound a whole bar of semiquavers' (in Hoyt and Cassirer 1965: 21). Similarly, Diderot expressed a preference for the automatic weaving of silk over human labour (Reilly 2011: 163).[18]

At first glance, the *Paradox* only offers oblique references to automata, which do not tally with the technological sophistication Diderot was familiar with. Unlike essays that appear later, for example by Heinrich von Kleist (1972 [1810]) and Edward Gordon Craig (1908), which argued that marionettes are superior performers to humans, Diderot does not wish to substitute actors with automata.[19] He rather conceives the actor by analogy with an automaton.[20] As such, the exact and reliable repetition of a score becomes the main criterion according to which Diderot evaluates the quality of the actor's performance: the actor is 'at his best mark' when he is 'invariable' (Diderot 1883: 9). Accordingly, the concern with the actor's experience of emotion could be seen as a result of the debates that arose in relation to what machines could or could not do and the constant redefinition of boundaries between organic and mechanical activities. Emotional experience is arguably the par excellence activity that cannot be simulated by a machine. If, however, performers do nothing else apart from feeling the emotions they are supposed to portray, then theatre becomes identical with real life. In the *Paradox*, Diderot seems well aware of this possibility and is keen to preserve the distinction between theatre and life (1883: 81). In doing so, he insists on the artifice of theatrical performance and posits that such artifice can only be achieved through simulation. Accordingly, the actor's 'talent depends not […] upon feeling, but upon rendering so exactly the outward signs of feeling, that you fall into the trap' (Diderot 1883: 16). Diderot's emphasis on artificiality is also noted by Mark Franko, who observes that 'the end result Diderot is after is naturalness, always a relative concept in theatre history. But the important point is that he claims it can be best achieved through a technique of artifice' (1989: 68).

It could be argued then that through the *Paradox*, Diderot is reworking a prominent philosophical question regarding the boundaries between human and machine, which, during the eighteenth century, kept shifting. In the *Paradox*, Diderot asks this question in relation to human rather than mechanical performers and rehearses a rhetorical move that is crucial to materialist philosophy. By arguing for the mechanisation of acting, it seems that Diderot has to reach one of the two following conclusions: either he will have to argue for the replacement of humans by automata, as became the case in other industries, and as it will be eventually argued in relation to theatre by Gordon Craig in 1908. Or he will have to prove that the actor is able to perform as well as a machine. Diderot goes for the latter and accordingly he contends that the *only* way to affect is through an automatic process. Although Diderot is not calling for the substitution of human actors by mechanical ones, he is following a methodology of onto-epistemic mimesis, whereby automata offer the criteria for defining and evaluating good acting. In this way, Diderot manages to put forward a philosophical position that accommodates both the human actor and the mechanical model. As a result though, acting becomes mechanised twice: first the actor's body is understood as a machine, albeit a vitalist one that needs to be fully controlled. Second, the criterion of good acting is the extent to which it can be rendered automatic. Diderot's conception of acting technique not only ousts emotions; it leaves no space for mistakes, accidental discoveries, or the unexpected. What is remarkable in Diderot's text, then, is neither his refutation of 'sensibility' nor his call for an acting technique. Rather what is truly outstanding is that in the *Paradox*, Diderot advances an understanding of technique in terms of the efficiency of the machine.

Such a move is paralleled by a wider reconceptualisation of technique during the Enlightenment period that becomes inextricably connected with technology. Tim Casey traces in the period leading up to the Enlightenment the emergence of a 'metaphysics of technique' whereby technique becomes 'mechanised' and linked to the production of 'desired results in the most efficient and trustworthy way' (Casey 1997: 76). The mechanisation of technique then entails 'the reduction of technical know-how to a set of mechanical rules whose routine operation, it is alleged, automatically and invariably leads to some predetermined result' (Casey 1997: 79). As we shall see in the next section, precision and exact repetition are the standards according to which acting will be evaluated during the nineteenth century. At the same time though, because the actor's instrument can never become a machine, the mechanisation of acting technique in twentieth-century actor training practice will become both accepted and challenged.

Part II

The actor's instrument

As I have indicated, the aim of this section is to trace how key ideas we find in the *Paradox* reproduce and evolve during nineteenth- and early twentieth-century theatre. Unlike Diderot's 'detachment' from the stage and the First's reference to past performances and hypothetical examples, the texts examined in this section emerge from direct and longstanding practical engagement. It is significant therefore that key ideas articulated in the *Paradox* are repeated or developed further with direct reference to the authors' own careers. These include the primacy of a prior design as a basis for the role (Coquelin et al. 1932: 33; Irving 1904: 41); the importance of the distinction between theatre and daily life (Coquelin et al. 1932: 45; Craig 1908: 13; Irving 1904: 51–2); an emphasis on the actor's selection of and control over the appropriate emotions (Coquelin et al. 1932: 71; Craig 1908: 6; Irving 1904: 42); and the significance of technical accomplishment, especially with regard to vocal and speech training (Coquelin et al. 1932: 58; Craig 1908: 6–7; Irving 1887: 10, 14, 17). Most importantly, even though the question of the actor's emotional involvement was still debated, an emphasis on technique is a central theme shared across these accounts.

Irving's preface to the English translation of the *Paradox* reads more like a critique rather than an endorsement of Diderot's text. Irving calls attention to the 'illustrations, real or imaginary' (1883: x) with which Diderot furnishes his arguments, undermining from the very beginning Diderot's authority and reminding the reader of his own status as a successful actor. Irving is also quick to emphasise the improvements in the actors' social and moral status that had taken place since Diderot's time (1883: xi). It is only after he distances himself from the author of the *Paradox* in these important respects that Irving deals with the main debate presented in the text. And, again, Irving refutes Diderot's thesis by stressing the importance of sensibility for the actor's artistic process and performance. It is all the more important then, that the point that Irving does concede to Diderot concerns the question of technique: 'if tears are produced at the actor's will and under his [sic] control, they are true art; and happy is the actor who numbers them amongst his gifts' (Irving 1883: xx). Despite the prevalence of the First interlocutor in the dialogue, Irving sides with the compromise offered by the Second and argues that an actor may identify with the emotional world of the play as long as he retains the technical aspects of his craft, such as a sense of timing and proper intonation (Diderot 1883: 87–8). Indeed, in a lecture he gave in 1900, Irving permits emotion only as a direct result of technical mastery: 'the actor or actress worth of the name are not the slaves but the masters of the emotion they portray' (Irving 1904: 51). In other words, Irving nuances Diderot's argument by claiming that sensibility is not the antithesis of reason; it is rather the characteristic of 'untrained actors' (1883: xv). As such, the question is not whether actors should feel the emotions they portray but rather whether they can control their emotional expression. In this manner, sensibility becomes recast as a technical accomplishment and this proves an enduring idea, at least amongst English-speaking practitioners.

In an interview that was included in the English translation of Coquelin's text, Madge Kendal confirms Irving's view and boasts that over a series of performances of the same play 'she wept real tears in the same place, in the same scene' (Coquelin et al. 1932: 103). Having cited the *Paradox* earlier in her interview, she concludes with an unmistakable Diderotian idea: 'the actor's performance should vary as little as possible from one representation to another' (Coquelin et al. 1932: 103). In her Introduction to the same volume, Fogerty generalises Kendal's point by observing that the power of performance, at the beginning of the twentieth century, did not so much stem from the plot of the plays, with which audiences were well familiar anyway, but rather from 'what I may call the instrumentalism of the actors' (Coquelin et al. 1932: 20). Fogerty does not explain what she means by the term, but the context of the rest of the paragraph suggests that what she has in mind is some form of extra-ordinary skill related to vocal and physical expression.

Fogerty's argument is echoed by Craig's volume on Irving, which confirms the latter's technical prowess as well as the importance bestowed on technical ability. An influential theatre practitioner in his own right, Craig studied with Irving during an eight-year apprenticeship at the Lyceum Theatre between 1889 and 1897 (Craig 1930: 15). Craig's volume charts Irving's entire career and offers detailed descriptions of key moments in seminal productions at the Lyceum. On the whole, the account verges on the hagiographical, as Craig exudes unconditional awe for his mentor with the intention to induce a similar effect in the reader. What is interesting, however, is not whether Craig's evaluation of Irving is balanced but rather that his admiration is expressed with reference to Irving's technical abilities.

To begin with, Craig emphasises the long and careful process through which John Henry Brodribb, a young farmer from Cornwall, became the first British actor to receive a knighthood in 1895 (1930: 24–40). Whereas Irving's modest background is biographically correct, rhetorically it operates, as Esposti notes (2015: 6–9), as a reminder to Craig's readership that great actors are not born but made. Indeed, in an address at the University of Harvard, Irving claims that perfection in acting can be achieved in 'no less than twenty years' (1887: 6). Similarly, Craig attests that even at the height of his career, Irving was committed to long preparations for his roles, which were then rendered on stage through calculated and measured performance. Craig brings attention to Irving's 'perfection of craftsmanship' (1930: 58) and gives detailed accounts of Irving's rhythmic and well-designed facial and bodily movements, carefully-choreographed and minutely-executed scores of action (1930: 70–86), as well as his idiosyncratic yet perfect speech (1930: 62–9). Irving, according to Craig, managed to achieve artificiality to such a degree that instead of stifling his playing, it endowed it with the power of a natural phenomenon:

> From the first to last moment Irving stood on stage each moment was significant … every sound, each movement, was intentional – clear-cut, measured

dance: nothing real – all massively artificial – yet all flashing with the light and pulse of nature.

(Craig 1930: 78)

Craig's description has significant parallels with Diderot's *Paradox*. As Patrick Le Boeuf notes, 'Craig acquired this volume as early as 1896 and annotated it at various times' (2010: 114). Le Boeuf further observes that next to the passage where Diderot describes the actor encased in a basket standing on top of the poet's shoulders, 'Craig inscribed the initials U-m-', asserting that Craig's key concept was inspired by Diderot (2010: 105). It could be argued therefore that Irving, in being 'the nearest thing ever known to what I have called the Übermarionette' (Craig 1930: 32), also constitutes an instantiation of Diderot's perfect actor. Emulating Diderot's ideal, Irving's process begins in prior design and culminates in a well-executed technical performance that is entirely artificial.

What is more, Irving's relationship to his audience also resonates with Diderot's text. As we saw, according to Diderot, the actor's performance and the audience's response are two entirely discrete processes. Emotional engagement is aroused in the spectator by the technical skill of the actor, who remains emotionally unaffected. In a similar fashion, Craig recounts that Irving met the reactions of his audience with '*good-natured contempt*', which protected him like 'a suit of armour' (Craig 1930: 35–6, emphasis original). Craig describes how Irving maintained his composure upon entering the stage in roles that drove audiences to a frenzy of applause. He also responded with equanimity to both praise and critique. Similarly to Diderot then, Craig describes a fundamental disconnect between actor and spectator, whilst identifying technical skill as a means to inoculate the actor's process and performance from the audience's response.

We see therefore that during the nineteenth century good acting becomes synonymous with technical perfection. This is articulated in terms of the arguments Diderot advanced in the *Paradox* and becomes further supported by contemporaneous examples of practices of both performance and preparation. If good acting is premised on the acquisition of technique, the logical conclusion is that this can be achieved through training. And training needs to involve more than the standard practice of 'learning on the job'. It is notable that in Fogerty's text, these two key ideas emerge side-by-side: the actor can reach a state of 'instrumentalism' by learning to master her resources in a systematic fashion. Having been trained at the Paris Conservatoire in the 1880s (Sanderson 1984: 47), Fogerty argues that the chief problem with the available training in the UK was the lack of pedagogical technique. Instead of following a carefully laid out programme of study, the actor is taught 'ad hoc' (Coquelin et al. 1932: 30). However, after systematic training, 'the actor would be able to 'pla[y] on his instrument, through the medium of an important part' (Coquelin et al. 1932: 22). Similarly, Craig envisages that a training programme would offer a 'place where men and women eager to do well should be trained by the best masters until they were sound, reliable executants' (1930: 120).

What is further interesting is that both Fogerty and Craig understand training as a disciplinary mechanism that will enable the actor to control her expressive medium. 'The average student', proclaims Fogerty, 'has a stiff uncontrolled body, a mind preoccupied with self, and a voice utterly beyond his own control' (Coquelin et al. 1932: 21). A similar, if not more extreme, version appears in Craig's well-known essay 'The Actor and the Über-marionette' (1908). A polemic against naturalism, as well as the celebrity status enjoyed by actors during the time, Craig's essay argues that the continuation of theatre as an art form is premised on the substitution of actors by an Übermarionette.[21] Echoing Diderot, Craig begins his essay with the assertion that 'art arrives only by design. Therefore in order to make any work of art it is clear we may only work in those materials with which we can calculate. Man is not one of these materials' (1908: 3). The essay then continues repeating the point that no matter how perfect the conception of the poet or indeed the actor's conception of a role, its rendition by the human body is bound to suffer from the unpredictability of the flesh. A perfect rendition of the role, says the painter to the actor, would be possible

> *if* you could make your body into a machine, or into a dead piece of material such as clay, and *if* it could obey you in every movement for the entire space of time it was before the audience, [...] you would be able to make a work of art out of that which is you.
>
> (Craig 1908: 8, emphasis original)

Craig not only adheres to ideas of mastery and predictability, evoked in Diderot's text. He explicitly compares the actor's resources to inorganic matter: against inorganic matter, – which is presumably fully controllable – human materiality is unpredictable. Yet, it can be safely assumed that through his engagement with materials as a designer and artisan, Craig would have become aware of their own tendency to 'misbehave'. For example, whereas in the 1908 essay Craig proclaims that materials can be calculated and clay is 'dead', accounts of his design for *Hamlet* at the Moscow Art Theatre between 1908 and 1912 (Innes 2004 [1998]: 168–9; Stanislavsky 2008b: 285–97), demonstrate that materials would not bend to his artistic will as easily as Craig assumes in his essay.[22] An understanding of matter as pliable or dead tallied with neither the actual conditions in eighteenth-century workshops nor the production process of early-twentieth-century theatres. It is all the more revealing therefore of an approach to inorganic and organic nature that is guided by a desire to gain control and mastery.

A similar tendency to master both organic and inorganic matter is evident in the work of Craig's mentor. As mentioned already, Irving was not only a celebrated actor, he was also an acclaimed theatre manager who brought many innovations to the nineteenth-century stage, especially in light design and infrastructure. Bram Stoker, the manager at the Lyceum, offers a comprehensive list of the lighting innovations Irving made to the theatre both in terms of the technological equipment as well as the way this was operated. According to Stoker (1911), Irving's innovations included: two mains for gas supply, so that if one system went off the other one would kick in and keep the auditorium lit; a prompt box that enabled the control of every single light from a centralised system; coloured lights; and the darkening of the auditorium. What is more, Irving was involved with all aspects of lighting at the Lyceum: 'he thought of it, invented it, arranged it, and had the entire thing worked out to his preconceived ideas under his immediate and personal supervision' (Stoker 1911: 912). In true Enlightenment spirit, Irving's theatre employed technology and technique towards producing carefully pre-conceived roles and theatre designs, reducing safety hazards and overall improving the conditions for both audience and actors. The kind of exactness, reliability and predictability that Irving demonstrated in his acting, as extolled by Craig, was also expected of all the other resources that made up the theatrical events at the Lyceum. Acting technique and stage technology combined to put an end to chance and accidents. Far more importantly than the question of emotional sensibility, in Irving we find a substantiation of the perfect actor *and* craftsman, a perfection premised on the control of both organic and inorganic resources.

Irving may be seen as an heir of Diderot's actor in one more crucial respect. As we saw, according to Diderot's conceptualisation, the performance and its reception are two clearly demarcated events. Craig's description of Irving's relationship to his audiences also confirms this demarcation. However, in addition to an emotional attitude of 'good natured contempt', which assumedly allowed him to remain impervious to the reactions of audiences, Irving instituted another, arguably more powerful, means of separation. Although Irving was not the first theatre practitioner to darken the auditorium, he established the practice at the Lyceum and is credited with popularising it (Palmer 2017). At the end of the nineteenth century, the dimmed auditorium received a mixed reception (Burdekin 2018) and it would take until the beginning of the twentieth century for the practice to become fully established. Nonetheless, the dimming of the lights at the Lyceum set forth two interrelated processes: against its dim surroundings, the spectacle on stage became further accentuated; and the spectators' attention was effectively directed to the stage and away from one another. The darkened auditorium, in other words, had both an aesthetic and a disciplining function. I shall examine the way lights became incorporated directly into the actor's process in the next section.

Part III

The actor's instrument in a pool of light

As mentioned already, Stanislavsky was well familiar with the lighting practices of his time. Laurence Senelick's (1976) reproduction of the minutes of the production meetings for *Hamlet* at Moscow Art Theatre (MAT), reveals that Stanislavsky directly experimented on stage with Craig's suggestions for the lighting of the design and the blackouts, both on stage and in the auditorium, that would enable scene changes. Furthermore, in his autobiographical account, *My Life in Art,*

Stanislavsky states that he followed closely the installation of the lighting equipment when MAT moved to a new building in 1902 (2008b: 215). In *An Actor's Work*, Stanislavsky presents a set of concepts and a series of practical exercises with the aim to teach actors to concentrate their attention. The lighting states described include: blackout; flickering lights; a narrow, medium and large pool of light; a mobile spotlight; an immobile table lamp on the stage; as well as discrete lamps at different parts of the theatre.

These resources are utilised with the aim to demonstrate key areas of the actor's work. The static on-stage lamp offers an immediate focal point both representing and facilitating the actor's ability to concentrate on a specific object (Stanislavsky 2008a: 92) as well as the skill to endow the object with imaginary qualities (Stanislavsky 2008a: 110). The narrow, medium and large wash respectively showcase 'immediate, mid and distant focal points' (Stanislavsky 2008a: 95). By extension, the pools of light are utilised by Stanislavsky as a means to enable the actor to visualise the range of her own focus, respectively in small, medium and large 'circles of attention' (2008a: 98–102). In juxtaposition, the flickering lights 'illustrat[e] the actor's concentration when it is unfocused' (Stanislavsky 2008a: 95). The mobile spotlight demonstrates the circumference of the actor's focus as one moves about on stage (Stanislavsky 2008a: 103). It also offers a visualisation of the actor's internalisation of what Stanislavsky calls a 'state of public solitude': the ability to behave in front of others as if one were on one's own (2008a: 103). Individual spotlights of varying intensity are utilised to personify different key roles in the theatre production, such as the critic and the director (Stanislavsky 2008a: 95–6). Blackout is frequently employed as a way to reset the lights between the aforementioned states. It is also used in an observation exercise where the students are asked to look at an object for a specified amount of time and then describe it in darkness (Stanislavsky 2008a: 96–8).[23] In this manner, different lightning states and combinations of darkness and light serve as a means of training arguably the most important resource of the actor's craft. In Chapters 4 and 5, I discuss further the pedagogical implications of Stanislavsky's idiosyncratic use of technology. Here, I wish to bring attention to three aspects of the text related to the discussion so far.

The first aspect of the exercises worth considering is the difference between the performance of the students and the performance of the technology. Throughout the section, technology operates seamlessly and transparently. The lights are switched on and off as if by magic and there is no reference to the significant preparation and technical support that the experiment would require.[24] This can be seen as a continuation of a tendency in nineteenth-century theatre to conceal 'particular forms of labour, […] technologies of production, and, finally […] the theatrical spectators themselves' (Nield 2017: 205). What merits additional attention here is that in Stanislavsky's descriptions, the student actors are depicted to struggle and falter. Chiming with Fogerty's diagnosis that the body of the student actor is uncontrolled, and Craig's proclamation that 'Man' is no material for art, the student actors' inability to master and control their power of concentration becomes all the more pronounced against a technology that apparently operates without a glitch. In this respect, the section presents a faithful reproduction of the dichotomy between docile matter and volatile body, implicitly pitting the students' faltering abilities against the impressive capacities of the technology. Similarly to the function of automata during the eighteenth century, it could be argued that technology once more sets the standards for human performance. Indeed, in Stanislavsky's remarkable pedagogical application of technological ingenuity, we could trace a process of onto–epistemic mimesis: humans are asked to replicate a specific capacity or behaviour of a machine with the aim to train an aspect of their organism. The process of mimicking the behaviour of the technological entity engenders an understanding of how the chosen aspect of the human organism operates as well as what it is. In this case, light serves as a visual manifestation of the actor's concentration, which can be 'trained', like a beam, to illuminate one's object of attention. Light also serves as a benchmark of achievement, with the actor expected to switch between different objects and variable ranges of focus as swiftly and seamlessly. In this way, the ability of light to control visibility sets forth a technique for controlling attention.

An additional, but nonetheless significant benefit of the exercises presented by Stanislavsky, is that the different lighting states not only make tangible the actor's work on concentration, they also exemplify the actor's relationship to the audience. As mentioned already, in this section Stanislavsky puts forth the concept of 'public solitude' and further stresses the institution of the imaginary, yet impenetrable, fourth wall. Roach notes the continuity between Stanislavsky's concept and the separation between performance and reception advanced by Diderot (2007: 155). However, what Roach misses is that this fundamental change in the theatrical experience is not only encountered in Diderot's text; it was materially realised in practice, specifically through the dimmed auditoria at the Lyceum and other theatres during the nineteenth century. It is because of the changes in lights that the seated area becomes, and is appropriately described by Stanislavsky as, a 'big black hole' (2008a: 90). Against such a clear demarcation between stage and auditorium, the student actors are explicitly taught to keep their attention on their side of the stage. This not only has a calming effect on Kostya's nerves, the student actor who describes the 'actor's work' in Stanislavsky's fictive diary. It also creates an aesthetic and phenomenological reality of solitude: as the audience becomes reduced to an undifferentiated 'black hole', the actor is 'cut off from everything else' (Stanislavsky 2008a: 99).

Ironically, however, in the very section where a 'proper' technology imparts such important pedagogical benefits, Stanislavsky demonstrates an ambivalent attitude towards the machine. As I have already intimated, although mechanised technique is argued by Diderot and becomes accepted by actors in the nineteenth century, mechanical acting also has negative connotations. Despite its focus on reliability and repeatability, Diderot is eager to emphasise the creative skills required by acting: 'profound judgement', 'an exquisite taste' and imagination (1883: 95–6). Diderot, in other words, stresses those operations essential for 'good acting' that would fall on the human side of the human–machine divide. It is in this vein that we can also understand Garrick's attitude, who despite being allegedly able to reproduce emotion at will, dismissed 'automaton Players who are literally such mere Machines that they require winding up almost every time before they act' (quoted in Roach 2007: 91). An almost identical caution is repeated by Stanislavsky, when the fictional Tortsov warns the students that 'if you speak a word, or do something mechanically onstage [...] you will perform like a machine that's been wound up, an automaton' (2008a: 84). Indeed, as Pitches mentions, for Stanislavsky the term mechanical is 'deeply pejorative' (2006: 22) and, in fact, mechanical acting is often positioned as the antithesis of his System. At the same time though, there are positive references to machines. For example, according to Tortsov, when 'all the parts of your physical mechanism [...] are supple, receptive, expressive, sensitive, agile, [they are] like a well-oiled and tuned machine in which all wheels and rollers are working in perfect harmony' (Stanislavsky 2008a: 580).

The same ambivalence towards the machine is also evident in the section examined here. At the beginning of the passage, there is a derogatory comment on automation, with Tortsov stating that 'a wagging tongue, hands and feet moving like an automaton cannot replace thoughtful eyes that give life to everything' (Stanislavsky 2008a: 95). Tortsov not only draws a sharp distinction between automata and actors, but explicitly denunciates the machine as something devoid of life that cannot compete with the animating force of the living human actor. Similarly, at the beginning of the section the students are reprimanded for exercising 'a deal of mechanical staring' (2008a: 94). At the very end of the session, though, and after many failed attempts to regulate his attention, Kostya becomes eventually able to modulate his focus 'immediately, machine-like. I limited my circle of attention to the confines of the mobile circle' (Stanislavsky 2008a: 105). Finding himself in an awkward social situation, Kostya discovers to his surprise that the newly acquired skill has been automated and enables him to maintain his composure. Arriving late and trying to find his seat in a busy auditorium with all eyes on him, the young student gets a first taste of the actor's paradox and the creative potential it opens: he is able to master a key aspect of his expressive instrument automatically *and* retain the ease and grace, which, according to Tortsov's earlier statement, are precisely those hallmarks that differentiate humans from machines. What Kostya further learns in this incident, and what Stanislavsky wants his readers to take away, is that this paradoxical combination of technique and grace allows Kostya to command not only his attention but also the attention of others and thus become watchable: presence is achieved by the mechanisation of technique. In this truly remarkable passage in twentieth-century actor training history, the actor's instrument is developed by and mapped onto the performance of a technological device, yet it is also clearly distinguished from the function of the machine.

Conclusion: how does performer training become technological?

This chapter endeavoured to position the beginning of modern actor training in relation to the technological advancements that became possible during the eighteenth century, as well as the mechanisation of technique that was consolidated during the same time. It also sought to draw out a common conceptual basis underpinning acting technique and theatre technology. Through an examination of the way 'good acting' is evaluated and presented in a range of different sources including Diderot's *The Paradox of Acting*; accounts of nineteenth-century theatre practice; early twentieth-century texts; and Stanislavsky's comprehensive description of the actor's concentration, I have argued that the control of the actor's fleshy reality becomes part and parcel of a pursuit for control of the entire stage and performance event.

Through an examination of the *Paradox* in relation to Diderot's work in the *Encyclopaedia* on the one hand, and the invention of automata on the other, this chapter foregrounded the way Diderot's understanding of acting was both deeply influenced by the development of technological artefacts during the eighteenth century and propounded the mechanisation of acting technique. Good acting, according to Diderot as well as the theatre practitioners after him, who are reviewed here, presupposes the development of an instrument, which draws on the very resources that make up the self but remains ontologically distinct from the machine. This has bequeathed contemporary practice not only the enduring metaphor of the actor as instrument, but also a guiding assumption of what training is: training is a subordinate clause, it is an 'in-order-to' aiming to achieve technical mastery. Training, in other words, is the means to the actor's 'instrumentalism'. In this way, despite being subservient to performance, training acquires an ontology and becomes a distinct field of artistic practice.

Even though the innovators examined here made a contribution to both acting and theatre design/technology, acting technique/performer training and theatre technology/scenography are routinely treated as separate subjects. Yet, as I have argued throughout the chapter, there are important connections between the two, both in discourse as well as in praxis. In this respect, Stanislavsky's experimentation with theatre lights is doubly significant. As I have demonstrated, the section on 'Creative Concentration and Attention' exemplifies the development of a fully-fledged actor-training pedagogy according to the behaviour and standards of a specific technology.[25] Despite the scholarly and practical attention that this aspect of Stanislavsky's work has received, technology has been bracketed out of most existing accounts. By foregrounding the very obvious, yet neglected, role of lights in this aspect of Stanislavsky's work, this chapter also aims to demonstrate an analytical attitude of 'technology spotting' as well as to present the important insights this attitude can yield.

Specifically, the texts and practices examined in this chapter show that technology is not simply an artefact that the actor may or may not use; it rather becomes the very ground on which acting becomes conceptualised. Indeed, as the next chapter will discuss in detail, it is precisely an approach to nature as a resource to be mastered and exploited that Martin Heidegger in 1955 will identify as the 'essence of technology'. And whereas Diderot, as well as Irving and Craig, are confident of the benefits of such an approach, once performance trainers begin to practically explore the development of a 'mechanised technique' they come up against those elements that cannot be mechanised. As we saw, Stanislavsky's work is under-pinned by an ambivalence towards the machine, which allows him to accom-modate, but never entirely resolve, a tension between a 'well-oiled and tuned machine' and '*the life of the human spirit*' (2008a: 580, emphasis original). The next chapter will argue that this tension persists and becomes further accentuated in the second half of the twentieth century. Contra Roach, who interprets the 1960s avant-garde experimentations in performer training 'as a reversion to vitalism' (2007: 221), I will contend that this strand of performer training is a continuation of the ambivalence towards the mechanisation of technique we find in Stanis-lavsky's work. If anything, it marks a renewed attempt to grapple with this tension, this time by searching for ways to 'de-mechanise' technique, albeit without ceasing to develop *techniques*. In order to offer a more thorough understanding of the neg-ative turn towards technique and technology, the next chapter reviews the work of Martin Heidegger and Herbert Marcuse, and examines the way a critique of tech-nology influenced performer training approaches during the 1960s and 1970s.

Notes

1 As Scott Palmer explains from the late eighteenth century onwards, key developments in the illumination of the stage took place. The use of the Argand lamp in theatres from the 1780s onwards produced more light while it consumed less oil (Palmer 2013: 63–4). This was followed 30 years later by the introduction of gas lighting around 1816. As Palmer notes, the installation of gas lighting in theatres underwent 'a continual process of change as the technologies of distribution and operating techniques had developed' (2013: 174). From 1881 onwards, gas was gradually replaced with electric lights (Palmer 2013: 173).

2 The volume appeared in French in 1894 and was translated in English in 1932. Fogerty was the founder and director of the Royal Central School of Speech and Drama, and Kendal (1848–1935) was one of the most celebrated actresses and theatre managers at the turn and beginning of the twentieth century.

3 As Roach explains, the essay in question was *Garrick, ou Les Acteurs Anglois* by Antonio Fabio Sticotti (1769). This was a translation of the English title *The Actor* (1755) by John Hill which was a translation of the French title *Le Comedien* (1749) by Saint-Albine (Roach 2007: 132). The *Paradox* first appeared as a review of Sticotti's book in 1770, was 'greatly expanded and put in dialogue form in 1773, and finally completed in perhaps 1778' (Roach 2007: 129).

4 Roach further argues that the concept of the ideal model may be better understood as an '"inner model", implying not only a refinement of nature, but the creation or collection of diverse images to form a picture in the mind of the artist' (2007: 125).

5 According to the First, sensibility is 'that disposition which accompanies organic weak-ness, which follows on early affection of the diaphragm, on vivacity of imagination, on delicacy of nerves, which inclines one to being compassionate, to being horrified, to admiration, to fear. To being upset, to tears, to faintings, to rescues, to flights, to excla-mations, to loss of self-control, to being contemptuous, disdainful, to having no clear notion of what true, good, and fine, to being unjust, to going mad' (1883: 56).

6 Roach identifies a third factor, i.e. Diderot's 'increasingly absorbing inquiries into physi-ology' (2007: 122). As I argued already, although I agree with Roach that Diderot's argument in the *Paradox* is influenced by physiological treatises of the time, my aim here is to foreground the impact of technological developments.

7 Payne mentions that in 1759 the practice of spectators sitting on the stage was discontinued after the petition of French theatre companies (2017: 143). It is likely that Diderot is drawing here from experiences that preceded the writing of the *Paradox*.

8 Roach makes the same point arguing that 'Diderot's ideal actor thus performs mechanically in one of the basic meanings of the word- capable of exact duplication, replicable by rule and measure' (2007: 133–4). Yet, he does not draw the obvious links with the *Encyclopaedia*, although he argues earlier in his chapter that Diderot's role in the *Encyclopaedia* was an important influence on the *Paradox*.

9 According to Koepp, the *Encyclopédie* offers evidence that the treatment of different crafts was uneven and indeed the editors were prone to identify positive characteristics in those crafts that were considered high-brow, such as goldsmiths and clockmakers, and accordingly accuse of backwardness low-brow crafts, such as butchers. Koepp attributes this discrimination to the relation between different crafts and the dominant culture: 'when the *Encyclopédie* offers negative depictions of workers, in general the editors mean the ones who shared the least (in terms of values, property, literacy) with the dominant, literate culture, and further, to the extent that workers/artisans/masters were actively literate, property owning, and so on, they were less likely to be criticised' (1986: 246n53).

10 John Pannabecker (1998) cautions against treating the *Encyclopédie* as a uniformed enterprise and assuming that Diderot managed to impose editorial coherence. Pannabecker takes as a case in point the entries on printing and demonstrates that some contributors favoured the formal representation sought by Diderot, whereas others foregrounded issues of health and safety and tried to capture the tacit knowledge inherent in artisanal processes. Although Pannabecker's work opens new areas of investigation for the *Encyclopaedia*, his argument does not undermine the view supported here, since my interest lies in Diderot's vision and how this vision was reflected in some of the plates.

11 As Palmer notes 'performances would be interrupted continually by the intrusions of the candle snuffer who needed to attend to and trim each individual wick in a constant battle against darkness' (2017: 45).

12 There are obvious power implications here. According to Koepp: 'what we have in the *Encyclopédie* is a subtle and comprehensive expropriation of that nonliterate knowledge and hence power by the literate culture, an attempt, largely successful, to remove the inefficient and inarticulate world of work from the hands and mouths of the workers and to place it in printed form before the eyes of an enlightened "management" whose ordered purposes it would serve' (1986: 257).

13 The plates were part of the tenth volume, and the ninth instalment of the *Encyclopaedia*. They were drawn by Bernard, whereas commentary was written by Radel, an 'architect-expert' under the supervision of de M. Giraud, 'the machinist of the Paris Opera' (Diderot et al. 1772: 4).

14 The plates as well as the written descriptions that accompanied them can be viewed on the ARTFL website, a project that digitised French resources held by North American Libraries: https://artflsrv03.uchicago.edu/philologic4/encyclopedie1117/navigate/27/24/ [accessed 3 March 2020].

15 Of special note here is the Tympanon Player, an automaton commissioned by Marie Antoinette and constructed in her own image in 1780. As Reilly observes, 'this mimetic replica of the Queen demonstrates that courtiers aspired to be as perfectly mechanical as their celebrated automata' (2011: 94).

16 Automata toured in the European metropoles and, for a considerable entry price, could be seen performing a range of actions and gestures, such as playing musical instruments and writing letters.

17 However, the waste produced was not a product of the actual food consumed by the duck, but a different substance that had to be added to the mechanism. Vaucanson was clear about this and asked not to be judged for not recreating biological processes that cannot be reproduced: 'I don't pretend to give this as a perfect Digestion, capable of producing Blood and nutritive Particles for the Support of the Animal' (Vaucanson in

Fryer and Marshall 1979: 267). It seems that defecating marked for Vaucanson the limits of mechanical reproduction.

18 Another example of such a tendency was the *serinettes*, small wooden boxes that often featured in Parisian front rooms. These not only reproduced the singing of canaries but were used to teach canaries to sing (Cottom 1999: 70).

19 Heinrich von Kleist's essay 'On the Marionette Theater' (1810) sits chronologically between the *Paradox* and Craig's essay. Taxidou notes that Craig was well aware of Kleist's essay, which first appeared in English in 1918 in *The Marionette*, a journal edited by Craig (1998: 166). Similarly to Diderot's text, Kleist's essay is structured as a dialogue between two interlocutors, one of them being a famous dancer. The essay does not reach the radical conclusion suggested by Craig, but it does argue that the self-consciousness that comes with adulthood gets in the way of grace, an affliction that affects neither puppets nor animals. As we shall see in the third part of this chapter, the problem of self-consciousness appears again in Stanislavsky's work, who proposes the development of a state of 'public solitude' as a solution to it.

20 Franko also notes that 'Diderot comes to picture him or her [i.e. the actor] as an automaton' (1989: 66). Crucially, although Franko makes this point with direct reference to the *Paradox*, he does not draw any links between such understanding and the automata that were a popular aspect of eighteenth-century culture.

21 Whether the Übermarionette was supposed to invoke an ideal to be achieved by human actors or an actual artefact meant to replace and/or cover human actors is an ongoing debate (see Esposti 2015; Le Boeuf 2010; Taxidou 1998).

22 In his account of the production, Stanislavsky reveals that certain aspect of Craig's design could not be realised by the means that were at the time available, whereas the construction of the screens involved a drawn-out process of trial and error. Stanislavsky notes the resistance of specific materials as well as the considerable technical labour that the realisation of Craig's artistic vision required (2008b: 295).

23 This is one of the main similarities between the meditation exercises we find in Ramacharaka's book *Raja Yoga* and Stanislavsky's work. However, the key difference is that in Ramacharaka's 'Mental Drill in Attention' students are instructed to observe an object and then proceed with writing down what they can remember. In a second exercise, students are instructed to enter a room, take in their surroundings, walk out and then write down what they can remember (1906: 114–15). Whilst the similarities between the two sections clearly demonstrate the influence of Ramacharaka on Stanislavsky, the changes that Stanislavsky brings to the practice are noteworthy. The fact that the exercise can be achieved in a far simpler manner, for example by looking or walking away from the object under observation, brings further attention to Stanislavsky's choice to substitute readily available physiological actions with a complicated technological one.

24 I presented a reconstruction of Stanislavsky's exercises at the TaPRA Interim Event of the Performer Training Working Group in a fully equipped black box theatre space at the University of York in 2017. The reconstruction utilised lights that were already rigged and involved only the changes between narrow, medium and general wash, blackouts and the 'darting' lights. Even so, the setting of the lighting cues necessitated a two-hour rehearsal with a theatre technician who also operated the lights during the presentation. Assuming that Stanislavsky had access to the means to realise these experiments, they would require considerable preparation and technical know-how. This is entirely absent from the text.

25 It is highly unlikely that lights are used in the same way in the teaching of Stanislavsky's System today. In her *Complete Stanislavsky Toolkit*, Bella Merlin notes the use of lights in Stanislavsky's work on concentration, but proposes a set of exercises that serve as 'an adaptation of this Circles of Attention light-show' (2007: 279) and solely involve instructions for directing the student's attention to different parts of her physiology and environment (2007: 280).

References

Baugh, C. 2005. *Theatre Performance and Technology: The Development of Scenography in the Twentieth Century*. Hampshire: Palgrave.

Burdekin, R. 2018. 'Darkening the Auditorium in the Nineteenth Century British Theatre'. *Theatre Notebook*, 72 (1), pp. 40–57.

Camp, P. 2017. 'Technologies of Performance'. In: *A Cultural History of Theatre in the Age of the Enlightenment*, Vol 4, edited by Mechele Leon. London: Bloomsbury, pp. 181–202.

Carlson, M. 1993. *Theories of the Theatre* (expanded edition). Ithaca and London: Cornell University Press.

Carnicke, S. M. 2008. *Stanislavsky in Focus*. London: Routledge.

Casey, T. 1997. 'Technology and the Metaphysics of Technique', *Research in Philosophy and Technology*, 16, pp. 73–86.

Coquelin, C., Fogerty, E. and Kendal, M. 1932. *The Art of the Actor*. London: Allen & Unwin.

Cottom, D. 1999. 'The work of art in the age of mechanical digestion', *Representations*, 66 (Spring), pp. 52–74.

Craig, E. G. 1930. *Henry Irving*. London: J.M. Dent and Sons.

Craig, E. G. 1908. 'The Actor and the Über-Marionette', *The Mask*, 1 (2), pp. 3–15.

Diderot, D. 1883. *The Paradox of Acting*, translated by Walter Herries. Pollock. London: Chatto and Windus.

Diderot, D., D'Alembert, R. L. J. and others (eds) 1772. [*Encyclopaedia*] *Encyclopédie, ou dictionnaire raisonné des sciences, des arts et des métiers*, Vol 10. Paris: Chez Briasson.

Esposti, Degli P. 2015. 'The Fire of Demons and the Steam of Mortality: Edward Gordon Craig and the Ideal Performer', *Theatre Survey*, 56 (1), pp. 4–27. doi: https://doi.org/10.1017/S0040557414000544.

Franko, M. 1989. 'Repeatability, Reconstruction and Beyond', *Theatre Journal*, 41 (1), pp. 56–74.

Fryer, M. D. and Marshall, C. J. 1979. 'The Motives of Jacques de Vaucanson', *Technology and Culture*, 20 (2), pp. 257–69.

Goodden, A. 2011. 'Diderot, Rousseau and the art of craft'. In: *New Essays on Diderot*, edited by James Fowler. Cambridge: Cambridge University Press, pp. 59–73.

Hoyt, S. N. and Cassirer, T. (translation, introduction and notes) 1965. *The Encyclopedia: Selections [by] Diderot, D'Alembert and a society of men of letters*. Indianapolis: Bobbs-Merrill.

Innes, C. 2004 [1998]. *Edward Gordon Craig: a vision of theatre*. Oxon: Routledge.

Irving. H. 1904. *Two Lectures: Colley Cibber's "Apology" delivered to the members of the O. P. Club, Sunday, April 24th, 1904 and The Art & status of the actor, delivered to the members of the Playgoers' Club, Sunday, April 1st, 1900*. London: Chiswick Press.

Irving, H. 1887. *The Art of Acting*. Chicago: The Dramatic Publishing Company.

Irving, H. 1883. 'Preface'. In: *The Paradox of Acting*, translated by Walter Herries Pollock. London: Chatto and Windus, pp. ix–xx.

Koepp, J. C. 1986. 'The Alphabetical Order: Work in Diderot's *Encyclopedie*'. In: *Work in France*, edited by Stephen Lawrence Kaplan and Cynthia Koep. Ithaca, NY: Cornell University Press, pp. 229–57.

Landes, B. J. 2011. 'Vaucanson's Automata as Devices of Enlightenment', *Sjuttonhundratal*, 8, pp. 50–59.

Le Boeuf, P. 2010. 'On the Nature of Edward Gordon Craig's Über-Marionette', *New Theatre Quarterly*, 26 (2), pp. 102–114. doi: 10.1017/S0266464X10000242.

Ley, G.1995. 'The Significance of Diderot'. *New Theatre Quarterly*, 11 (44), pp. 342–54.

Merlin, B. 2007. *The Complete Stanislavsky Toolkit*. London: Nick Hern Books.

Nield, S. 2017. 'Technologies of Performance'. In: *A Cultural History of Theatre in the Age of Empire*, edited by Peter W. Marx. London: Bloomsbury, pp. 203–26.

Palmer, S. 2017. 'Harnessing Shadows: a historical perspective on the role of darkness in the theatre'. In: *Theatre in the Dark*, edited by Adam Alston and Martin Welton. London: Bloomsbury Methuen Drama.

Palmer, S. 2013. *Light*. Hampshire: Palgrave Macmillan.

Pannabecker, R. J. 1998. 'Representing Mechanical Arts in Diderot's *Encyclopedie*', *Technology and Culture*, 39 (1), pp. 33–73.

Payne, D. 2017. 'Communities of Production'. In: *A Cultural History of Theatre in the Age of the Enlightenment*, Vol 4, edited by Mechele Leon. London: Bloomsbury, pp. 139–58.

Pitches, J. 2015. 'Introduction to Part III: Technique – Training the Actor's Body and Voice'. In: *The Actor Training Reader*, edited by Mark Evans. London: Routledge, pp. 55–65.

Pitches, J. 2006. *Science and the Stanislavsky Tradition of Acting*, Oxon and New York: Routledge.

Ramacharaka [William Atkinson]. 1906. *Raja Yoga or Mental Development*. Chicago: The Yogi Publication Society.

Reilly, K. 2011. *Automata and Mimesis on the Stage of Theatre History*. Hampshire: Palgrave.

Riskin, J. 2003. 'The Defecating Duck, or, the ambiguous origins of artificial life', *Critical Inquiry*, 29 (4), pp. 599–633.

Roach, J. 2007 [1984]. *The Player's Passion*. Ann Arbor: The University of Michigan Press.

Sanderson, M. 1984. *From Irving to Olivier*. London: The Athlone Press.

Schaffer, S. 1999. 'Enlightened Automata'. In: *The Sciences in the Enlightened Europe*, edited by William Clark, Jan Golinksi and Simon Schaffer. Chicago: University of Chicago Press, pp. 126–65.

Senelick, L. 1976. 'The Craig-Stanislavsky "Hamlet" at the Moscow Art Theatre', *Theatre Quarterly*, 22 (6), pp. 56–71.

Sennett, R. 2008. *The Craftsman*. London: Penguin.

Sewell, H. W. Jr. 1986. 'Visions of Labour: Illustrations of the Mechanical Arts before, in, and after Diderot's Encyclopedie'. In: *Work in France*, edited by Stephen Lawrence Kaplan and Cynthia Koepp. Ithaca, NY: Cornell University Press, pp. 258–86.

Stanislavsky, K. 2008a. *An Actor's Work*, translated by J. Benedetti (1st edition). Oxon: Routledge.

Stanislavsky, K. 2008b. *My Life in Art*, translated by J. Benedetti (1st edition). Oxon: Routledge.

Stoker, B. 1911. 'Irving and Stage Lighting', *The Nineteenth Century and After: A Monthly Review*, 69 (409), pp. 903–12.

Stucky, N. and Tomell-Presto, J. 2004. 'Acting and Movement Training of the Body'. In: *Teaching Theatre Today: Pedagogical Views of Theatre in Higher Education*, edited by Anne L. Fliotsos and Gail S. Medford. New York: Palgrave Macmillan, pp. 103–24.

Taxidou, O. 1998. *The Mask: a periodical performance by Edward Gordon Craig*. Amsterdam: Harwood Academic Publishing.

Vartanian, A. 1981. 'Diderot's Rhetoric of Paradox, or the Conscious Automaton Observed', *Eighteenth-Century Studies*, 14 (4), pp. 379–405.

von Kleist, H. 1972 [1810]. 'On the Marionette Theatre', *The Drama Review: TDR*, 16 (3) pp. 22–6.

Werner, S. 1993. *Blueprint*. Birmingham, Alabama: Summa Publications.

White, A. 2014. 'Stanislavsky and Ramacharaka: The impact of Yoga and the Occult Revival on the System'. In: *The Routledge Companion to Stanislavsky*, edited by Andrew White. New York: Routledge, pp. 287–304.

3

BEYOND TECHNIQUE

Critiquing technology and actor training in the 1960s

Introduction

The previous chapter traced the emergence of the idea of the actor's instrument. With reference to Dennis Diderot's *The Paradox of Acting* as well as nineteenth- and early twentieth-century theatre practice, the chapter argued that an overly positive disposition towards technology led to an understanding of and a call for an acting technique that was modelled on the efficiency of the machine. Yet, the chapter also pointed out that during the establishment of actor training in the early twentieth century, the idea of the machine became both embraced and negated. This chapter continues this trajectory and examines the way the actor's instrument and training is approached in the second half of the twentieth century. It focuses on a current of twentieth-century theatre practice that approaches technique with suspicion, if not hostility. In contrast to the positive outlook towards technique and technology that characterised the actor's work in the nineteenth and early twentieth century, this chapter aims to foreground the links between developments in actor training during the 1960s and a wider critique of, and often against, technology.

In addition to presenting a critical stance towards ideas and practices of technical accomplishment, this chapter is also concerned with techne, another key term that is etymologically and semantically cognate with both technology and technique. Ihde explains that in Ancient Greek philosophy:

> Techne was simultaneously a craft and art object – it could be a marvellous shield, a finely wrought statue, or a vessel for drinking. Art and technology were not separated, and, indeed, intrinsic to the judgement of any such object was not simply its utility, but also its beauty. But, techne clearly was a produced artefact, a virtual 'technology'.

(1993: 26)

As I will discuss, during the mid-twentieth century techne attracts renewed theoretical attention and, in a certain sense, acquires a reparative potential: since techne constitutes an activity of making similar to, but distinct from, the productive force of technology, it could provide an alternative to the technological rationality that was perceived to dominate Western societies and subjects.[1] This understanding of techne will be discussed in relation to the work of Martin Heidegger (1889–1976) and Herbert Marcuse (1898–1979) on the one hand, and the work of 1960s theatre practitioners, on the other. As I will demonstrate, both Heidegger and Marcuse offered deeply influential analyses of technological domination and Marcuse, in particular, was widely read by and popular with the American counter-culture. Drawing on ancient Greek philosophy, they also saluted techne as a way of transcending a technological way of being in the world. Nonetheless, an obvious, but rarely acknowledged, fact is that neither Heidegger nor Marcuse was an artist. Yet, their work engaged with the arts and Marcuse's writings, in particular, resonated with the work of theatre practitioners of the time. How realistic were, nonetheless, their expectations that the realm and processes of art-making could become a means for transcending technological rationality? And how did these expectations play out in the actual endeavour of theatre groups to revitalise theatre praxis in the 1960s? As the rest of the chapter will discuss, because the stakes during the 1960s were nothing less than a radical reinvention of society and of theatre as an art form, performer training acquired a central function in the endeavour for artistic and social regeneration. The additional aim of this chapter, then, is to explore not only how performer training has been influenced by a critique of/against technology, but also how it measured up against the claims made by intellectuals and artists of the time that art could offer an alternative.

With reference to the wider scene of American avant-garde theatre, this chapter will pay particular attention to the work of the Open Theatre and its artistic director Joseph Chaikin (1935–2003). This choice of focus has been determined both by the critical appraisal the group received for its artistic accomplishments, which, as I will explain later, was not always the case with other avant-garde performances, as well as their explicit commitment to the performer's work (Hulton 2010) and the development of a training approach that still has a legacy today (Babb 2006). Historiographical analyses of their work also exemplify a particular bias towards the study of technology, which is of particular interest to this book. As I will discuss in the following section, to a significant extent scholarship on avant-garde theatre tends to highlight the importance of ritual, myth and the actor's presence, whilst overlooking or downplaying how a critique against technological rationality also shaped the group's approach. In response to this bias, this chapter aims to foreground the role that a critique of technology had in the development of the Open Theatre's work and training. In doing so, I will draw links between Marcuse and Heidegger's critique of technology and the Open Theatre's development of a theatrical language that gave expression to the political and psychical alienation of American technologised society. Marcuse's influence on Chaikin is documented and Bigsby frequently stresses the impact of Marcuse's thinking on American experimental theatre practitioners (1985: 10, 39, 71, 79) and Chaikin specifically (1985: 102). Nonetheless, in discussions of avant-garde theatre, Marcuse's ideas are not presented in depth and equally the position of technology in the work of the Open Theatre has not been analysed. A philosophically informed analysis will also be complemented by paying attention to the role that a specific artefact had within the group's work. As I will discuss, television not only defined American culture in the 1950s and 1960s; it constituted a recurring point of reference in the group's work and has not been subjected to date to in-depth analysis.

Closer attention to the intersections between the group's work, a critical stance towards technology, as well as the position of a specific artefact may allow us, I will argue, to appreciate the importance of the overall project the Open Theatre was committed to, and its potential relevance today. It can also offer a better under-standing of a philosophical critique of technology that on paper may appear to be too abstract or too deterministic. It can, finally, enable us to evaluate how the redemptive potential of techne, advocated by Marcuse and others, was realised within the work of a specific group. To put it another way: my argument is that the Open Theatre was not only influenced by but managed to create an aesthetic form and artistic ethos that embodied a philosophical critique of technology. The development of the actors, both as persons and artists within the group, was inex-tricably linked to this critique. Yet, the group was in the end short-lived and, as I will explain later, its disbandment was presented as a means to resist becoming 'an institution, a success in the good old American way' (Coco et al. 1983: 27). In the light of the group's professional career and artistic vision, I will conclude that the Open Theatre both confirms Marcuse's and Heidegger's instinct about the poten-tial of techne to realise alternative social relations and at the same time demonstrates the fundamental difficulties of such a realisation.

The argument will unfold in the following way. The next section offers an over-view of avant-garde theatre in the 1960s and discusses how it is often associated with particular emphases on the actor's presence, in terms of training and prepara-tion and on myth and ritual, in terms of content and form. It will be argued that although these emphases are historically correct and in line with the pronounce-ments of practitioners, the picture is more complicated. The second section will present a critique of technology as developed by Marcuse in *One-Dimensional Man* (2002 [1964]), a book that proved highly popular with the counter-culture and which Chaikin read. The presentation of Marcuse's text will be supplemented with reference to another highly influential critique of technology, Martin Heidegger's essay 'The Question Concerning Technology' (1977).[2] The two texts together will allow us to understand what, from a mid-twentieth century vantage point, was perceived to be 'wrong' with the world and how technology was implicated in this perception. In the third section, I will trace the way this critique emerges in devel-opments in actor training within avant-garde circles and the work of the Open Theatre in particular. The chapter will conclude with a consideration of larger questions: can techne offer an alternative to a technologised world as suggested by Marcuse and Heidegger? To what extent is such an alternative premised on technical mastery? How might such mastery be achieved through training? What is the legacy of the training approaches developed in the 1960s and can these approaches be relevant or valid as a form of critique today?

American avant-garde theatre in the 1960s

The American experimental theatre scene in the 1960s is often captured under collective nouns, such as 'avant-garde theatre' (Aronson 2000; Innes 1993); 'the avant-garde' (Schechner 1981; 2015); underground theatre (Bottoms 2006); off-off or beyond Broadway scene (Bottoms 2006; Bigsby 1985); and radical theatres (Harding and Rosenthal 2006; Sainer 1997 [1975]). The use of umbrella terms, such as 'avant-garde theatre' has been challenged. Either because it sets in train a process of canonisation, which effectively obscures practitioners whose work does not fit with the canon (Bottoms 2006), or because it brings to the analysis a set of unexamined assumptions with regard to what the avant-garde is (Harding 2016). The term will be used here because, unlike the other proposed terms, it encapsulates both revolt and protection. Specifically in relation to the practices examined in this chapter, the avant-garde not only denotes the forefront of artistic experimentation; in creating spaces for artistic expression outside the mainstream it also 'guarded' artists against the ills of technologised culture. The term therefore serves here as a shorthand that captures the wider ethos as well as the cultural milieu in which the work of the Open Theatre developed. In this respect, it also bears noting that although the adverb 'American' denotes a geographical location, it is better understood as a cultural rather than geographical denomination. If anything, groups – such as the Living Theatre, the Performance Group, and the Open Theatre – travelled extensively, performed abroad and had ongoing contacts with European theatre practitioners, primarily Jerzy Grotowski (1933–99), Eugenio Barba (1936–) and Peter Brook (1925–).

Overall, avant-garde theatre practice in the 1960s took place within a wider counter-cultural youth movement that swept through the United States as well as parts of Europe. Theatre practitioners and artists were often directly involved in political activism whilst performances addressed political issues, most prominently the war in Vietnam. Indeed, avant-garde theatre in the 1960s was fuelled by an appreciation of performance as a catalyst for social change as well as an appreciation of performance-making as a possible ground for exercising radical democracy. 'For a brief moment', Bigsby observes, 'the theatrical event and the political event genuinely seemed part of a continuum and it was only logical and natural for people to flow between them' (1985: 11). As such, the 1960s avant-garde scene challenged key aspects of the theatrical enterprise, not least the hierarchy of text and language, the role of the audience and the use of space. Furthermore, and as Jean Benedetti attests, 'the finished work, the packaged "product" the emblem of consumerism was mistrusted' and artistic work was 'referred to as "research" or "work in progress"' (2005: 221). An emphasis on process as well as an enthusiasm for trying out and developing new performance techniques entailed a renewed interest in performer training practice, which subsequently influenced further developments in North America and Europe.

The tone across histories of 1960s avant-garde theatre varies. Some sources are celebratory of the experimental spirit and political commitment that marked the approach of the groups (Sainer 1997 [1975]) and/or trace the significance of the work for contemporary practice (for example Babb (2006) and Hulton (2010) in relation to the Open Theatre). Other accounts are a lot more critical. For example, Richard Schechner (1981; 2015), a key player within the scene at the time, claims not only that the revolutionary spirit was in the end short-lived, but that financial difficulties, political conservatism and personal conflicts undermined any meaningful continuation; like a firework the spark of the avant-garde was bright but brief. Of particular relevance here is that one of the key reasons for the perceived failure of the avant-garde to live up to its promises is attributed, according to Schechner (1981), to the lack of a training method that could disseminate the insights and technical skills developed by practitioners in the 1960s to later generations.

Beyond the problems outlined by Schechner in terms of legacy, other scholars are critical of the avant-garde project in and of itself, suggesting that the theatre experiments of the time were often characterised by political naivety and artistic inadequacy. In his historiographical evaluation of the off-off Broadway scene, for instance, Bigsby identifies 'an altogether insufficient rigorous aesthetic' (1985: 60) as one of the main causes for the demise of the avant-garde. In other words, the quality and impact of the artistic product failed to match the promises of the rhetoric. Although the aim of this chapter is not to offer a renewed appreciation of avant-garde theatre production in the 1960s, the evaluation of the avant-garde project as a whole and the work of specific groups is pertinent here for two reasons.

One reason pertains to performer training history and practice. As the experimental theatre practice in the 1960s constituted a vital period for the development of actor and performer training, it is important to understand what drove these developments and whether the way training was conceptualised in the 1960s has any valence today. The other reason pertains to historiography. As Bonnie Marranca (2006: 14) has argued, performance practice in the twentieth century appears to have been captured in two histories: one situated in the field of visual arts and the other in the field of theatre. Marranca observes that (ibid.), since these two histories are yet to be integrated into a comprehensive whole, it is easy to lose sight of the important exchanges and cross-fertilisation that took place between them.

Of particular relevance to this chapter is the position of technology within these two histories. Accounts that deal with instances of 'performance' in galleries and non-theatrical spaces by visual artists and music composers readily discuss experimentation with technologies. Notable examples are the work of Nam June Paik with television and video circuits; and the collaboration between John Cage, Robert Rauschenberg and various members of the Judson Dance Theatre with engineers from the Bell Laboratories, initially for an event entitled 'Nine Evenings of Theatre and Engineering' (1966) and later renamed to 'E.A.T' (Experiments in

Arts and Technology). On the other hand, established histories of avant-garde theatre, for instance by Aronson (2000), Bigsby (1985) and Innes (1993), map a territory of influences, commonly including Artaud's Theatre of Cruelty, Zen and the Beats, Black Mountain College and John Cage. Although this set of influences is historically correct, they are skewed, since in an effort to emphasise the ritualistic and mythological bend of much avant-garde theatre work, analyses fail to properly account for the importance that technology had at that time within society in general, and the work of specific avant-garde theatre practitioners in particular. For example, Innes argues that 'what defines' avant-garde practice both in the early and the mid-twentieth century 'is not overtly modern qualities [...] but primitivism' (1993: 3). There is a clear bias amongst theatre scholars, in other words, to overlook the influence that technology was exerting on avant-garde practices. Unless one studies sources of both 'theatre' and 'performance' history, it would be impossible to gain an understanding of the shared ground underpinning the diverse experimentation that was taking place within the same cultural milieu.

A particular point merits reference here. A key aspect of avant-garde rhetoric and practice was a repudiation of technological rationality, that is an understanding of persons, populations and societies in terms of efficiency and productivity. Technological rationality, as we saw in the previous chapter, began to be established in the eighteenth century and came to full fruition with the Industrial Revolution. The post-WWII development of the American military-industrial complex as well as the war in Vietnam constituted the political manifestation of this approach and offered a set of clear targets against which avant-garde experimentation was positioned. At the same time, however, a significant part of the population that came of age in the 1960s, at least in the United States, grew up and enjoyed living in conditions of unprecedented affluence. Avant-garde artists were thus caught in a bind: technology could and certainly did wreak havoc; technology could and certainly did make life easier.

An avant-garde sensibility dictated, therefore, an opposition to technological rationality, and at the same time sought to develop relationships to technology that were, or at least seemed to offer, an alternative to the dominant version. In some cases, avant-garde practitioners attempted to wrench technology back from military-industrial operations and put it to the service of a humanist ideal towards an egalitarian, non-materialist society. For example, according to The Living Theatre co-founder Julian Beck, 'industrial society' and 'capitalistic morality' had respectively 'numbed' and 'clamped shut' the body (Beck 1972: section 32, np). At the same time though, computers and cybernetic technologies were hailed as an essential component of the new world, since they were expected to free people from unnecessary tasks and allow them to enjoy life (Beck 1972: section 121, np). Although Beck's vision may come across, and has been dismissed, as naive (Bigsby 1985: 71), there was also at the time significant artistic experimentation with technologies, primarily within visual arts circles.

For example, Nam June Paik's 'prepared' television sets, and the guerrilla television groups that emerged in the 1960s, were highly influential and ushered in 'multimedia' and 'video art'. These works simultaneously demonstrated an explicit critique of technology, as a political and socio-economic force, and an actual tinkering with technological devices. As mentioned, although these practices are promptly noted by scholars of visual arts (Joselit 2007) and 'performance' (Marranca 2006), they have been entirely ignored by theatre historians, who by comparison are pre-occupied with the emphasis that theatre practitioners of the time placed on the actor's presence and the live encounter between actors and audience. Some scholarly analyses deal very little with technology or not at all. Others position technology as a force antagonising the 'liveness' of theatre practice. I will review each of these positions in turn, along the way making the argument that the relationship of avant-garde theatre practitioners with technology was more nuanced.

The majority of scholarly material on experimental theatrical practice in the 1960s makes only passing references to the various ways in which technology defined American culture. Notably, in *American Avant Garde Theatre*, Arnold Aronson acknowledges that

> America was the land of radio, television, movies, automobiles, airplanes, skyscrapers, supermarkets, neon lights, planned obsolescence, atomic weapons, rockets, computers and rock 'n' roll. It was a land where, at least through the 1960s, technology was promoted by government and commercial enterprise alike as a panacea, a means toward a better life, a virtual utopia.
>
> (2000: 41)

Yet, this long list is followed by the rather cryptic conclusion that 'the avant-garde theatre that emerged did not always reflect the new technology, but it often captured the rapidly shifting consciousness of the new age' (Aronson 2000: 41). What is more, in the chapter that examines the Living Theatre, the Performance Group and the Open Theatre, Aronson focuses on the groups' emphasis on ritual and their process of collective creation. He does not explore whether technology had an impact on their work or, indeed, whether significant features of the work were in any way related to the technological development he outlines earlier in the book.

Similarly, in *Avant Garde 1892–1992* Christopher Innes introduces the Open Theatre by offering the following trajectory: the group 'developed from a close acting workshop to ritualistic performances of archetypal material with *The Serpent* in the same year as Schechner's *Dionysus*' (1993: 178). In the rest of the section, Innes examines *The Serpent* and makes the rather startling conclusion that the Open Theatre 'turned productions into a form of psychotherapy' (1993: 179). The way Innes introduces the group omits not only the first six formational years of the group's process, between 1963 and 1969, but also a highly significant aspect of *The Serpent*: the juxtaposition of the myth of Genesis with the respective assassinations of J. F. Kennedy, Robert Kennedy and Martin Luther King. Most importantly, Innes fails to acknowledge that, as Dorinda Hulton (2018) has observed and I will discuss in more detail later, the assassination scenes were developed out of television footage and utilised techniques of video and film editing, such as fast forward and replay.

In addition to Aronson's and Innes' canonical histories, other titles mention technology but only as a component of popular culture against which theatre practice was positioned. For example, in her monograph on Joseph Chaikin, Eileen Blumenthal positions Chaikin's emphasis on presence in an antithetical relation to the popularity of recorded media. According to Blumenthal, presence is 'the fundamental difference between the stage and film or television' (1984: 40). More recently, Marianne Weems, the artistic director of the Builders Association, also suggests that 'the Performance Group and the Living Theatre were frequently ideologically opposed to media and based their work on physical ritual and the sanctity or at least undeniable presence of the performer' (Weems in Marranca 2009: 184). Claire Bishop, finally, makes a similar point with regards to the work of Jerzy Grotowski and Peter Brook, both of whom had significant exchanges with the Open Theatre and the Performance Group. Remarking on Grotowski's and Brook's respective focus on the actor's live performance, Bishop states 'for both directors, what motivated this desire for proximity was new technology: theatre was unable to compete with the seductions of cinema and television, but what it could offer was immediacy, proximity, and communion' (2018: 30).

Indeed, in his well-known aphorism, cited by Bishop and others, Grotowski claimed that 'theatre can exist without make-up, without autonomic costume and scenography, without a separate performance area (stage), without lighting and sound effects etc. It cannot exist without the actor-spectator relationship of perceptual, direct, "live" communion' (1991 [1968]: 18). A less well known, but equally influential statement was published in the same year in *The Tulane Drama Review*. In his co-authored article on theatre buildings, architect, polymath and avant-garde guru Buckminster Fuller begins by claiming that:

> Theatre, at mid-twentieth century, finds itself in a position of 'change or die'. The rapid development of television and cinema have been to it what photography was to representational painting: they can do many of the same things better and more simply. The only means of survival clearly lies in making the very most of the unique quality of theatre – the relationship between a live audience and live performers.
>
> (Fuller and Sadao 1968: 117)

In the light of these statements, it is easy to see how scholars and practitioners may conclude that 1960s experimental theatre practice was underpinned both by an antipathy towards the 'big' technologies that made up the military-industrial operations of the United States, as well as an antagonism towards the more 'domestic' technologies, such as television, radio and cinema, that made up the daily life of millions of Americans. The relationship, however, is more complicated.

To begin, we have to bear in mind that despite his coinage of 'poor theatre', Grotowski's work, as well as celebrated productions such as *Akropolis* and the *Constant Prince* – which were presented in New York in 1969 – were marked by sophisticated textual dramaturgy, a radical rethinking of the playing area and carefully designed costumes. Even though Grotowski *argues* for a theatre denuded of 'the trappings' of language and other technologies, both language and technologies were employed, and indeed developed to a high standard. An instructive example is Grotowski's reference to the use of lights, where he describes how the abandonment of 'lighting effects [...] revealed a wide range of possibilities for the actor's use of stationary light-sources' (1991 [1968]: 20). A closer look at Grotowski's rhetoric reveals, therefore, that 'poor theatre' did not banish theatrical technologies as such, but rather proposed to approach them in new ways. Equally, in their manifesto of 1968, Fuller and Sadao do not advocate shunning technology but *replacing* the design of conventional theatre buildings with new ones. Indeed, a prototype of Fuller and Sadao's proposal for an open plan, flexible playing area was later realised in the Wooster Street garage, the training and performance space of the Performance Group and, afterwards, the Wooster Group.

It has to be stressed, therefore, that although scholarly work seems to favour the negative disposition of experimental theatre practitioners towards technology and although this may appear consistent with the pronouncements of some of the practitioners, the actual experimentation was far more nuanced and often concerned with a realignment between live action and technology. As such, the theatrical act was being redefined *vis-à-vis* the technologies of the time and, accordingly, the technologies of the time were explored from different angles and for different effects, even if they were not directly used. This position will be exemplified in more detail later in the chapter with reference to television.

Accordingly, instead of understanding the intersections between technology and the development of the actor's presence in a linear, antagonistic manner, the proposition here is to examine the actor's training *in relation* to the way technology was understood within a counter-cultural critique. This chapter then proposes to explore the work of avant-garde practitioners 'against the grain', a tactic, which according to James Harding, needs to include a reading 'not merely against the grain of avant-gardes but also against the grain of the implied or even expressed intent of avant-garde artists' (2016: 23). In response to the accounts that either overlook technology or simplistically position it as the polar opposite of live theatre practice, the remainder of this chapter aims to offer an in-depth exposition of the way technology was critiqued and the way this critique found its artistic expression within the development of Open Theatre's innovative training approach.

Critiquing technology: Martin Heidegger and Herbert Marcuse

Positioning Heidegger and Marcuse's names side by side may provoke thoughts of a proverbial funerary turn or two. In response to the publication of Heidegger's seminal *Being and Time* (1928), Marcuse relocated to Freiburg and studied with

Heidegger between 1928 and 1932. His aim was to combine Heidegger's existential philosophy with Marx's socio-economic analysis, producing a fusion that has been retrospectively called 'left Heideggerianism' (Wolin 2001). Nonetheless, Marcuse eventually broke contact with Heidegger. The reason for the estrangement between the two philosophers was Heidegger's support of the Nazi party during 1933–4 – the year Marcuse, a German of Jewish origin, fled Germany. The men resumed contact after the war but Heidegger's refusal until the end of his life to explain, let alone condemn his political affiliations put an end to the relationship. Although Marcuse repudiated Heidegger's influence (Olafson 2007 [1977]), and although their political leanings were diametrically opposite, there are significant resonances between their thinking, which have been pointed out by recent commentators (Feenberg 2005; Wolin 2001; Zimmerman 1990).

In a certain sense, Heidegger's and Marcuse's respective work, especially their critique of technology, may be seen as complementary: where Marcuse's analysis sheds light on a concrete social context, Heidegger explains that technology is a form of being in the world. As Heidegger's text only alludes towards specific socio-historical processes, it can frustrate the reader who seeks an explanation of how his critique of technology may play out within a particular society. Marcuse's analysis, on the other hand, concentrated on the way the effects of technological rationality were produced and manifested within the socio-economic environment of the global superpower that the United States was in the 1960s. As such, it may be seen as an application of Heidegger's thinking on a specific geographical and socio-economic environment. Most importantly, both thinkers advance two connected ideas, which are of particular relevance here: there is no critical or existential outside beyond technological rationality; art can offer the space for developing alternative possibilities.

'A comfortable, smooth, reasonable, democratic unfreedom prevails in advanced industrial civilisation, a token of technical progress' (Marcuse 2002 [1964]: 3). Thus opens Marcuse *One-Dimensional Man*, a diagnostic analysis of American society in the 1960s, which proved highly successful with the counter-culture and offered the theoretical ground for civic revolt. According to Marcuse, the problem centred on the shrinking of the political, social and psychic reality to a limited sphere dedicated to increasing productivity whilst repressing human potential. The trade-off was a comfortable life, 'much better than before', which, however, 'militates against qualitative change'. As a result, there

> emerges a pattern of *one-dimensional thought and behaviour* in which ideas, aspirations, and objectives that, by their content, transcend the established universe of discourse and action are either repelled or reduced to terms of this universe. They are redefined by the rationality of the given system and of its quantitative extension.
>
> (Marcuse 2002 [1964]: 14, emphasis original)

According to Marcuse, both language and art have been co-opted by a repressive system and robbed of their ability to express any experience that falls outside this one dimension. As a result, persons are condemned to being alienated not only from their labour, as in traditional Marxist thought, but also from their own selves. Within this universe, individuals can no longer determine their own needs, since these are dictated by extraneous agendas and interests, which ultimately serve political and social domination. Marcuse therefore is unequivocal that

> No matter how much such needs may have become the individual's own, reproduced and fortified by the conditions of his existence; no matter how much he identifies himself with them and finds himself in their satisfaction, they continue to be what they were from the beginning – products of a society whose dominant interests demand repression.
>
> (2002 [1964]: 7)

Alienation is, therefore, one of the chief maladies diagnosed by Marcuse and one of the key junctures where his thinking meets Heidegger's.

Heidegger begins his essay on technology with the rather paradoxical claim that the essence of technology is 'by no means anything technological' (1977: 4). Instead of identifying technology with technological artefacts, Heidegger concentrates on the way technology manifests as a way of being in the world. As Andrew Feenberg explains, 'world' according to Heidegger is 'a nexus of meanings enacted in practice' and technology is positioned as 'the underlying basis of modernity' (2015: 230). For Heidegger then, technology is not a symptom of our times, but the very mode in which Western modernity has been constituted, and, as a result, the very mode in which a world becomes meaningful to human subjects. As such, technology is ontological, since it 'reveals' the way human beings can experience the world *as* a world to which they bear a relationship. In order to support this claim, Heidegger begins with an important inversion between science and technology. As presented in the Introduction, Heidegger, as well as contemporary philosophers such as Don Ihde, maintains that although technological instruments appear to follow scientific development, the opposite is true. Crucially, however, for Heidegger such inversion is not only a question of sequence, i.e. whether a technological artefact precedes a scientific theory; it is foundational, since science has to presuppose a particular way of approaching nature. Technology is not a generic term for the artefacts produced out of scientific advancements; it is a primary way of relating to the world, and as such determines and predates science.

The 'technological' way in which nature is approached Heidegger calls 'standing reserve', a cyclical and value-free process whereby 'the energy concealed in nature is unlocked, what is unlocked is transformed, what is transformed is stored up, what is stored up is, in turn, distributed, and what is distributed is switched about ever anew' (1977: 16). The overall mode that determines an approach to nature as 'standing reserve' Heidegger calls 'Enframing' (Gestell). Enframing denotes the foundational manner in which humans relate to the world, a manner according to which 'reality acquires its identity from what can be done with it' (Verbeek 2005: 54). Enframing thus suggests that humans approach nature with an *a priori* inclination towards appropriation, exploitation and domination. More importantly, Heidegger argues that this disposition may also extend to the self: 'he [man] comes to the point where he himself will have to be taken as standing-reserve' (1977: 27). Enframing, therefore, becomes a totalising attitude that treats as resources-to-be-exploited not only physical entities, but social, interpersonal and even psychical spaces. And because such attitude is foundational, humans are not even aware that their actions and relations are determined by it. Heidegger, thus, positions humankind on 'the brink of the possibility of pursuing and pushing forward nothing but what is revealed in ordering and of delivering all [...] standards on this basis' (1977: 26). Reality becomes constricted to what can be quantified, calculated and exploited.

As mentioned already, barring the occasional example, Heidegger's analysis is not grounded within a specific social context. What is more, the poetic, slightly apocalyptic, and, according to some commentators, obscure tone of the writing raises the question of whether Heidegger's thinking can be applicable as a form of social critique at all. In this respect, Marcuse's book could be seen as the last nail on the coffin of Western (American) modernity: it not only proves the usefulness of Heidegger's thought as a critical lens, it further demonstrates that Heidegger's worst fears had been confirmed. Drawing on his understanding of Marx, Marcuse identifies technological rationality as the very heart of a capitalist socio-economic system, and argues that it is so corrosive that the individual cannot even lay claim to an internal territory that may remain free, or at least separate, from such thinking. Rather, such thinking is so totalising that 'this private space has been invaded and whittled down by technological reality' (Marcuse 2002 [1964]: 12). Echoing Heidegger, Marcuse claims that 'the instrumentalisation of things' becomes 'the instrumentalisation of man' (2002 [1964]: 163). 'Instrumentalisation' according to Marcuse, or 'Enframing' according to Heidegger, 'claim[s] the *entire* individual' (Marcuse 2002 [1964]: 12, emphasis original). Individuals are thus locked in an inauthentic, that is heteronomous, relation to the world, since their physical and psychical needs, material and emotional desires, social relations and labour conditions are determined by instrumentalisation.

It is precisely this internalisation of instrumentalisation that makes both Heidegger and Marcuse pessimistic about the emergence of a different kind of order. Marcuse makes an additionally alarming observation, which, as I will demonstrate, is particularly relevant to the Open Theatre specifically, and avant-garde artistic practice in general: he does not claim that opposition does not exist; he rather laments that it ultimately becomes co-opted. Forms of cultural, political or even spiritual resistance only achieve 'harmless negation, and are quickly digested by the status quo as part of its healthy diet' (Marcuse 2002 [1964]: 16). The result is a closed off universe that promises 'an ever-more-comfortable life for an ever-growing number of people who, in a strict sense, cannot imagine a qualitatively different universe of discourse and action' (Marcuse 2002 [1964]: 26).

Techne: artworks and aesthetic sensibility

In view of the stark conclusions reached by both philosophers, it is highly significant that both Heidegger and Marcuse identify in art a vital function. Heidegger closes 'The Question Concerning Technology' arguing that a confrontation with technology needs to happen within the field of art, because techne is 'akin to the essence of technology and on the other hand, fundamentally different from it' (1977: 35). What technology and techne have in common is that they both involve active manipulation of matter, a *making*. The crucial difference, however, is that technology involves a making that is blind to the potentialities of materials and rather follows a logic of control and domination, eventually extending from physical to human nature. Drawing on Greek philosophy, Heidegger argues that techne, on the other hand, involves a dialogic process of making between maker and matter that allows space for the expression of both. As Feenberg explains, within Heidegger's formulation of techne:

> A reciprocal interaction and exchange takes place joining maker and materials in a unity in diversity, a totality. It is at this level that activity and receptivity complement each other rather than appearing as alternatives, that the subject is in harmony with the object it transforms without wholly supressing its independence, that identity and nonidentity are reconciled. The object belongs to a human lifeworld as a subject with its own potentialities.
>
> (2005: 130)

According to Heidegger then a solution to Enframing is premised not on banishing technology but on developing a relationship to the world that is mapped onto the kind of reciprocity between object and subject we find in techne.

Also drawing on Greek philosophy and echoing Heidegger, Marcuse similarly argues that artistic or craft making is underpinned by values intrinsic to the art form. Technological making, by contrast, manifests in dominating, controlling and exploiting resources. As a result, 'things no longer have intrinsic potentialities transcending their given form, but are simply there, unresistingly available for human use' (Feenberg 2005: 87). According to both Heidegger and Marcuse, technological rationality is understood as a degeneration of the fundamental human activity of making. A way to transcend technological domination, then, is to reclaim an 'artistic' way of making, which, according to Marcuse's analysis, can provide 'a model of a transformed instrumentality different from the "conquest" of nature characteristic of class society' (Feenberg 1999: 155). In other words, art like technology involves making, which necessitates the use of resources and the mastery of both materials and technique. Yet, artistic making is qualitatively different from technological making, because it emerges from a different relationship to the world and eventually can transcend the established technocratic order. Heidegger's essay finishes with the tantalising but rather underdeveloped assertion that techne can be the 'salvation' to technology, an idea which will be revisited in the last chapter.

Marcuse takes this idea further and positions techne within a social and cultural sphere. In his analysis, techne is discussed in the following two main ways: with respect to the possible effect of an artwork, and as a form of praxis. Although Marcuse does not distinguish explicitly or sufficiently enough between these two understandings, I will discuss them separately. As mentioned already, Marcuse is pessimistic about the ability of an artwork – be it a novel, a painting or a theatrical performance – to engender effective critique, let alone action. Marcuse thinks that the potential of art-as-a-cultural-product to usher in another relation to the world is stifled, since the artwork is a product of, and thus subjected to, the taming that characterises one-dimensional society:

> the absorbent power of society depletes the artistic dimension by assimilating its antagonistic contents. In the realm of culture, the new totalitarianism manifests itself precisely in a harmonizing pluralism, where the most contra- dictory works and truths peacefully coexist in indifference.
>
> (Marcuse 2002 [1964]: 64)

Works of art, therefore, however challenging they might appear to be to the dominant culture, are rendered ineffective since they fail to change the terms of the discourse. At the same time, Marcuse acknowledges that artworks, even though they may not be able to realise alternative worlds, have the potential to *present* them, and the experience of such presentations *is* real. In a passage, which Chaikin will also repeat in his own book eight years later, Marcuse writes:

> Like technology, art creates another universe of thought and practice against and within the existing one. But in contrast to the technical universe, the artistic universe is one of illusion, semblance, *Schein*. However, this semb- lance is resemblance to a reality which exists as the threat and promise of the established one.
>
> (Marcuse 2002 [1964]: 243 and cited in Chaikin 1991 [1972]: 23)

Art produces a reality that exists only in illusion, but exists nonetheless.

The other way in which techne is encountered in Marcuse's analysis is as a form of aesthetic sensibility. In this understanding, techne is discussed not in relation to the finished product and its reception, but rather as a kind of disposition that under- pins and guides human action: one that 'perceives potentialities in the objects themselves, as potentialities of those objects, and not as arbitrary desires or wishes of the subject' (Feenberg 2005: 96). Moreover, in Marcuse's formulation, aesthetic sensibility is uncoupled from the practice of a specific artistic discipline and is pre- sented as a form of life praxis (Marcuse 1969: 32). In *An Essay on Liberation* (1969), which outlines the concept, Marcuse notes that change effected by political action is not enough because it fails to upset the foundations of the dominant system (1969: 54–6). The only solution, then, is a radical refashioning of the human sensorium, which will allow human subjects to 'break with the familiar, the routine ways of seeing, hearing, feeling, understanding things so that the organism may become receptive to the potential forms of nonaggressive, nonexploitative world' (Marcuse 1969: 6).

Marcuse turns an ontological understanding of technological instrumentalisation into a biological one: 'the so-called consumer economy and the politics of corporate capitalism have created a second nature of man which ties him libidinally and aggressively to the commodity form' (1969: 11). It is precisely because technological rationality is understood to be so deeply rooted, lodged in the very systems of perception, that Marcuse calls for a new sensibility: an ability to perceive the world differently and to perceive more than the reality that is manifest through technological rationality. Accordingly, Marcuse foresees that once such sensibility is attained, a different relation to technology will be possible, one that will fulfil 'technology's promise' and put it exclusively at the service of human life (1969: 19). Marcuse calls this new kind of perception 'aesthetic' in order to evoke two key aspects of the word: 'pertaining to the senses' and 'pertaining to art' (1969: 24). An aesthetic sensibility, to put it otherwise, needs to be realised through the senses and will switch 'society's capacity to produce' from a technological to an artistic kind (Marcuse 1969: 48). As Bradley Macdonald explains, Marcuse's understanding of art is underpinned by a tension: on the one hand, according to Marcuse, 'art clings to the society from which it arose' by relying on existing production and symbolic systems for its circulation; on the other hand, through its aesthetic function 'it opens a dimension for creating sensibilities which point beyond the current social conditioning and modes of repression' (2011: 43). In Marcuse's utopia then, techne is restored as a primary relation to the world.

As I will discuss in the next section, Marcuse's analysis resonated with the renewed interest in training that marked not only theatre in the 1960s, but culture in general. Being immersed in the youth movement of his day, it could be argued that Marcuse developed the theoretical ground for the need for a new perception, having sensed it within and feeding it back to 1960s counter-culture.[3] Nonetheless, as Feenberg – who studied with Marcuse – observes, Marcuse's concept 'raises as many problems as it solves' (2005: 94). Feenberg explains:

> On the one hand, it [Marcuse's aesthetics] grounds the argument in experience, a potentially universal domain in which all can participate and which can support a rational discourse. On the other hand, it valorises one of the dimensions of experience that is most difficult to universalise rationally, art. Is Marcuse's aestheticism compatible with democracy? Democratic public reason is an intersubjective process, but insofar as the aesthetic is disclosed to an attuned sensibility, it appears private.
>
> (2005: 94)

A key issue emerging from Feenberg's critique, and of particular relevance to this chapter, is that of education. Marcuse's argument makes it clear that the 'new sensibility' needs to be cultivated but does not outline how or what would constitute such cultivation. Yet, the question of education is absolutely crucial to the overall project: Marcuse *has* to assume that an aesthetic sensibility can be trained; otherwise, he will have to grant concessions to notions of talent, grace or personality which preclude democracy.[4] To put it simply: aesthetic sensibility is premised on developing it. When, therefore, Marcuse does not explain how this is to be done, he leaves a significant lacuna. Presumably, this question was picked up by those involved in training.

Training for liberation: avant-garde theatre and training practice

The dominant approach to actor training in the United States until the 1960s consisted of derivatives of Stanislavsky's system and variations of Method Acting.[5] During this time, several new approaches were grafted out of the combination of existing knowledge and the popularisation of new disciplines. In a publication on actor training in 1972, Richard Brown offers an extensive list of the range of subjects that were by that time explored in training studios: 'Alexander [Technique], T'ai Chi Ch'uan, Yoga, the work of Slater, Horney, Berne, Laing, May, Lowen, Rogers, Reich, Levi-Strauss' (1972: viii). Accessibility to a range of non-theatrical disciplines coupled with a suspicion towards theatrical text and character also led to a drastic reconsideration of the nature of the theatrical role; as Schechner argued in *Environment Theatre*, a role is a 'theatrical entity, not a psychological being' (1994 [1973]: 165). As such, the emphasis now was on the development, composition and precision of a physical score, a set of actions through which the performer came to live and represent on stage.[6]

Although sources from the time, for example Beck (1972) and Schechner (1994 [1973]) often resound with a revolutionary enthusiasm for breaking new ground, the avant-garde project was not free of tension. One such tension revolved around the importance of training for enabling the actors to express new forms. For example, Paul Goodman, whose plays were staged by the Living Theatre, remarked that the emphasis in his play *The Young Disciple* on 'the pre-verbal elements of theatre' required actors to 'open their throats to such sounds or loosen their limbs to such motions' (Goodman 1965: 62 cited in Bigsby 1985: 81). Yet, he remarked that 'the actors we have are quite unable both by character and training' to engage with such actions (ibid.). A key mission of the avant-garde theatre groups, therefore, was not only to offer actors a space beyond commercial structures but also the necessary training to give expression to new forms. Despite this aspiration, however, the means adopted to develop such new skillset remained questionable. Grotowski, who was an important point of reference for American avant-garde practitioners, was highly critical of the remit and tone of their training experiments, pointing out that they lacked rigour and commitment (Munk et al. 1969: 182). According to Grotowski, the kind of authenticity American avant-garde practitioners were after could only be achieved through discipline. Reviewing the *Commune* by the Performance Group in 1971, Richard Gilman's similarly argued that the performers' lack of technical ability in fact hindered rather than enabled the expression of authenticity. Without having the necessary skills to move beyond their existing vocal and movement vocabularies, the performers ended up repeating counter-cultural clichés devoid of meaning.

There was, in other words, a discrepancy between the search for a new form of theatrical praxis and the ability to communicate it effectively. Although such discrepancy may have resulted from the absence of methodical work and commitment amongst the group members, it also reveals a deeper tension, which I would argue, lies at the heart of the avant-garde project. If, at least according to Heidegger and Marcuse, 'the instrumentalisation' of humankind constituted a kind of historical *modus operandi* for advanced industrial societies, then within theatrical praxis such instrumentalisation was even more pronounced. Indeed, as we saw in the previous chapter, from Diderot onwards, one of the key emphases that characterised performer training was an understanding of the actor as an 'instrument'. This conception has been, of course, articulated within theatrical contexts and refers to a kind of artistic instrumentalisation that serves the emergence of the theatrical world; a world, it should be stressed, that, according to Marcuse, can provide an alternative to established hegemonies. At the same time, however, we can appreciate that precisely because of texts such as Marcuse's, references to and understandings of the actor as an 'instrument' could have evoked in the 1960s the spectre of technocratic instrumentalisation. Julian Beck's defiant admission that the 'Living Theatre actors were awkward [and] untutored' (1972: section 7, np) can thus be understood as a repudiation of a whole discourse that turned actors into instruments. Similarly, it can be argued that Richard Schechner's admonition to performers that 'your body is not your "instrument"; your body is you' (Schechner 1994 [1973]: 145) was not only aimed at established actor training practice. It attempted to reclaim the performer's process from a wider rhetoric and history of instrumentalisation.

The question, however, was whether new approaches to training as well as new understandings of what training is for were rigorous enough and could serve the needs of performance. As Gilman's review, Goodman's remark and Grotowski's critique attest, the ability of avant-garde theatres to effect change was premised on the actors' skill to engage the spectators. And the acquisition of such skill depended on training. Whether radical or not, theatrical activity turns by default certain resources into instruments of expression, and through this process sets in motion an act of instrumentalisation. We might say that within the avant-garde groups, the training process acquired a different inflection and became rearticulated from a mechanism for technical efficiency to a journey of personal and collective discovery. Yet, this formulation did not prove wholly satisfactory and raised a key question: 'Is excellence in art to be so easily identified with wholeness as a human being […]?' (Gilman 1971: 325). Here is therefore the bind: if, on the one hand, avant-garde theatre training shuns notions of technique, the communication of its intentions might also get lost. If, on the other hand, it concedes to the importance of training for the mastery of technical skill, how can such mastery be differentiated from the kind of master-ful management of human and natural resources, which according to Heidegger and Marcuse had compromised natural habitats and the human lifeworld? As the next section is going to argue, Chaikin was acutely aware of this problem. In fact, I would argue that one of the chief reasons that the work of the Open Theatre merits close examination was precisely the group's ability to marry a philosophical critique with what were at the time ground-breaking technical skills. Contributing to existing examinations of the Open Theatre's training, the next section aims to offer a different perspective, focusing on the way the group managed to critique the instrumentalisation of American society *through* the development of what Hulton calls the 'actor's resources' (2010).

The Open Theatre

The Open Theatre emerged in the early 1960s out of an acting class on non-naturalistic dramaturgies led by Nola Chilton, which was disbanded when Chilton left the country. The group consisted of writers and actors who had 'a strong grounding' in Method acting (Blumenthal 1984: 53) and attended Chilton's class in order to engage with other styles. From the very beginning, then, the development of the actors' artistic skills and personal resources was at the centre of the group's mission. Although the group was set up as a collective, Joseph Chaikin provided both artistic and professional leadership and was responsible for key decisions with regard to the choice of workshop material, the performance programme and even, at a certain point, the group's membership. The Open Theatre eventually became renowned for several stylistic elements and competencies: extensive physical and vocal skills that went beyond conventional character work; the collective creation of evocative performance scores; the actors' ability to engage in two different actions at once. Accordingly, the group's work has received critical attention that has primarily focused on ritual, ensemble practices and the actor's presence (Blumenthal 1984; Aronson 2000). In contributing to this body of work, I am taking here a different perspective, one that centres on the way a critique of technological rationality influenced the group's work and training.

Chaikin believed that the apparent limitations of dominant training methods were a symptom of a deeper malady. He perceived that the emotional and behavioural registers from which American subjects drew for the expression of private emotional experience were considerably narrow; and this was the same for actors in the representation of theatrical characters. He became convinced that the training that was available to actors in the 1960s 'has been able to have access to the popular version of our sadness, hurt, anger, and pleasure. That's why our training has been limited' (Chaikin 1991 [1972]: 6). As a result, though, 'there are zones of ourselves which have never lived yet' (Chaikin 1991 [1972]: 13). Training and theatrical performance, then, could only replicate the kind of inauthentic experience that tied American subjects to material affluence. In response, the Open Theatre sought to engender a 'liberated consciousness' that went beyond the sanctioned registers of 'the contemporary bourgeois ego' (Chaikin 1991 [1972]: 9).

Chaikin's overall evaluation of 1960s American theatre and culture has clear resonances with Marcuse's critique. Chaikin not only accepts the basic premises of *One-Dimensional Man*, he further confirms Marcuse's argument that art, in this case theatre, had lost its potential to exercise effective critique. What is more, Chaikin seems to be taking Marcuse's analysis to its logical conclusion: if the actor's training is based on the language, emotions and behaviours of the popular culture of TV commercials and programmes, it would only produce actors defined by the false needs of a material society. The aims and remit of the actor's education had to be radically reconfigured, and Chaikin perceived that such a refashioning would extend beyond the development of skills. The actor's training had to be a process of remaking and redefining a self and as such was bound to have not only artistic but also political and ethical implications. In a section with clear Marcusian undertones, Chaikin observes:

> the industrial mainstream of society is always a pressure to make of us 'achievers', to make of us 'goods'. Many of our appetites are developed by the industrial society, and most of our models are not freely picked by us. We are trained and conditioned to be present only in relation to the goal.
>
> (1991 [1972]: 65)

In response, Chaikin attempted to engage actors in a process that, on one hand, would 'renounce the set up that sees people as "goods"' (Chaikin 1991 [1972]: 11) and, on the other, would restore the actor's sense of astonishment. An idea with Brechtian undertones, Chaikin wanted to enable actors to de-familiarise themselves from acculturated and normative behaviours whilst becoming in touch with a sense of wonder. And this is another crucial respect in which Chaikin's work meets Marcuse's thinking: it can be argued that what the Open Theatre was after was the kind of 'aesthetic sensibility' that Marcuse saw as the only way to transcend instrumentalisation. Or in Chaikin's words: the Open Theatre was set up as 'a place of re-perceiving' (Coco et al. 1983: 46).

As mentioned already, Chaikin was not alone in critiquing American society, and many of his observations were shared by other avant-garde practitioners. What makes the work of the Open Theatre particularly interesting, though, is that the training they eventually developed did not so much go against the type of 'false consciousness' Chaikin criticises, but rather *through* it. Put otherwise, the Open Theatre did not shun the kind of stifled subjectivity which Chaikin as well as Marcuse and others saw as the underbelly of the American dream: they used it as a primary source. Although the group developed many exercises, here I will concentrate on two: 'Machines' and 'Perfect People'. Crucially, these exercises, which stayed in use for years and featured in training as well as performance work, tell a different story about the group's relationship to technology. Whereas the majority of scholarly analyses of the group's work give a sense of movement away from technology, these exercises demonstrate a confrontation with technology on an aesthetic, thematic and ethical level.

'Machines' and 'Perfect People'

As Robert Pasolli describes, 'Machines' was inspired by Viola Spolin's 'parts of the whole' exercise where actors would play the parts of existing machines. Pasolli argues that the Open Theatre took this exercise further by developing machines that did not exist, by using the machine as a metaphor to stage 'social roles', and by embodying the properties of a mechanic entity and thus becoming part of the set (1970: 18). As Pasolli's description attests, the exercise was part and parcel of the ensemble aesthetic that the group developed and we can assume that it enabled actors to develop rapport, a sense of attunement and an ability to play together. When seen in the light of the previous discussion, additional elements come to the foreground.

To begin with, in the actor's attempt to embody parts of machines, we can identify an impulse to humanise technology and render mechanical effects through organic means. When the exercise was applied to performance – the example Pasolli (1970: 18) gives is the recreation of the electronic circuitry of a telephone operation system through the actors' voice and body in *Interview* (1966) – we can read this as an example of a 'poor theatre' aesthetic, where the actor's organism is prized as the primary means of theatrical expression. As Pasolli attests, however, the Open Theatre 'has done a great deal with machines as metaphorical statements' (1970: 18) and explored social systems and roles *as* machines. In this attempt, we can trace a different logic at work: if, in the first rendition of the exercise, machines were played by actors, in this second application, humans are performed as machines. Indeed, Pasolli attests that the 'Machines' exercise formed the basis of scores for improvisation on the theme 'A Man Sometimes Turns into the Machine He Is Using' (1970: 51). Theatrical characters therefore were no longer treated as psychological entities but approached as mechanical instruments. Such an approach arguably freed the group from psychological acting, but it also made a wider point. By representing humans as instruments, it could be said that the Open Theatre put flesh and bones onto a philosophical discourse that detected the mechanisation of humankind.

A similar exercise in tone and remit, 'Perfect People' aimed to give expression to the 'conditioned person' (Pasolli 1970: 38). According to Pasolli, 'perfect people are the sanitised, regularised, and glamorised types which the image makers have us all secretly believing we ought to be' (1970: 38). 'Perfect People', in other words, aimed to give expression to a form of inauthentic existence determined by false needs. Moreover, as Pasolli notes, the sources for this material were the mediatised images that were in circulation at the time in television, commercials and magazines. Here, too, we can identify the kind of double movement that underpins 'Machines'. By giving expression in 'Perfect People' to a set of cultural icons which exist only through mediatisation, the actors humanise them. At the same time, though, the point is made that human subjects can barely exist beyond and outside these mediatised roles. Indeed, as Pasolli explains, the exercise was used 'to awaken actors to degrees of aliveness' (1970: 38) making them aware of their 'reliance on conventional acting'. The exercise therefore aimed to sensitise the Open Theatre members to the kind of stock-in-trade acting that was utilised for the production of these images – which were, in fact, produced by other actors assumedly trained in the established actor training approaches of the time. This palimpsest of (Open Theatre) actors playing (commercial) actors who play social roles demonstrated that the production of 'Perfect People', on stage and in real life, involved the impoverishment not only of acting technique, but actual 'real' people. In this manner, the development of acting technique engaged with both the mechanisation of the acting as well as of society at large.

It could be argued, then, that contrary to the search for the character's depth, which was the nominal acting approach at the time, the Open Theatre both revitalised the actors' presence on stage, making their performances compelling, but also gave expression to a life devoid of liveness, a language devoid of meaning, and feeling devoid of experience. In this manner, the actors could both 'explor[e] how people become automatons' (Blumenthal 1984: 90) and develop a new acting style. Exercises such as 'Machines' and 'Perfect People' thus offered the space to engage with a kind of instrumentalisation that Diderot would have hardly foreseen. As we saw in the previous chapter, Diderot, as well as actors in the nineteenth century, maintained that the expression of emotion should result solely from technical accomplishment, which would enable the actor to repeat the score of her role with exactness and precision. However, from the vantage point of the 1960s, the efficiency and productivity achieved by techniques of automation in many aspects of social life and labour produced not an enlightened society, but psychic alienation, social repression and political hegemony. The group both critiqued technologisation *and* achieved the precision of physical expression exalted by Diderot. What these exercises demonstrate, then, is that in addition to exploring myth, collective creation and techniques for enhancing the actor's presence, there was a concomitant current in the work of the Open Theatre that addressed and engaged with technological rationality at an aesthetic and thematic level. Most importantly, these exercises exemplify the unique achievement of the group: the ability to combine a critique of instrumentalisation with technical mastery. This achievement becomes further exemplified if we look at the function of television within the group's work and history.

Perfect People – Perfect Actors?

As mentioned already, the development of a vibrant, psychophysical presence that marked the work of the group has often been positioned in opposition to recorded media, particularly television. Indeed, in the *Presence of the Actor*, Chaikin refers to

> The University of TV. TV Programs become recommended personal fantasies to be shared by all, and TV is successful because many millions of people at once are given a very similar repertoire of fantasy and experience. It becomes one of the most effective ways of manipulating the imagination

through establishing a common premise and promoting a uniform inner life.

(1991 [1972]: 75)

Television, therefore, was a key way of achieving social coherence; indeed, it can be seen as a form of behavioural training that could reach and shape millions of people. Chaikin's observation is not hyperbolic. According to Aniko Bodroghkozy, following a steady penetration in households during the 1950s, 'by the early 1960s the medium had achieved a near saturation rate of 92 percent' (2001: 25). As a result, for Chaikin's generation, television had a function unlike any other preceding technology: it 'forged baby boomers into a special community – one that recognised itself as such by the way its members all shared a common TV culture' (Bodroghkozy 2001: 22). Yet it also forged a paradox: upon coming of age, the generation weaned on TV eventually rejected it 'as a commercial, network-dominated industry hopelessly corrupted by the values of the establishment' (Bodroghkozy 2001: 46). At the same time, the technological device instigated experimentation. This ranged from advice on how to use static as a means of enhancing acid trips (Bodroghkozy 2001: 49–50) to art practices that enacted a 'thoroughgoing transformation of the apparatus from the inside out' (Joselit 2007: 11). Specifically in relation to Nam June Paik's 'prepared televisions', Joselit identifies the changes the artist effected on the medium:

> signals were bent into abstract patterns through changes in internal circuitry; external media or audiotape were linked to the television signal to disrupt it; and TVS were altered so that visitors could manipulate the image on the screen by, for instance, speaking into a microphone.
>
> (2007: 7)

Paik's experimentation, as Joselit attests, not only aimed at tinkering with the mechanics of the medium, it constituted 'an alternate vision of the television network whose purpose is to re-educate perception' (Joselit 2007: 11).

This double movement between critique and appropriation, aiming at re-educating perception, can be traced in the work of the Open Theatre. In *The Presence of the Actor*, Chaikin makes frequent references to television and these references, at least at the time, had a particular rhetorical effect. First, they marked what the work of the Open Theatre stood against and this could be achieved precisely because television was a common denominator of American life. Television offered a point of reference that Chaikin could take for granted – even if he did so in an effort to distance his work from it. At the same time, television also provided content for exploration and techniques for representation that remained a constant thread in the group's work. I have already mentioned that the primary source for 'Perfect People' was television and commercials. Similarly, *America Hurrah* (1966), a trilogy of plays that marked the first public success of the Open Theatre, included a short play entitled 'TV'. According to Pasolli, the play featured two groups: 'one group are employees of a television rating service' and 'the other group are actors who perform the TV shows' (1970: 91). Each group utilised markedly different acting styles, in the process depicting 'real life' as 'flat, insipid, tedious', whilst 'the TV life is dynamic, lively, full of emotional display'. The play finished when the TV people took over the stage as well as the action (Pasolli 1970: 92).

The Serpent (1967), the group's most celebrated performance, included scenes from the television footage of the assassinations of J. F. Kennedy, Robert Kennedy and Martin Luther King. As Bodroghkozy reports, J. F. Kennedy's assassination and funeral were televised over 'four days of continuous uninterrupted coverage' (2001: 32), further intensifying the impact of the event. It is therefore significant that *The Serpent* not only staged the content of these events, it sought to recreate the mediated manner in which these events were communicated, producing, according to Hulton, 'a dramaturgy that could be described as a theatrical equivalent of filmic montage' (2018: np). As shown in video footage of the performance, the assassination was recreated by positioning four actors kneeling on the floor, representing the passengers in the open limousine that carried the Kennedys. A chorus group stands behind them playing the crowd. The action is divided into ten sections, each representing a frame of the footage. A voice calls out numbers one to ten − first in order, then backwards and then randomly − while the actors duly recreate the image of each frame. After the repetition of the scene, the chorus begins to chant whilst the four actors at the front continue with the frame-by-frame staging of the assassination (www.youtube.com/watch?v=JBmM31N2AJo). The scene both marks the technical accomplishment of the group − the ability of the actors individually to hit each frame with precision whilst remaining rhythmically and compositionally tuned as a whole group − as well as an overall pre-occupation with the content of mediated images.

On the basis of this, there emerges an important distinction between the life(style) that arguably television promoted and the Open Theatre critiqued, and the representational techniques, which television made possible, and the Open Theatre embraced. In this respect, the work of the Open Theatre has similarities with other artists of the same generation who also made a distinction between the content and the device. Whereas the content of the television was derided, rejected and more or less seen as emblematic of all that was wrong with 'Media-America' (Joselit 2007), the technological artefact was harnessed for counter-cultural ends. Although the Open Theatre did not use the actual device directly, there is a similar tactic of appropriation, whereby the technological possibilities of the medium, for example the ability to break an action into discrete frames, are used to expand the theatrical language and the actor's skills.

There is, finally, an additional way in which television is significant in relation to the work of the group. As a highly popular and well-financed medium of the time, it embodied the industry actors ultimately aspired to 'break' into. For avant-garde theatre, television was not only the demonised other; it also posed a real threat since it could seduce actors away from experimental practices and into commercial structures. In Marcusian terms, television was, therefore, a means through which the status quo could 'swallow up' opposition by capturing within the 'small screen' not only ideas but the artists themselves. It is highly ironic then that the *America Hurrah* trilogy, which included the play 'TV', marked the group's first success but also revealed its fragility. As the performance gained critical acclaim, the actors of *America Hurrah* began to be preoccupied with publicity events, splitting the group into winners and losers. What is more, two of the actors, bolstered by the performance's success, started working on commercial programmes on TV (Blumenthal 1984: 62). Chaikin's comments on television, in general, and the particular events that followed *America Hurrah* might come across as elitist, assuming, for example, a crude divide between 'low' and 'high' culture.[7] It is also evident, though, that within the overall spirit in which the Open Theatre was set up, television and media were experienced in negative ways. After the success of *America Hurrah*, the writer of the script Jean-Claude van Itallie observes that the group 'felt "watched", and this created a subtle pressure even in the work process' (Coco et al. 1983: 31). Actor Joyce Aaron equally observes that the group's first commercial success meant that a new set of imperatives started creeping into the work (Coco et al. 1983: 37). Television and media, therefore, exposed the actors as all-too-human, susceptible to factors beyond the pursuit of the group. The training succeeded and failed at the same time: the strength of technical accomplishment also rendered them vulnerable to weakness of character.

The rift caused by the group's first recognition eventually healed; the group reformed and the experimental ethos was further galvanised (Pasolli 1970: 95). Yet, as Gordon Rogoff remarks, the group 'was doomed to succeed' (Coco et al. 1983: 30). The pressures of publicity were repeated with the critical appraisal of *The Serpent*, first abroad and then in the United States. In addition to these pressures, the group's continuing commitment to in-depth training entailed a growing reliance on external funding and the inevitable engagement with the agenda of cultural organisations. Funding, in other words, constituted another version of officialdom, which would also compromise the integrity of the work. As a solution to its growing institutionalisation, the Open Theatre was eventually disbanded (Blumenthal 1984: 25).[8] The biography of the group seems to suggest that there was in the end no way out of the 'set-up', since they either had to choose 'success' and ultimately become absorbed into the system they had tried so hard to resist or stop working. They chose the latter, and one might justifiably ask what kind of conclusion this story leaves us with.

From one point of view, we would have to concede that the group did manage to create a viable and effective language for representing the crisis of American society as well as for pointing to alternative ways of existing. Crucially for this discussion, they managed this by developing a form of techne that put the instrumentalisation of the actor's resources at the service of the actor's development. And the actor's development was part and parcel of a wider project that aimed not only to critique instrumentalisation but also engender an alternative way of being in the world. In a certain way, the work of the Open Theatre can be seen as a confirmation of the kind of vision Heidegger and Marcuse outlined: a form of technical mastery which, however, eschews the trap of technological instrumentalisation. Or did so for ten years. The recurrent struggles and eventual disbandment of the group also show how fragile the whole endeavour was. Are we then to conclude that this vision is by definition short-lived? Or might the Open Theatre exercises offer creative fulfilment and have socio-cultural relevance today?

Roger Babb traces the legacy of the group through the collectives that were set up after the group's dissolution and the teaching practice developed by some key members who 'educated several generations of theater students', primarily in Higher Education Institutions across the United States (2006: 106). Babb observes the way former Open Theatre members used and/or developed further seminal exercises, such as the 'Sound and Movement'. He also points out that there has been a wider diffusion of the group's aesthetic:

> many of the innovations that Chaikin and the Open Theatre developed to escape the conventions of American realist acting in the 1960s, such as an emphasis on improvisation, transformations, sound and movement, non-verbal modes, and a collage-like, nonlinear structure of images, became part of the normative vocabulary of experimental theater in the United States in the following years.
>
> (Babb 2006: 122)

However, it is noteworthy that according to Chaikin, training exercises should be entirely contingent upon their context: 'you make a path/where there is no path/ and this path/is good for nothing/else except/to get you where you are going. Never before and never again' (Chaikin cited in Beck 1972: Section 32 np). Accordingly, Chaikin argued that 'forming an exercise is one of the most important things a theater person can do' (in Blumenthal 1984: 69) suggesting, in this way, that each form of theatre needs its own set of techniques. We might assume then that in terms of content the Open Theatre vocabulary is no more appropriate for current practice than Method Acting was for them. What however may remain is the ability, indeed the need, for self-determination and autonomy. I would argue that the legacy of the Open Theatre needs to be evaluated in relation to the radical shift they made in the ontology of training: away from an understanding of training as an 'in-order-to', expected to serve a set of heteronomous demands, and towards an approach that views training as a form of creative praxis, in and of itself. Indeed, training in the Open Theatre was understood as nothing less than training in 're-perceiving', as a way of transcending established modes of perception and social relations.

Conclusion: the promise of avant-garde actor training

The chief aim of this chapter was to demonstrate the way a critique of technology underpinned and shaped the overall ethos of 1960s avant-garde theatre and the training approach of the Open Theatre. I have argued that the critical reception of the work of the Open Theatre provides one more instance of a scholarly bias to overlook technology in order to pursue arguments of presence and primitivism. Such bias not only impoverishes the historical and contextual significance of the group, it also entrenches false dichotomies between bodies and devices, live and mediated action, nature and culture. By supplementing existing accounts that tend to prioritise notions of presence, myth and ritual, and/or position the development of the actor's psychophysical resources as anti-technological, this chapter has argued that technology, in the form of automobiles, TV sets and military weapons, not only was a key aspect of American life, but that it formed a mode of being in the world that had ethical, political and personal consequences.

Drawing on a Heideggerian understanding of technology as a way of having a world, this chapter foregrounded a key tension at the heart of training in and for avant-garde performance: the need to develop the actor's resources towards the creation of a new theatrical language on the one hand, and the danger of naturalising a way of seeing oneself as an instrument, on the other. It is against this tension, I would contend, that the work of the Open Theatre acquires particular significance, since its actors attempted to develop their expressive instrument without instrumentalising the self. If anything, the development of their resources aimed to expose processes of instrumentalisation that by that time had become established in American theatre and society. The group was by necessity short-lived, and some of its actors – from a certain perspective – eventually 'succumbed' to the lure of the 'set-up'. It might be argued, nonetheless, that what can guide contemporary practice is the way a particular group attempted to claim a creative and artistic space that both eschewed technological 'Enframing' and developed a language that allowed them to comment on that condition. The work of the group shows that the relationship between technology and training extends way beyond the use, or absence, of specific devices; rather training is implicated with the trainees' way of being (as artists, people and theatrical characters) and such ways of being necessarily take place in a technologised world.

The question that emerges, of course, is how training can or should respond to current technologies, which arguably produce a world markedly different from the one in the 1960s. This question will be addressed in the last two chapters of this book. Before I engage with that question, another story has to finish. The chapter that follows deals with the criticism that Heidegger and Marcuse's view of technology has received and the development of a post-Heideggerian approach to technology, one that treats it not as a totalising force but as a means of mediating the world. The next chapter draws on postphenomenology in order to discuss the use of material objects in performer training as well as to advance an understanding of the instrumentalisation of the actor's psychophysical resources in terms of tool-use and tool-making. It also revisits questions about the actor's professionalisation within the contemporary arena of the creative industries.

Notes

1 A commitment to art as a way to usher in non-exploitative systems of production as well as to enhance the daily life of individuals was developed in both theory and practice in the late nineteenth century through the Arts and Crafts movement, both in the UK and the United States. Bradley Macdonald (2011) traces the resonances between Marcuse's understanding of art and William Morris' thinking.

2 The essay was first presented as a lecture in German in 1955 and translated in English in 1977 (Lovitt 1977: x).

3 Marcuse openly endorsed and frequently participated in student political activism. He was also involved, as was Feenberg, in the Paris events in May 1968 and the *Essay on Liberation* is dedicated to 'young militants' (Marcuse 1969: x).

4 This is the interpretation advanced by Richard Wolin who claims that Marcuse supports a kind of enlightened intelligentsia, akin to the one described by Plato (2001: 171–2). Feenberg convincingly explains how and why Wolin's conclusion is misguided (2005: 143 n).

5 In his historical examination of actor training in the United States, Peter Zazzali identifies the 1960s as a turning point for actor training provision, with 'a shift in emphasis from private acting studios to university-sponsored conservatoires' (2016: 28). Zazzali notes that the former were heavily based on Stanislavsky's System, or aspects thereof, and aimed to prepare actors to act for the camera. The latter had a pronounced psycho-physical orientation, stressing the training of the actor's voice and movement and aiming to prepare actors for the stage.

6 Physical action was not emphasised in avant-garde circles only. Stella Adler as well as Uta Hagen also focused on action as the primary means through which a role is created and communicated. However, action, as understood in variations of Stanislavsky's System is always tied to the external behaviour and/or internal landscape of the character. Avant-garde practices moved beyond the assumption that a theatrical character equated a person, and invitations for action could include animals, natural forces, or 'social types'.

7 This criticism is often levelled at exponents of the Frankfurt School. Marcuse addresses it in *One-Dimensional Man*, arguing that the popularisation of 'high art' did not result in its democratisation, but rather in the flattening of its 'antagonistic force' (2002 [1964]: 67). It could be that Chaikin's stance towards American popular culture, and television, in particular, was inflected by a similar disdain.

8 Blumenthal explains: 'from a tiny-budget group [...] the Open Theatre had become a $100,000 a year organisation, which leased its own loft, hired teachers, subsidized its own productions, and even bought health insurance and paid salaries [...] (1984: 25). One of the organisations that subsidised the group was the Ford Foundation (Blumenthal 1984: 28), a Foundation, built on the very systems of management and automation the Open Theatre sought to critique.

References

Aronson, A. 2000. *American Avant Garde Theatre: a history*. London: Routledge.

Babb, R. 2006. 'Ways of Working: Post-Open Theatre Performance and Pedagogy'. In: *Restaging the Sixties: Radical Theaters and Their Legacies*, edited by James Martin Harding and Cindy Rosenthal. Ann Arbor: University of Michigan Press, pp. 106–24.

Beck, J. 1972. *The Life of the Theatre*. New York: Limelight Editions.

Benedetti, J. 2005. *The Art of the Actor*. London: Methuen.

Bigsby, C. W. E. 1985. *A Critical Introduction to Twentieth-Century American Drama, Volume Three: Beyond Broadway*. Cambridge: Cambridge University Press.

Bishop, C. 2018. 'Black Box, White Cube, Grey Zone: Dance Exhibitions and Audience Attention', *The Drama Review*, 62 (2), pp. 22–42. doi.org/10.1162/DRAM_a_00746.

Blumenthal, E. 1984. *Joseph Chaikin: exploring at the boundaries of theater*. Cambridge: Cambridge University Press.

Bodroghkozy, A. 2001. *Groove Tube: Sixties Television and the Youth Rebellion*. Durham and London: Duke University Press.

Bottoms, S. 2006. *Playing Underground: A Critical History of the 1960s Off-Off-Broadway Movement*. Ann Arbor: University of Michigan Press.

Brown, Richard B. (ed.) 1972. *Actor Training I, The Institute for Research in Acting*. New York: Drama Book Specialists.

Chaikin, J. 1991 [1972]. *The Presence of the Actor*. New York: Theatre Communications Group.

Coco, W., Rogoff, G., van Itallie, J. C., Aaron, J., Yankowitz, S., Zimet, P., Gilman, R. and Chaikin, J. 1983. 'The Open Theatre [1963–1973]: Looking Back', *Performing Arts Journals*, 7 (3), pp. 25–48.

Feenberg, A. 2015. 'Making the Gestalt Switch'. In: *Postphenomenological Investigations*, edited by Robert Rosenberger and Peter-Paul Verbeek. Lanham: Lexington Books, pp. 229–36.

Feenberg, A. 2005. *Heidegger and Marcuse*. New York: Routledge.

Feenberg. A. 1999. *Questioning Technology*. London: Routledge.

Fuller, R, B. and Sadao, S. 1968. 'A Theatre', *The Drama Review: TDR*, 12 (3), pp. 117–20.

Gilman, R. 1971. 'The Commune', *The Drama Review: TDR*, 15 (3), pp. 325–9.

Grotowski, J. 1991 [1968]. *Towards a Poor Theatre*. London: Methuen Drama.

Harding, M. J. 2016. *The Ghosts of the Avant-Garde(s)*. Ann Arbor: University of Michigan Press.

Harding, M. J. and Rosenthal, C. (eds) 2006. *Restaging the Sixties: Radical Theaters and Their Legacies*. Ann Arbor: University of Michigan Press.

Heidegger, M. 1977. 'The Question Concerning Technology'. In: *The Question Concerning Technology and Other Essays*, translated by William Lovitt. New York: Harper, pp. 3–35.

Hulton, D. 2018. *Joseph Chaikin*. Digital Theatre +.

Hulton, D. 2010. 'Joseph Chaikin and Aspects of Actor Training: Possibilities Rendered Present'. In: *Actor Training* (2nd edition), edited by Alison Hodge. London: Routledge, pp. 164–83.

Ihde, D. 1993. *Philosophy of Technology: An introduction*. New York: Paragon House.

Innes, C. 1993. *Avant Garde Theatre 1892–1992*. London: Routledge.

Joselit, D. 2007. *Feedback: Television Against Democracy*. Cambridge, Mass: The MIT Press.

Lovitt, W. 1977. 'Introduction'. In: *The Question Concerning Technology and Other Essays*, Martin Heidegger. New York: Harper, pp. xiii–xxxix.

Macdonald, B. 2011. 'Morris after Marcuse: Art, beauty, and the aestheticist tradition of ecosocialism', *The Journal of William Morris Studies*, 19 (3), pp. 39–49.

Marcuse, H. 2002 [1964]. *One-Dimensional Man*. London: Routledge.

Marcuse, H. 1969. *An Essay on Liberation*. Boston: Beacon Press.

Marranca, B. 2009. 'Mediaturgy: a conversation with Marianne Weems', *International Journal of Arts and Technology*, 2 (3), pp. 173–86. doi.org/10.1504/IJART.2009.028924.

Marranca, B. 2006. 'Performance, a Personal History', *PAJ: a Journal of Performance and Art*, 28 (1), pp. 3–19. doi.org/10.1162/152028106775329679.

Munk, E., Coco, B. and Croydon, M. 1969. 'Notes from the Temple: A Grotowski Seminar. An Interview with Margaret Croyden', *The Drama Review: TDR*, 14 (1), pp. 178–83.

Olafson, F. 2007 [1977]. 'Heidegger's Politics (1977): An Interview with Herbert Marcuse'. In: *The Essential Marcuse*, edited by Andrew Feenberg and William Leiss. Boston: Beacon Press, pp. 115–27.

Pasolli, R. 1970. *A Book on the Open Theatre*. New York: Avon.

Sainer, A. 1997 [1975]. *The New Radical Theatre Notebook*. New York: Applause.

Schechner, R. 2015. *Performed Imaginaries*. London: Routledge.

Schechner, R. 1994 [1973]. *Environmental Theatre*. New York: Applause.

Schechner, R. 1981. 'The Decline and Fall of the (American) Avant-Garde: why it happened and what we can do about it', *Performing Arts Journal*, 5 (2), pp. 48–63.

Verbeek, P. 2005. *What Things Do*, translated by Robert P. Crease. Pennsylvania: The Pennsylvania State University Press.

Wolin, R. 2001. *Heidegger's Children*. Princeton: Princeton University Press.

Zazzali, P. 2016. *Acting in the Academy*. London: Routledge.

Zimmerman, M. 1990. *Heidegger's Confrontation with Modernity*. Bloomington, Indianapolis: Indiana University Press.

4

USING AND MAKING TOOLS

Introduction

The previous two chapters examined performer training through the lens of two respective, and to a great extent contrasting, philosophical understandings of technology. The aim was to demonstrate that performer training is intertwined with questions, developments and concerns about technology in much more immediate ways than has been previously assumed. These chapters also demonstrated that technology, and its influence, may manifest in a variety of ways and what is needed is an ability to recognise its presence, whether this manifests in the use of a specific artefact or not. This chapter also deals with the trope of the actor's instrument and examines the pedagogical and embodied processes in which this instrument becomes constituted through the employment of a range of tools.

It presents postphenomenology; an empirically driven philosophical approach that seeks to articulate the relationships between users, artefacts and the world. It deals with a strand of philosophy of technology that has been developed in response to and as a turn away from the so called 'classical' approach of the mid-twentieth century, and utilises specific methods of this strand in order to explore the use of tools in performer training. The main impetus of postphenomenology is to develop an analytical framework, which, by focusing on the interactions between user, artefact and world, can sketch ways of relating to technology, and the world at large, that offer an alternative view to an understanding of technology as a totalising force. Postphenomenology builds on Heidegger's basic insight that technology is a way of having a world, but stipulates that Heidegger's evaluation of technology, especially in his later work, did not appropriately discriminate between different kinds of use and different kinds of technology (Verbeek 2005; Ihde 2010). The key problem with analyses of technology put forward by the classical tradition is, therefore, methodological. Peter-Paul Verbeek explains:

> Classical philosophy of technology prestructured its analysis in such a way that it could not *but* discover alienation. It failed to see that the diagnosis that technology *presupposes* a dominating manner of thinking or a functional orientation of social life does not necessarily imply that dealing with concrete technologies can only *produce* this domination and functionalism.
>
> (2005: 7–8, all emphases original)

Postphenomenology then sets out to correct this inherent methodological bias of the classical tradition by focusing the analysis on specific technologies and the contingencies of their production and use. It insists that in its concrete manifestations technology is not predestined to produce alienation; rather the shifts and changes between 'material configurations' and 'learned and acquired human embodiment practices' (Ihde 2012: 184) can engender new ways of sensing, thinking and living. One of the aims of the chapter, then, is to test the postphenomenological argument specifically in relation to the use of tools in performer training.

Although resources on performer training are replete with discussions of and instructions for the use of various objects, and although, as we shall see below, performer trainers often refer to the use of 'tools' and 'toolkits', there is very little consideration of this area of practice in terms of a larger analytical or discursive framework, let alone in relation to technology. With the exception of a few studies, notably Margolies (2016) and Camilleri (2019), an examination of the use of objects in performer training has been confined within the histories and analyses of specific regimes. Nonetheless, and as I will discuss in more detail below, the term 'tool' is used extensively in performer training parlance and with reference to several pedagogies; it also denotes a range of different things, including: objects, skills and techniques. What is more, performer training practice not only uses a variety of artefacts, including, as we shall see, hand-held tools and electric systems, it also makes tools. And as I will demonstrate, *it makes tools out of the very organism of the trainee's bodymind.*

Instructive, in this sense, is Mark Evans' analysis of the idea of the 'toolbox' (2009: 130). Positioned in a section on technique and instrumentality, Evans regards the concept of the 'toolbox' as a metaphor denoting the collection of technical skills a performer develops throughout their training. Evans further argues that the idea of the 'toolbox' serves as a distancing device between the trainee and the learning process: 'the "toolbox" operates to disassociate the student as "subject" from their body's pain or discomfort, or from the psychic pressure of the tutor's "crits" [critique], through configuring the body (and its actions) as instrumental' (2009: 131). The 'toolbox', then, operates as a shorthand, signalling both a depository of techniques and a mechanism of inscription that professionalises the trainee's body and subjectivity according to a set of values. Evans, however, acknowledges that the 'toolbox' also evokes a sense of selection and appropriation. On the basis of his in-depth ethnographic work in conservatoire and drama schools in the UK, Evans stresses 'the students' belief that the tutors supply the exercises, the techniques, which is then their responsibility to evaluate and use creatively' (2009: 132).

Although Evans does not position his study in relation to debates on technology, his argument that the 'toolbox' has both an inscriptive and an emancipatory dimension resonates with philosophical understandings of technology. The obvious difference, of course, is that what Evans has in mind are exercises, biological entities and organic resources, whereas what philosophers of technology have in mind are material artefacts. As a result, Evans does not consider what role material tools might have in the trainee actor's 'toolbox', and similarly the majority of philosophers of technology do not examine the instrumentalisation of psychophysical resources.

This chapter then returns to the actor's instrument with the aim to consider the process of instrumentalisation from a pedagogical perspective, i.e. the way an object or organic resource becomes and/or operates as a tool during and/or through the training process. What is more, the chapter aims to consider *both* material objects and psychophysical resources *within the same* theoretical framework. As such, the chapter moves simultaneously in two directions. In terms of performer training, the aim is to bring attention to the affinities and continuities between the appropriation of material objects and the development of psychophysical resources. In other words, the aim is to liberate the toolbox from its quotation marks and consider it not only as a powerful metaphor, but also as conglomeration of real, embodied interactions within bodies, between bodies, and between bodies and objects.

In terms of postphenomenology, the chapter seeks to test whether the argument, that a close examination of tool-use reveals different relationships to the world, remains valid once tool-use extends to the whole organism. If we accept that in performer training practice tools are not only balls, sticks and scarves, but also the breath, the vocal folds, the spine, concentration and so many other aspects of the performer's bodymind, where does this leave the postphenomenological argument that an examination of different kinds of tool-use may reveal alternative relations to the world? To put it another way: if the performer's very self, or aspects thereof, become instrumentalised (turned into tools) in what ways might such an instrumentalisation (tool-ification) be different from Heidegger's fear that an exploitative attitude will eventually define the way human subjects view and treat themselves? Where and how might we trace the agentic power of embodiment – that both Ihde and Evans consider possible – within a mechanism of inscription? As such, this chapter aims to consider relations to technology from a perspective that contains both the embodied and the technological, and specifically in relation to pedagogical processes and aesthetic formation.

In order to achieve this aim, the analytical framework of this chapter will also include the philosophy of John Dewey (1859–1952), specifically the rendition of his thinking by the philosopher of technology Larry Hickman (1992). As we shall see, Dewey propounds an understanding of technology that is far more inclusive than the one accepted by most scholars of technology and hence allow us to treat the use of material objects and organic resources as part of a wider phenomenon of tool-use. Dewey is not the only thinker that considered the dexterity and acuity of the human body as a form of technological intervention that enacts changes in the surrounding environment; seminal thinkers such as Andre Leroi-Gourhan and Karl Marx traced similar connections. Likewise, Philip Brey quotes Lewis Mumford who considered the body as 'a primary, all-purpose tool': 'man's total equipment for life' (Mumford 1967: 7 quoted in Brey 2000b: 68).

Despite the presence of this idea in the work of other philosophers, Dewey's thinking is singled out for the following three reasons. One is that Dewey is acknowledged as the forefather of postphenomenology. As Don Ihde explains, the tradition of pragmatism, of which Dewey was a key exponent, enacted an important shift in steering philosophy away from abstract theorisation and towards a preoccupation with instances of human activity and practice. In this manner, pragmatism, and Dewey's work in particular, endowed postphenomenology with 'a sensitivity to both praxis and materiality' (Ihde 2012: 128) and offered historical and philosophical heft to the postphenomenological argument that philosophical examinations of technology need to engage with instances of concrete manifestations thereof. The other reason is that unlike other philosophers that also identified the human body as a site of technics, Dewey engaged with a psychophysical practice. Specifically, he studied for a period of over 20 years with Frederick Matthias Alexander (1869–1955), the founder of the Alexander Technique and one of the most influential practitioners of the field that would later be called 'somatics'. As Eric McCormack (1958) argues in an unpublished PhD thesis, Dewey's work with Alexander was a key component of his philosophy, and, I would argue, of his understanding of technology specifically. In his 'Introduction' to Alexander's title *Constructive Conscious Control of the Individual* (1924), Dewey positions 'the work on the self' that Alexander Technique advocates within a wider framework of tool-use and mastery:

> Through modern science we have mastered to a wonderful extent the use of things as tools for accomplishing results upon and through other things. The result is all but a universal state of confusion, discontent and strife. The one factor which is the primary tool in the use of all these other tools, namely ourselves, in other words our own psychophysical disposition, as the basic condition of our employment of all agencies and energies, has not been studied as the central instrumentality.
>
> (Dewey 1983: 315)[1]

As we see, Dewey positions the human organism on par with other tools, and, in fact, considers it as the first technology, a tool in and of itself. Dewey also draws an ethical distinction between the use of other tools and the use of the self, which needs to be sharpened, in order to ensure the intelligent use of everything else. Whereas the mastery of other tools is often the cause of concern, the intelligent use of the self by the self can remedy false approaches and ameliorate the ills caused by previous misuse. In Dewey's understanding of self-use, then, we can trace both a technological as well as pedagogical sentiment and it is in these two respects that his thinking resonates with key aspects of performer training.

An attempt to analyse the trainee's embodied process in terms of technology runs the risk of subsuming embodiment under technology, as is for example the case in popular versions of transhumanism, which envisage that the use of technology will eventually enable the transcendence of the body's materiality. As I argued in Chapter 2, an understanding of the actor as an instrument has evolved in tandem with the increased sophistication of machines and automata. Following this line of thought, it could be argued that contemporary references to tools, especially when these references involve organic resources, are a manifestation or remnant of such positive attitude towards instrumentalisation. If this is the case, references to instruments and/or an equation of embodied technique with technology risks aligning embodied practice with the insidious technologisation that avant-garde practitioners in the 1960s sought to resist and scholars rightly criticised. As I will demonstrate, however, the use of the term 'tool', and indeed the prioritisation of material artefacts within performer training practice, often takes place within long-standing and sophisticated somatic engagements. Accordingly, I would argue that when, for example, performer trainers refer to a stick as a teacher or partner, it would be reductive to view such references as a result of technological fetishisation. I would, instead, propose that an analysis focuses on the links between the development of embodied practice and the materiality of the object. This chapter, therefore, aspires to open up and add nuance to tool-use, as a pervasive practice and metaphor. By exploring tool-use through a postphenomenological lens, it will also seek to mobilise a different perspective in examining the defining operation of performer training: if performing necessitates that the trainee's self becomes an instrument of/for expression what relationship(s) to the world, the self and others does such instrumentalisation produce? Can the kind of instrumentalisation effected within performer training practice transcend the technological rationality that Heidegger and Marcuse identified as the enveloping worldview that defines Western societies?

I will begin by offering an overview of what is considered to be a tool in the philosophy of technology and performer training respectively and I will then review the Dewey-Hickman thesis, in order to put forward an understanding of tool-use and tool-making that is appropriately inclusive of the diverse practices across performer training. I will then present Don Ihde's framework of I-Technology-World relationships. Each of Ihde's categories will be presented in a separate section, following the order of Ihde's exposition, and discussed with reference to instances of performer training practice drawing from written accounts, email communications with practitioners and video material. Although these examples will by no means be exhaustive, the account will strive to balance diversity with consistency.

Towards achieving this balance, each category of Ihde's framework will be exemplified through a different instance of performer training practice that involves nonetheless the same object. Called the 'prop of all props', with reference to Meyerhold's Biomechanics (Pitches 2007: 99), sticks have been used by prominent performer trainers throughout the twentieth and twenty-first century, for example by Phillip Zarrilli (Zarrilli et al. 2013); Peter Brook, David Zinder, Phillip Gaulier and Monica Pagneux (Crook et al. 2015: 362–5). They also feature prominently in philosophical discussions on embodiment and technicity, especially with reference to their use as an assistive technology for the blind (for example Brey 2000a; Ihde 1990). Sticks, therefore, can serve as a constant point of reference that traverses different pedagogies as well as accounts of technology. In addition to sticks, the examination will also include organic resources as well as different artefacts that have a relationship to the body other than handling and are encountered in different pedagogies. The chapter will conclude with a consideration of two key issues. It will first evaluate the postphenomenological argument that a close examination of tool-use reveals different relationships to the world with specific reference to performer training. Specifically, it will test the extent to which this argument can still have purchase when the 'world' of Ihde's tripartite framework includes the field of the creative industries, within which trainees will eventually be expected to operate. It will also introduce the question of whether postphenomenology can serve as a lens for examining digital technologies, transitioning, in this manner, into the issues that will be considered in the last two chapters of the book.

Intra- and extra-organic tools

As noted in the Introduction, the rule of thumb according to which technology is identified is the involvement of tools in human activity. For example, Andrew Feenberg attests that 'technology is an elaborate complex of related activities that crystallises around tool-making and -using in every society' (1995: 18). Similarly, Carl Mitcham argues that technology is 'stipulated to refer to the human making and using of material artefacts in all forms and aspects' (Mitcham 1978: 232 quoted in Hickman 1992: 7). In a similar vein, Ihde (1990) bases his classification of the I–Technology–World relationships, which forms the basic analytical method of postphenomenology, on a distinction between what he calls 'mediated' and 'non-mediated' experiences of the world. Accordingly, Ihde equates mediated experience with the use of technology and non-mediated experience with a lack thereof. Notwithstanding those technologies essential to survival, such as clothing and footwear, Idhe begins his account with the non-mediated experience of walking to the beach and taking in the scenery. The account progresses by describing an experience of looking through a glass window; an experience so slightly mediated that it is almost imperceptible that various technologies are in operation (for example, technologies around glass manufacture that moderate refraction and thus make the technology, i.e. the window in this case, literally transparent). Ihde finally considers the use of eyeglasses and thus the account arrives at a fully-fledged example of technological use (1990: 45–9).

Of course, it could be argued that there is no such thing as a non-mediated experience. As Asle Kiran points out 'the manners in which we deal with the world is [sic] mediated in many ways – through symbols, language, culture, history, embodiment and technology' (2015: 125). Embodiment, therefore, can be seen as a form of mediation in and of itself, especially through what sociologist Marcel

Mauss called 'techniques of the body': 'the ways in which, from society to society, men [sic] know how to use their bodies' (Mauss 1992 [1934]: 455). However, let us agree for now with Ihde that there is a valid distinction to be made between an experience, or an activity, that directly involves or requires the use of a material artefact and one that does not. Accordingly, we could identify in performer training practice a particular sensitivity towards the effects of different kinds of mediation and, in some cases, a preference for non-mediation. For example, the common practice of removing one's shoes at the beginning of a training session could be interpreted, through the lens of Ihde's distinction, as the removal of a technology, aiming to foster a non-mediated contact with the floor. Indeed, Ben Spatz refers to the studios that often host performer training practice as intentionally '*emptied*' spaces 'zones in which technology has been cleared away, in order to bring forth and make space for embodied technique' (2015: 14, emphasis original).

As noted already, despite an emphasis on embodiment, the performer training studio is occasionally refilled with a range of material objects, and constitutes, as I will discuss in the next chapter, a technology in and of itself. What is more, performer training demonstrates an attitude towards tools that is far more inclusive than the one that scholars of technology would be willing to admit. In 2015, the Training Grounds section of the *Theatre Dance and Performance Training Journal* put to performer training practitioners the question: 'What are your/the tools of training?'. The responses, depending on individual expertise and background, included: identifiable objects (sticks); parts of the body (hands, toes, eyes, ears); dispositions such as 'foolhardiness, commitment and conviction', 'tangible tools, for example rhythm, speed, balance' as well as 'consciousness', i.e. a series of 'recognitions' that the trainee undergoes (Roberts et al. 2015: 355–62).

A similar inclusivity can be noted with reference to the work of the same practitioner. For example, in *The Complete Stanislavsky Toolkit*, Bella Merlin outlines a series of exercises based on Stanislavsky's System that involve a wide set of resources, ranging from biological processes such as breathing and relaxation, work with objects and text, as well as the 'subconscious', which Merlin considers to be part of the 'meat of the toolkit' (2007: 311). In a similar vein, John Lutterbie, who examines acting from the perspective of Dynamic Systems Theory, points out that 'what makes actors unique is the way they are able to use tools they have in common with everyone else'. He identifies six such tools: 'movement, language, gesture, memory, attention, and executive control' (Lutterbie 2011: 104). To complicate matters further, as Margolies (2016: 43) notes, a significant part of performer training practice involves exercises with 'imaginary objects', towards developing physical skills and/or a rich emotional life. For example Meyerhold's etudes 'Throwing the Stone' and 'Shooting an Arrow' feature an imaginary stone and arrow respectively (Margolies 2016: 43); whereas Mike Alfreds' exercises 'Creating a Mimed Activity' and 'Developing the Handling of Mimed Objects' (2013: 378) involve the development of a score of physical actions related to the handling and/or use of imaginary artefacts. The evident observation to be made in relation to these examples is that performer training employs an impressively diverse range of tools that are not limited to material objects. In fact, what has been recognised as a tool includes material objects, imagined objects and body parts, as well as cognitive, behavioural and emotional traits or dispositions. What is more, the term is used to refer to skills as well as the ways, i.e. the exercises and techniques, with which such skills are expected to be trained.

These accounts demonstrate, therefore, that performer training practice may involve activities that strictly speaking do not involve the use of a material artefact. They are thus, in Ihde's terms, non-mediated and should be positioned as the 'other' of technological mediation. Yet, they include the use of resources that are explicitly referred to as tools, fitting in this way the category of mediated activity. We should therefore conclude that either in performer training parlance the term 'tool' is used loosely and somewhat inaccurately or that there is a need for an additional category of technological mediation: activities where engagement with the world *is* mediated but *not* through material objects. The absence of such a category in existing postphenomenological thinking presents a methodological difficulty in the attempt to apply postphenomenology to the examination of performer training: to what extent can postphenomenology be used in performer training analysis? Is it suited to analysing some aspects of the practice but not others? To put it another way, does the use and making of tools in performer training practice necessitate the employment of two separate analytical frameworks: one for the use of material objects and another for the tool-ification of organic resources? As explained already, the way I propose to deal with this impasse is to include in a postphenomenological framework the work of John Dewey, both because Dewey's work constitutes the basis of postphenomenology but also because, as I will argue below, his understanding of technology has close affinities with performer training practice.[2]

As Larry Hickman notes, Dewey does not offer a body of work that deals exclusively or directly with technology, rather technology is at the very heart of his entire thinking.[3] He further argues that

> the feature of Dewey's critique of technology that renders it unique is his contention that tools or instruments cut across traditional boundary lines such as those between the psychical and the physical, the inner and the outer, and the real and the ideal.
>
> (Hickman 1992: xii)[4]

Dewey considered tools to be both intra- and extra-organic. In this manner, his thinking both recognises a difference between objects and biological/cognitive functions *and* accommodates the acknowledgement that conceptual material, such as theories and hypotheses, are tools with which we 'do' something, for example draw inferences or make plans. Furthermore, it should be emphasised that although the prefixes 'intra' and 'extra' denote a sharp distinction between inner and outer, organism and environment, Hickman reminds us that Dewey believed that there 'was an extremely malleable and permeable membrane that separates the "internal" from the "external" with respect to the organism only in the loosest and most tentative of senses' (1992: 11). As Garrison and Watson explain further, the corner-stone of Dewey's thought is that organism and environment are involved in an ongoing 'transaction', rather than inter-action, which pre-supposes exchanges between two separate entities (2005: 252–5). Transaction thus suggests that the process of encounter and exchange between organism and environment is mutually constitutive.

The counterargument could be made here, that similarly to the answers given by performer trainers, Dewey's radical inclusivity could result in everything being regarded as a tool and hence everything being regarded as technology. This would not only prevent us from separating tool-use from other human activities; it could also lead to a kind of totalitarianism that sees no lifeworld beyond technology. It is crucial, then, that Dewey drew a second distinction: one between tool-use that is mechanical, habitual or routine and tool-use that is 'inquerential'. In other words, Dewey distinguished between a kind of tool-use that has an epistemic dimension or goal and instances of tool-use in 'which knowing is not operative' (Hickman 1992: 11). As Hickman explains, the distinction between an 'inquerential' form of tool-use and a 'mechanical' one is entirely contingent on the situation and the user; the fixing of a broken light switch by an electrical engineer would involve a mech-anical use of tools; the same task undertaken by a layperson would involve an inquerential form of tool-use, since the layperson would have to 'inquire' how to fix the light, i.e. what tools to use and how (Hickman 1992: 21). In this vein, Dewey considered 'technology' to include only those instances that involved an 'inquerential' use of tools and accordingly excluded those cases where tools were employed in a habitual or mechanical fashion. As Hickman explains, 'when what is commonly called technology fails to be intelligent, it does not strictly speaking deserve the name "technology". It should instead be termed repetition or habitual behaviour' (1992: 11).

Dewey-Hickman's conception of tool-use resonates with performer training prac-tice in two significant respects. It considers both material 'extra-organic' objects as well as 'intra-organic' or – what Michael Passmore calls – 'internal' processes to be tools (Roberts et al. 2015: 362). Indeed, as Hickman points out, contrary to Ihde's distinction between unmediated and mediated activities, 'for Dewey the distinction would not have been between the instrument and the non-instrumentally perceptual, but between instruments of different functional types: those that are relatively exte-rior to the organism and those that are not' (Hickman 2008: 104). Dewey's concep-tion of technology further foregrounds in tool-use a pedagogical and exploratory potential. Specifically, his demarcation between 'intelligent' and 'routine' use of tools chimes with a similar distinction in performer training between unreflective repeti-tion of an exercise/score/method and mindful engagement within a learning/creative process. According to Grotowski, for example, 'only the exercises which "investi-gate" involve the entire organism of the actor and mobilise his [sic] hidden resources. The exercises which "repeat" give inferior results' (Grotowski 2015: 86). A Deweyan perspective then legitimises the pervasive use of the word 'tool' in performer training as encompassing of both material *and* psychophysical resources, and is indicative of the epistemic potential of embodied (inter)action. Having brought together material objects and psychophysical resources under one conceptual roof and in relation to a process of inquiry, the next section explores the different instantiations of the relationship between users and tools in performer training practice.

I–Technology–World relationships in performer training

One of Ihde's major contributions to contemporary analyses of technology is his classification of three types of relationships among I (user) – Technology (technological artefact) – World (social, cultural and political setting). Each category, developed by Ihde through close phenomenological description and with reference to specific examples of contemporary and historical practices, aims to highlight a particular way in which the user relates to the technological artefact. As a result, although the same artefact may be used in different ways and/or the same use may involve different techniques, Ihde's categories aim to capture the 'constants' that underpin different experiences of technological mediation.

The Embodiment Relationship

According to Ihde, the 'Embodiment Relationship' involves the use of a technological artefact that withdraws from the user's attention as the latter is directed towards the world. As such, in this relationship the technological artefact becomes part of the user's embodiment, so that it no longer needs attention and the user can direct her efforts to the particular action the artefact is expected to facilitate. In other words, although it is possible that the technology may occupy the user's thematic focus, its function is premised on the artefact's withdrawal from the user's direct attention. As Philip Brey puts it, the tool becomes 'a medium positioned between individual and world *through* which the individual perceives his or her world' (2000a: 47, emphasis original). As noted already, a classic example of the embodiment relationship is the use of eyeglasses; although I can consciously bring my attention to them, their optimal function is to correct my vision and enable me to see. If the glasses call attention to themselves, because they are broken or smeared, then their function is no longer 'transparent', i.e. the eyeglasses do not function as they should, because they no longer remain outside the realm of my immediate awareness, since my attention needs to be directed to them rather than the aspect of the world they are supposed to enable me to see. Drawing on Merleau-Ponty's analysis of the blind man's stick, Ihde argues that through optimal function, and on the proviso that the user is skilled enough to use the artefact, 'perception may be materially extended through the "body" of the artefact' (Ihde 1990: 40).

Developing Ihde's analysis, Brey returns to the same example and explains that the relation to the artefact is made possible by the artefact's inclusion into the user's body schema. Body schema is a concept encountered in Merleau-Ponty's work and developed further in more recent phenomenological and cognitive studies. According to Brey, 'the body schema is an organising structure contained in one's body that presents one with a unified understanding of one's body, which is experienced as a unified whole or "Gestalt"' (2000a: 51). Following this line of thought, Brey argues that the operation of body schema as a pre-reflective, but malleable, *sense* of one's body leads to a qualitative difference in the way one relates to a tool that is the hallmark of the embodiment relation: the tool 'is then experienced and used as another means by which one engages with the world, rather than as an object in the world that one engages' (2000a: 52). The body schema, then, gives a holistic sense of one's body from the 'inside' and as distinct from other objects in the space, but it can also include in its remit material objects. Once it becomes part of the body schema, a material object would no longer be experienced as an entity out 'there', but rather it will be included within the body's spatial and sensorial reach: 'as such it comes to function as a direct expression of ourselves, as an integral part of our bodies' (Brey 2000a: 52).

An example of the 'Embodiment Relationship' in performer training is discussed in detail by Rebecca Loukes in her account of an exercise with bamboo sticks, developed within Phillip Zarrilli's 'psychophysical training'.[5] As the stick is held between the centre of Loukes' and her partner's palms,

> We look into each other's eyes while keeping our awareness 'open' to the space around us. We sense our feet on the floor and through the palms to the cane, and through the cane to the partner. We begin to move, but allow the movement to emerge through the sensing feet, though the body to the cane through the cane to the partner and beyond into the space.
>
> (Zarrilli et al. 2013: 243)

Echoing Brey and drawing on yet another articulation of the relationship between a cane and a blind person, Loukes positions the aforementioned exercise within a wider discussion of the way tools can 'extend the body' (Zarrilli et al. 2013: 243). She argues that, through optimal engagement, the stick becomes an extension of her body, acting as a conduit for her relationship to her partner and the world.

There is, however, a point of contention. How far or in what sense could we say that the stick, during the actual exercise, is incorporated into Loukes' body? On the one hand, Loukes maintains that her experience of working with the stick constitutes a case of incorporation (Zarrilli et al. 2013: 244). On the other hand, Helena De Preester (2011, 2012) asserts that we need to be cautious of claims of incorporation; the tool might be 'incorporated' in the user's body schema (as Brey suggests), but this is not the same with an experience of incorporating the tool into one's body. De Preester argues that incorporation can only take place when there is a change in one's sense of 'body ownership'. She points out that even when an artefact is experienced as part of the user's body schema, the user does not consider the artefact to be a part of one's body: 'the embodiment of tools is *not* to be equated with the acceptance of tools as *body parts*' (De Preester 2012: 388, emphasis original). Incorporation then suggests replacement, often with regard to prosthetic use of artificial limbs, whereas extension 'involve[s] (bottom-up) changes in motor and perceptual capacities, but without changes in body-ownership' (De Preester and Tsakiris 2009: 317).[6] In the light of these arguments, should we then consider Loukes' claim of incorporation inaccurate? Or does Loukes strive to articulate an experience that is not fully captured by an understanding of the tool as extension?

There are two additional aspects in Loukes' example that warrant attention, both because they are defining in a performer training context and also because they suggest additional perspectives of the user–tool–world relationship: Loukes' engagement with the tool is *intersubjective* and *expressive*. As noted earlier, the stick is used in a partner exercise and it could be argued that Loukes' body schema in this instance extends and includes not only the stick but the other person too. It is telling in this sense that Loukes describes the exercise in the first plural pronoun and outlines a mode of awareness that progressively includes the entire structure: '*We* sense *our* feet on the floor and through the palms to the cane, and through the cane to the partner' (emphasis added). Similarly, in his discussion of the ethics of actor training, Zarrilli notes the intersubjective character of the training that Loukes received. He stresses that 'the actor's work begins with work on the "self", but can/should never be defined by our work on "the self". Rather, the actor's work is always informed by "being with/for" Others' (2014: 121). There is an important difference then between performer training processes and the normative descriptions of the embodiment relationship: whereas in Ihde's and Brey's respective accounts the relationship takes place between one user and the artefact, the stick is between Loukes and her partner. Accordingly, movement in the space originates through the entire Loukes–stick–partner structure. What is more, a crucial part of the exercise is to develop an embodied relationship to the partner, which can then be transferred to the performer's relationship to the audience in performance (Zarrilli 2014). In performer training then, it would be more accurate to put the embodiment relationship in terms of a 'We–Tool–World' formulation.

Moreover, it bears stressing that the sensory-motor and perceptive processes involved in the movement serve primarily expressive purposes. In this respect, it is worth noting that De Preester and Tsakiris mention at the end of their article that 'specialised tool-users, such as musicians, report about the relation between themselves and their instrument as an experience of completion or wholeness' (2009: 318). They further hypothesise that such experience may be due to 'the fact some tools such as music instruments, allow (and are designed for) *expression*' (De Preester and Tsakiris 2009: 318, emphasis original). The musical instrument in this way extends not only the 'sensorimotor body' but the 'expressive body'. In a later article, De Preester further elaborates that 'the experience that expression is possible via a non-corporeal object might be decisive for experiencing it as a body part and not as mere tool' (2011: 124).

De Preester and Tsakiris do not explain what an 'expressive body' might be, and indeed if the neurophysiological constitution of the expressive body is in any way unique or different. A proxy to such an answer can be found in Zarrilli's suggested fourfold model of the performer's embodiment, consisting of: 1) the ecstatic surface (sensorimotor) body; 2) the recessive (visceral) body; 3) the aesthetic inner (subtle) body-mind; and 4) the aesthetic outer (fictive) body (Zarrilli 2009: 52). Zarrilli explains that whereas bodies 1 and 2 are part of everyday embodiment, body 3 is developed through training, whereas body 4 is constituted in performance. According to this model, Loukes' experience takes place within the process of the constitution of this third body. It could be thus argued that if such body becomes possible through an exercise of which the stick is an integral part, it is plausible that the stick is experienced as part of this *third* body.

Here, then, we see how performer training contributes to the postphenomenological tripartite between person, tool and the world, a more nuanced understanding of embodiment as a processual and emergent phenomenon. As I have already argued in the Introduction, despite the evident focus on embodiment, in postphenomenological accounts embodiment is assumed as a rather stable and, in a sense, sedimented experience. For example, Robert Rosenberger, uses the term

> sedimentation to refer to the degree to which particular structures of experience have become set within a user's bodily perceptual habits. It is the degree to which it has become automatic for a user to approach a particular device through a particular organization of experience, with a particular field composition, and particular aspects of usage taking on particular levels of transparency.
>
> (2019: 307)

In other words, in postphenomenological accounts, embodiment relationships are often discussed with reference to a kind of 'routine' embodiment that the user will unproblematically 'find' once the artefact functions satisfactorily. In performer training, on the other hand, an embodied relation with tools is 'inquerential' or to paraphrase Grotowski, 'investigative', conceived as a fluid and emergent process, and aiming to institute change. Of course, the differentiation between a routine and inquerential action may not be as clear as Grotowski or Dewey implies. Brey, for example, notes how 'a long stick' may be used to enable one's reach of a remote object, in the process extending one's 'action horizon' (Brey 2000b: 68). Such process may be routine, but it may also involve inquiry, for example, a process of trial and error with how the stick needs to be handled. In Loukes' case, however, the employment of the stick is not extending her reach within an already known action or goal. Rather the inquerential use of the tool aims at the constitution of a new way of experiencing and relating to the world.

And it is precisely at this junction that a transition from a material to a non-material tool can be achieved. Through the mediation of the stick, Loukes is being trained in a non-quotidian mode of awareness, which will, in turn, become a non-material tool that she will eventually be able to use in performance. This is another fundamental point where postphenomenological analysis and performer training practice diverge. In postphenomenological accounts the embodiment relationship is rendered possible only when artefact and user are in contact or at least in interaction: the moment the eyeglasses are taken off, the embodiment relationship between wearer and glasses ceases and with it the sensory extension the artefact facilitates. In the case of performer training, however, the material tool only serves the development of, and will be eventually substituted by, the constitution of an organic one. In the remainder of her account, Loukes outlines the way she utilised in performance the particular skill produced through training, but without using the sticks. This took the form of an 'active relationship with the space' and 'the embodied, experienced situation' of the performance score (Zarrilli et al. 2013: 250). In the development of an organic tool, the embodiment relationship between trainee and artefact achieves a *legacy*.

We see therefore that an application of a key postphenomenological framework to an aspect of psychophysical performer training leads us to a series of conclusions that can be productive for both fields. Contra to the common postphenomenological expectation that in the embodiment relationship the tool will give rise to a kind of embodiment that is already there, an instance of performer training demonstrates that the tool contributes to the emergence of a new experience of embodiment. What is more, this new state of embodiment, is expected to become differentiated from other states and readily available to such an extent that it can be eventually employed with the ease and the transparency of a material tool. Material and psychophysical tools are therefore different, but they also share a reciprocal relationship, whereby material objects are used to cultivate organic resources and concomitantly the employment of these organic resources in performance or rehearsal is then understood as a kind of tool.

The Hermeneutic Relationship

The second category in Ihde's I–Technology–World typology is the hermeneutic one. Ihde explains that 'in its broadest and simplest sense it [hermeneutic] means "interpretation", but in a more specialised sense it refers to *textual* interpretation and thus entails *reading*' (1990: 80, all emphases original). As such, Ihde positions the origins of the hermeneutic relation in the development of writing, which he considers to be 'a technologically mediated language', which, in turn, gave rise to all sorts of technological artefacts (1990: 81). Ihde further points out that in certain forms of writing, such as charts, there is an isomorphism between the actual elements of the chart and what the chart refers to. In printed text, however, such 'representational isomorphism disappears' (1990: 81). As the distance between the shape of the written elements and the aspects of the world they are supposed to represent grows, 'what now presents itself is the "world" of the text' (Ihde 1990: 84).

It is precisely at this point that Ihde locates the hermeneutic function: a piece of text needs not only to be read, it also needs to be interpreted (1990: 84). Once this function is established – and in literate societies it is established to such an extent that this process becomes transparent (Ihde 1990: 84) – it can also be transferred to other kinds of instrumentation, beyond the strictly textual ones. Ihde gives the example of the thermometer. In this case, a hermeneutic relationship operates due to the use of a specific instrument. It also presupposes that a specific aspect of the world has been rendered into a kind of 'text' that the user is able to 'read'. For example, the use of the thermometer depends on apprehending the Celsius/Fahrenheit scale. In view of this process, Ihde points out that the hermeneutic relationship can also be traced in non-industrial and non-literate cultures. He specifically gives the example of shamanism and argues that 'the patterns of the entrails, bones, or whatever are taken to *refer* to some state of affairs, instrumentally or textually' (Ihde 1990: 89, emphasis original). He further emphasises that in shamanic practices, and in the absence of the mediating effect of the alphabet, the hermeneutic relationship operates on the premise of an 'entire gestalt' (Ihde 1990: 89) that guides the interpretation. The function of the hermeneutic relationship, in other words, is premised on a matrix, be that textual or material, secular or spiritual, that guides the interpretation.

The most evident example of the hermeneutic relationship in performer training manifests in exercises with play texts that aim to train the performer's ability to access the textual artefact with the aim to interpret it. Reviewing her training in Method Acting, for example, Lauren Love remarks that 'a good part of my work involves a hermeneutic study of the author's text. I try to discover the deeper truths at which the playwright may only hint [...]' (2002: 281). In this instance, performer training exercises may be seen as the gestalt that will alert the actor to the text's deeper meaning. For example, the popular technique of 'actioning the text' involves the use of a linguistic and kinetic gestalt in the form of verbs embodied in action, through which actors construe the relationships between characters. A script, then, like a thermometer, points towards a world that emerges through the hermeneutic function and training offers the gestalt according to which the script can be interpreted. Nonetheless, the 'hermeneutic paradigm' is operative beyond working with text. Specifically, I will argue that the hermeneutic relationship is the prime relationship in which the epistemic and pedagogical dimension of training manifests.

In an explanation of a series of biomechanical exercises that involve the balancing of a stick on/with various parts of the body, Pitches contends that, 'here, the stick is acting as an *index* of your own balance as a performer, it is *reading you* and *reflecting back* your centre of balance' (2007: 100, emphasis added). A similar relationship with a stick, although of a different size and in a different training context, is noted by Roberta Carreri. Considering a three-year process of working with sticks as part of her training with Odin Teatret, Carreri stresses the importance of the stick's dimensions in enabling her to evaluate the development of her strength:

> the fact that I started with a big stick and then moved on to a smaller one might appear strange. It seems more logical to do it the other way round. However, a smaller stick, which is lighter, would not have offered the resistance that I needed. I could *assess* my strength more easily if I had to confront a precise resistance.
>
> (Carreri 2014: 71, emphasis added)

Similar to Pitches' description, Carreri here recounts an instance of stick-use that was intended to evaluate a specific aspect of her embodiment. Finally, recounting the training she has developed as a result of various influences, Anne Furse also attests that working with bamboo sticks 'can bring deep physical awareness and material for collaborative "*reading*" to the practitioner' (Crook et al. 2015: 364, emphasis added).

These three cases are paradigmatic of influential pedagogies and, significantly, in all three of them the stick is used in different ways and is also a different kind of stick: broom handles that have been shortened for Biomechanics, found sticks in Carreri's work with the Odin, and bamboo canes in Furse's training. What, however, pervades all three accounts is that a relationship between stick and body, which arguably 'belongs' to the embodiment category, is explained in hermeneutic terms.[7] Note, for example, in both Pitches' and Furse's respective quotes the explicit use of the word 'read' as a descriptor of what the stick 'does', as well as Carreri's explanation of the stick's function in terms of assessment. In all these cases, the stick serves as an instrument that reveals aspects of the user's embodiment. Or as Thomas Wilson puts it: 'it betrays your inattentions, reflects your preoccupations, and magnifies your choices' (Crook et al. 2015: 365). Not unlike a thermometer, then, we could say that the stick offers a way of reading the individual's 'temperature' of movement, rhythm, strength and balance. Unlike the thermometer, though, such reading is not directed outwards and towards an aspect of the world; the stick, rather, externalises and renders visible internal processes.

In this manner, within the hermeneutic relationship the use of a tool can serve as a way to benchmark the trainee's progress within a particular pedagogy. In relation to the processes mentioned above, the set of interactions between stick and trainee could signpost the progressive acquisition of skill, for example, in terms of the frequency and length of time the stick is balanced or held as well as other somatic markers that are involved in the accomplishment of the task. What is more, and by contrast to the embodiment relationship that takes place in a closed circuit between user(s) and artefact, the hermeneutic relationship can be accessed from 'outside', as long as one has knowledge of the gestalt that guides the interpretation. Note for example that Furse refers to a 'collective reading', suggesting that interactions with the stick would be meaningful to more than one trainee familiar with the pedagogy. Indeed, I would argue that an informed participant or observer, be that the trainer or another trainee, would engage in a hermeneutic relationship automatically, looking for clues in the interactions between body and stick specific to the pedagogical context in which the interactions take place. In this manner, a pedagogy can be understood as a conglomeration of reference points, a gestalt to use Ihde's term, through which a trainee's process can be read and made sense of. Although such reference points may be different from one regime to another, their presence are constitutive of any pedagogy.

In his discussion of movement training for actors, Mark Evans similarly points out that an important part of training consists in the 'students learn[ing] to have their bodily surface *read* by the tutor' (2009: 129, emphasis added). In the process,

Evans identifies the operation of a set of norms, which are akin to the gestalt that underpins the hermeneutic relationship: 'what the tutors looks *at* [...] becomes what the students look *for*' (Evans 2009: 129, all emphases original). Here again we see the process of training rendered in terms of inquiry. What the trainer looks at is a set of clues specific to skills or competencies associated with a particular regime, which, accordingly, the trainee will first recognise, then learn to embody or express, and eventually turn into intra-organic tools she can have at her disposal. If the embodiment relationship is foundational in the way the trainee relates to objects and eventually her own resources, the hermeneutic relationship provides the criteria that guide this process.

And it is precisely in this normative dimension of the hermeneutic relation that Evans locates the inscriptive function of training. According to Evans, the trainee 'succumbs' to scrutiny and becomes located within 'an economy of looks' that value certain set of skills or attributes (2009: 129). This is indeed correct, and Evans is right to point out that training not only trains a set of skills but also, deliberately or not, fosters an awareness of the norms according to which the actor will be eventually looked at within the industry. However, I would add to Evans' analysis that the hermeneutic act is not exclusively visual. More like a shaman, rather than a reader, the trainer also becomes attuned to the trainee, since the clues emerging from the trainee's embodiment of a specific regime or exercise are likely to have a holistic, synesthetic character. The trainer sees, but also hears, and senses, and moves *with* the trainee in a hermeneutic act that is not only inscriptive but also caring, since the trainer is not an indifferent observer, but deeply invested in the process. Furthermore, in Pitches', Carreri's and Furse's respective accounts, we can trace a process of reflexivity, whereby the trainee, through the material object, is prompted to exercise the kind of observation that would otherwise be provided by the trainer. In this instance, the hermeneutic relationship, precisely because it institutes a distance between a set of phenomena and the meanings that such phenomena may acquire, becomes foundational of self-directed or auto-didactic learning. The distancing effect established through the hermeneutic relation can, therefore, also be achieved by the trainee, who can become, in this way, able to negotiate her relationship with the suggested tools by selecting, tweaking or rejecting them. I will return to this relationship in the last chapter with specific reference to the use of audio-visual sources.

The Alterity Relationship

Alterity is the last relationship put forward by Ihde and aims to capture those instances where the technology can be experienced as 'other' in a positive sense. Following Heidegger's analysis that a tool attracts the conscious attention of the user only when it is misplaced or breaks down, Ihde argues that in the alterity relationship the tool also becomes the terminal point of the user's attention but in a positive sense. Through reworking Levinas' concept of alterity, Ihde discusses phenomena where 'technologies emerge as focal entities that may receive the multiple attentions humans give the different forms of the other' (1990: 107). He considers two groups of artefacts. One is the sort of automatic technologies that can or seem to work without human intervention. Spinning tops and automata fall in this category. In this case, the artefact both exhibits signs of 'a life of its own' and 'may become the focal centre of attention as a quasi-other to which I relate' (Ihde 1990: 100). The other group involves artefacts that become a terminal reference point for the user's experience: 'the world in this case may remain context and background and the technology may merge as the foreground and focal quasi-other with which I momentarily engage' (Ihde 1990: 107). The television, the computer, and as I will discuss in the next chapter, the mobile phone, exemplify this category.

Ihde explains that in the alterity relationship a degree of interpretation is still involved, since the technological artefact is offering access to and/or a reading of a particular aspect of the world. Yet, he also points out that what defines the relation is that the artefact is experienced as a quasi-other. Verbeek further explains that the reason for such experience 'is that technologies on the one hand possess a kind of independence and on the other hand can give rise to "interaction" between humans and technologies' (2001: 131). What emerges therefore is a form of 'technological intentionality'. Drawing on the phenomenological understanding of intentionality, which denotes the about-ness or of-ness of human consciousness, technological intentionality suggests two things. First, it points towards the way human intentionality in an activity that involves technology is bound to be mediated by the technological artefact. Second, and more radically, however, in the alterity relationship, Ihde understands technological intentionality in terms of the artefact not the user. He gives the example of a recording in a busy lecture theatre by an audio recording device and points out that the outcome will be very different from the experience of a human listener. Whereas a person might tend to block out the overall hubbub and hear the voice of the lecturer, the recording device lacks this selectivity (Ihde 1990: 103). However, even if the device might not pick up the lecturer's voice, it could offer other information, for instance on the acoustics of the room, which may be missed by a human listener, who chooses to focus on the voice of the lecturer (Ihde 1990: 103). By identifying intentionality as a modality of technological artefacts, Ihde aims neither to anthropomorphise nor attribute to them some kind of 'consciousness'. Rather he points out that in the same way that human perception is selective, has a set of abilities, and a set of restrictions, so do technological artefacts (Ihde 1990: 103).

The alterity relationship can be traced in several examples of performer training practice, and, as I will discuss below, tools are often understood as partners or teachers. Perhaps the most obvious example of the alterity relation is to be found in the field of puppetry, where the overall intention is that the trainee, and eventually the audience, experiences the puppet as an animated quasi-other. My intention here, however, is to discuss the alterity relationship in terms of the use of tools aimed at developing generic skills, such as physical dexterity or concentration, that can be employed across a range of performance genres. To begin, the alterity relationship can be identified in the use of sticks. With reference to their use in ensemble work, Tom Wilson points out that:

the stick is a partner. It is the first partner. The easiest of partners and the hardest of partners: it does exactly what you ask of it. […] Alone: the stick becomes your teacher.

(Crook et al. 2015: 365)[8]

A similar assertion is made by Biomechanics teacher Alexei Levinski who identifies three possible relations between the actor and the stick: the actor may 'master', 'tame' or make 'friends' with the stick (Levinski 1996 quoted in Margolies 2016: 43).[9] Both in Wilson's and Levinski's assertion the stick is positioned as an other and moreover the stick's behaviour is identified as a possible source of knowledge.

Engagement with objects is also an enduring thread in Stanislavsky's System and twentieth-century teachings thereof. As Stanislavsky advocates, the actor must 'revitalise the object' and, building on its characteristics, endow it further with an imaginary life (2008: 111). Accounting on her own ten-month training at the Moscow State Institute of Cinematography, Merlin describes a careful process of observing an object's real attributes and gradually endowing it with dramatic poten- tial that serves the given circumstances of the play. She thus advocates that objects provide actors with opportunities for developing clear actions and may also serve as scene-partners: 'you can respond to any object with the same attention that you'd respond to a human partner. And focusing all your attention on an object can often alleviate potentially difficult given circumstances' (Merlin 2001: 72).

The 'endowment method' is also encountered in the work of Mike Alfreds, but he adds an important twist: instead of the actor bestowing an imaginary life-history and/or characteristics on the object, Alfreds proposes that actors become sensitised to the object's latent qualities (2013: 380). In the exercise 'Endowing props with a life of their own', he identifies material resistance as a source of creative knowledge and advises the trainer/director to allow the actor to 'have a problem with an object; it won't do what they want it to' (ibid.). As such, the object's 'refusal' to fulfil its purpose or resistance to perform its function, can alert the actor to a set of characteristics that transcend the object's daily use. Material resistance, in other words, can render the actor perceptive towards a series of possibilities that remained latent during quotidian use.

Although Alfreds is not drawing on Ihde, his formulation bears a striking resem- blance with Ihde's configuration of alterity. As explained already, Ihde argues that a thematisation of the object need not exclusively produce a negative experience. Ihde builds his argument in response to Heidegger's insight that a tool becomes present to the user only when it breaks down or becomes misplaced. If the tool works as expected, it withdraws. Ihde, however, argues that a foregrounding of the tool is not limited to cases of breakdown or malfunction and can involve a positive experience. As such, the alterity relation serves as a means to 'circumvent the tend- ency succumbed to by Heidegger and his more orthodox followers to see the otherness of technology only in negative terms or negative derivations' (1990: 98). In this respect, Alfreds' exercise may be seen as a confirmation of Ihde's thesis: the object's resistance may not only engender novel forms of interaction; it will result in the 'actor [...] playing a scene with a prop as partner' (Alfreds 2013: 380). What is more in Alfreds' exercise the alterity relationship is premised on the object's characteristics rather than the actor's ability to bestow meaning. What we see therefore is that once material objects are identified as constituent parts of training, what also opens up is a space that accommodates and invites the object's behaviour. This becomes further accentuated in the following instances of practice.

In the examples discussed thus far, the alterity relationship between tool and trainee takes place through the active handling and manipulation of the object. There are cases, however, when the trainee is expected to learn from an object not through handling it, although handling may be involved, but through observing and eventually embodying the object's behaviour. This, I would suggest, is not only a change in the modality in which the tool–user relationship takes place; it also foregrounds the pedagogical function of alterity, in the sense that the object's material behaviour is approached as an opportunity for learning. A well-developed example of such an approach can be found in the training of Jacques Lecoq (1921–1999). Movement is at the centre of Lecoq's training, aimed not only at developing a set of virtuosic abilities, but also at alerting the trainee to the movement that surrounds her. Everything moves, according to Lecoq, and everything is imbued with life. Accordingly, this means that the behaviour of matter is pregnant with dramatic potential.

Steph Kehoe, a Lecoq-trained director and trainer of the method, explains the three stages that comprise the overall process of working with materials:

> *observation* (if possible in the studio when working with materials [...]); *embodiment* (put the movement, the rhythms, the breath into your own body – without judgement or interpretation); then *transposition* (which is finding the right theatre language, style, size, duration to make the material 'play' so this might mean speeding up the 'real' time or slowing down real time or over-articulating pauses etc – but you are still drawing from the authentic rhythm/movement.
> (Kehoe 2017 email communication with the author, all emphases original)

The first part of the process described by Kehoe can be seen in a video held by the National Audiovisual Institute showing Lecoq working with a piece of cellophane that he quickly crumples.[10] A group of students is gathered around the material, while it slowly unfolds. Lecoq, standing on the side, comments on the affective dimension of the material's response ('It's painful? What pain'); makes guesses about how the cellophane's 'drama' might progress; and finally states that he used this kind of movement in a tragic chorus. The video then shows an extract from the students' work, where a chorus surrounding the tragic hero embodies the movement qualities of the cellophane.

In Lecoq's teaching, then, we can trace a trajectory, which starts with a preoccupation with manifestations of movement in materials, progresses through the trainee's embodiment of the suggested movement-qualities and rhythms, and culminates in the use of these qualities as a form of dramatic language. Metaphor plays a crucial role in this process, in that Lecoq enables the students to see a series of dramatic, and in a certain sense abstract, states in the material world. 'As such, in elastic materials that tend to return to their original shape, Lecoq identifies a sense of nostalgia; in materials that try to bounce back but do so less successfully, Lecoq sees a 'tragic dimension', whereas in 'breakages, splinterings, cracked glasses, shattered window panes, explosions, [...] we are looking at ourselves, at the variety of our internal cracks and divisions' (Lecoq 2002: 89). What is of further interest here is that, as the exercise with the cellophane exemplifies, the material's behaviour is positioned as a form of demonstration, not unlike the way a teacher or an advanced student might demonstrate a particular movement or step. Yet, the use of an object both depersonalises the movement from individual competencies and traits, and directs the students' attention to the possibilities of matter. Indeed, in the video discussed above, we could say that the cellophane enjoys the kind of focal attention usually directed at the instructor. In this process, the cellophane becomes a quasi-teacher.

A similar understanding of a material entity as a teacher can be found in the description of the use of lights in Stanislavsky's seminal *An Actor's Work* (2008). Electric lights are different from all the other tools considered in this chapter in two crucial respects: lighting is a technology, which, unlike the stick, requires considerable infrastructure and advanced scientific knowledge. (Of course, one could retort here, that the same applies to the manufacture of cellophane.) Furthermore, electric light is radically different from the human body and other material objects in its consistency, manifestation and effect, since it is weightless and ungraspable. It is thus instructive that in Stanislavsky's account the ability of electric light to spread, illuminate and flicker is mobilised for training the actor's concentration and attention, and this, as I will discuss below and in the next chapter, has implications about the way these faculties are construed.

As a detailed exposition of the section is offered in Chapter 2, here I offer a summary with the aim to foreground the alterity relationship. The section begins when Tortsov, the master-teacher in Stanislavsky's fictional training diary, makes the point that the actor's tendency to be preoccupied with what is happening in the auditorium can be combated, if the actor becomes '*engrossed in what is happening on stage*' (Stanislavsky 2008: 90, emphasis original). This is followed by a demonstration of a series of lighting states, including total blackout, light from a small lamp, general and medium wash, as well as spotlights of various sizes (Stanislavsky 2008: 90). The trainees are then positioned on stage whilst different lighting states operate. In each case, they are asked to spread their focus as close or as far as the range of the illumination provided by the lights (Stanislavsky 2008: 90–102). Similarly to the exercise with the cellophane, in this instance training takes place by asking the students to observe an-other entity; and after the demonstration, the students are taught to control an aspect of their organism by following the controlled behaviour of this entity. The light in this case is clearly positioned as a quasi-other by means of which the actor can become able to concentrate on progressively larger segments of space, or in Stanislavsky's terminology, work with varying 'Circles of Attention'.

Drawing on Ihde's analysis, it could be argued that Stanislavsky is exploiting the intentionality of the artefact in order to train the intentionality of the students. He is using the propensity of electric light to illuminate a certain part of the space, whilst leaving the rest in darkness, in order to teach students a similarly selective focus. In the same manner in which Lecoq utilised a piece of cellophane to demonstrate a material manifestation of movement (the attempt of the cellophane piece to return to its original state), Stanislavsky uses electric theatre lights to put forward one of the most enduring aspects of his work. Light in this case is not only a tool that allows the actor to include in their focus progressively larger segments of the stage; it provides the actor with a clear physical proposition of how concentration works (it brightens the object it is focused upon) and a metaphor (concentration is a sort of illumination that the actor can 'train' in the same way a light technician can 'train' a beam of light).[11] Correspondingly, a state of distraction is also demonstrated through the use of darting light. Here is Tortsov's gloss followed by the description of Kostya, the fictional student keeping the diary:

> 'Now I will show you what should never happen onstage but which, unfortunately, *almost always does* with the vast majority of actors'. […] Following this introduction little beams of light suddenly darted about. They filled the entire stage and auditorium, illustrating the actor's concentration when it is unfocused.
>
> (Stanislavsky 2008: 95, emphasis original)

A technological entity becomes employed as a tool for learning, and in the process becomes a kind of teacher or indeed a saviour: when students are losing their concentration, Tortsov quickly advises them to 'latch onto your lifesaver, the bulb' (Stanislavsky 2008: 101).

However, there is a marked difference between the way the cellophane is used by Lecoq and the way lights are used by Stanislavsky. The difference is that in Lecoq's case the 'dance' of the cellophane is offered as an example of the movement that inheres in inorganic matter. The larger message here is that movement can be found anywhere and, as such, anything can serve as a source of inspiration for theatre-making. In other words, the students not only observe and embody the movement of a certain material, they are also trained in identifying the creative potential that may inhere in the world around them. As such, it could be argued that Lecoq's training inculcates an appreciation that movement is not limited to humans, and accordingly flattens hierarchies in terms of what is worth observing and what is worth knowing. In Stanislavsky's case there is a similar appreciation of the technological artefact as a possible source of knowledge, but here the technological artefact also provides a standard of performance. This becomes further accentuated by the students' marked difficulty to match the capacity of the

technology. The training in this case is underpinned by the assumption that technological advancement equates mastery and accordingly Stanislavsky's 'mini light-
show' (Merlin 2007: 279) operates as a paradigmatic performance of efficiency,
raising the expectation that the students have to achieve a similar level of control
and mastery over their own organism. Even though in both examples a form of
technology serves as a quasi-teacher, each example conveys a radically different
message with regards to the trainee's relationship to herself and the world.

Conclusion

What postphenomenology tells us…

This chapter focused on the use of tools in performer training through employing
Don Ihde's postphenomenological framework of 'I–Technology–World' relations
and by including Dewey's notion of intra- and extra-organic tools. The analysis
revealed not only a wide range of application of material objects for learning purposes, but also that different relations between user and artefact correspond to
different pedagogical configurations. As we saw, the embodiment relation takes
place between trainee(s) and artefact and primarily centres on the use of a material
object towards the rendering of an organic resource into a tool. The hermeneutic
relation underpins the interactions between trainee and trainer, or trainee and a
specific regime, and in this case the artefact serves as an 'index' of a set of criteria
according to which a pedagogy can be accomplished. The alterity relation is also
taking place between trainee and artefact but crucially the artefact is expected to
substitute or act as a teacher. A postphenomenological analysis reveals therefore that
engagement with material objects is not simply, or at least not in the cases considered here, an add-on to a form of practice that could be realised without them.
In the examples examined in this chapter, material tools are constitutive of the
trainee's embodiment, can serve as an indication of the trainee's progress and incul-
cate a disposition towards artefacts that suggests a wider attitude towards the
world.

A postphenomenological analysis also made evident an approach to material
objects that transcends established kinds of use and/or involves an active process of
repurposing. We saw, for example, that in Carreri's case the stick's length was an
important aspect of the effect she wanted to achieve. The same applies to Biomechanics. As noted already, the sticks used in Biomechanics are broom handles,
which, as Biomechanics teacher Terence Mann (Chapman) explains, 'are made
shorter; cut with a saw to a length of one metre then sanded to a smooth finish at
the part where they have been cut' (Mann (Chapman) 2017 email communication
with author). There is, in other words, a pre-occupation with the object's materiality even before the training begins, and this involves active selection, possibly
changes to the object itself, and certainly changes in the function it is expected to
serve. Alfreds, for example, explicitly calls for the object to pose a problem. Similarly, in Biomechanics as well as in Lecoq training, the alterations that render the

object useful in a training context are precisely those that would render it useless in a quotidian one; a crumpled piece of cellophane or a shortened broom handle would be considered damaged.

In this process of appropriation and tweaking, we can trace, therefore, an attitude of what Andrew Feenberg calls 'interpretive flexibility' (2005: 104), i.e. an appreciation that the use of technological artefacts is not set but open to and dependent upon an ability to tinker with, loosen and reconfigure their material and cultural determinations. In the examples examined here, we can trace forms of practice that push both the use of the object as well as the pedagogy in new and, in some cases, innovative directions. They demonstrate both a focused engagement with the 'material configurations' of the object as well as the emergence of new forms of interactions, which subsequently become crystallised in specific methods and exercises. The analysis then seems to confirm the key postphenomenological tenet: 'when they are used, technologies may make it possible for human beings to have a relation with reality that is much richer that those they have with a manipulable stock of raw materials' (Verbeek 2005: 66).

Indeed, the practices that emerge in a performer training context reveal a relation with material reality, including technology, that is underpinned by ingenuity, curiosity, playfulness and responsiveness; a relation to the world far removed from the bleak picture painted by Heidegger. In fact, the attention and value that performer trainers bestow on the materiality of the object can be seen as an instantiation of Heidegger's notion of techne. As we saw in the previous chapter, according to Heidegger the transcendence of calculative thinking is premised on the development of a predisposition that acknowledges and allows the expression of matter. The kind of in-depth engagements examined here confirm the Heideggerian insight that, 'through commitment to a particular activity, entities matter in a way that they couldn't before. Before, everything showed up as a resource to support optionalisation. Now some things show up as that without which one cannot be who one is' (Wrathall 2019: 35). In this sense, and as Murray suggests, the training workshop, laboratory or rehearsal studio can serve as 'a brief space of resistance' (Murray 2015: 57), a physical site and intersubjective realm that provides opportunities to communicate, collaborate and understand rather than exploit. We could further assume that, in this version, the instrumentalisation of the self serves creative expression and, whether manifesting in performance or through an exercise, such creative expression has no other intention beyond its own fulfilment. It would seem then that Ihde is right to argue that when we look closely at the range of relations that evolve in seemingly innocuous actions, such as throwing and catching sticks, a different relationship to the world begins to emerge. What however remains unresolved is the position of the trainee and/or performer in professional settings. As the story of the Open Theatre demonstrated in the previous chapter, the actor's expression takes place in and is supported by economic and political networks. Can the soft version of instrumentality that emerges once performer training practice is seen through a postphenomenological lens mitigate the hard realities of the creative industries?

...and what it doesn't

As performers and performer trainers are well aware, training is also expected to serve as preparation for employment, amidst developments that include, at least in the UK and the United States: a rise in student debt; gradual withdrawal of public subsidy for the arts and apprenticeship schemes; and high levels of un-, or unpaid, employment in the creative arts sector. Accordingly, in the last few years, training in the performing arts has been marked by a strong, and in certain cases institution-ally led, wave of entrepreneurialism, which has been embraced by scholars as well as industry professionals. Against the dire 'given circumstances' of the professional world, entrepreneurialism is positioned as a pragmatic solution. According to Peter Zazzali,

> actors are faced with the choice of either succumbing to the system's hege-monic forces, or they can manage their way around and within it by choos-ing an entrepreneurial path that both invites and deploys creative thinking, self-promotion, and civic responsibility.
>
> (2016: 175)

In support of his argument, Zazzali is drawing on a roundtable on entrepreneur-ship, which called for the use of 'tools' that will enable actors to 'understand [their] own personal brand' (McGraw in Simpson 2013: np). In an article on the same subject, Bryce Pinkham admitted that, although actors might resist the idea of selling oneself, he considers his 'acting career as my own start-up business. It's something I "go to work" to do. Every day, I attempt to promote, expand and grow Bryce Pinkham, Inc.' (2013: np). A practice that is gaining prevalence amongst creative workers, 'self branding entails that individuals think of themselves as prod-ucts to be marketed to a broad audience in the hopes of becoming more economic-ally competitive' (Whitmer 2019: 1). Whitmer notes that although the rhetoric and ideology underpinning self-branding were present from the beginning of the twen-tieth century, a confluence of factors has further legitimised it as a strategy for eco-nomic and professional survival: 'the increasing marketization of public life, rising precarity in work, and the spread of information and communications technolo-gies' (2019: 2).

Entrepreneurialism, however, does not guarantee empowerment. In fact, studies in the field of the cultural industries (Banks 2007; Hesmondhalgh and Baker 2011) demonstrate that entrepreneurialism often becomes the euphemistic term for unpaid internships and exploitative labour conditions. Mark Banks points out that creative workers are often expected to 'thrive on low or no pay, juggle multiple jobs and "projects", relentlessly self-promote [...] while always remaining alert to the possib-ility of being undercut or "let go"' (2007: 36). Furthermore, a set of responsibilities that used to belong to the state are now passed on to the individual and with them comes not only risk-taking but also self-exploitation and self-blame (Banks 2007; McRobbie 2002). For example, Zazzali takes for granted that we cannot 'simply' expect that governments will see the value of the arts and properly support them. He contends that 'it is the responsibility of theatre artists – and those that train them to create a demand in the marketplace for their work' (2016: 174). Entrepreneurialism therefore is underpinned by and sustains a paradox. On the one hand, it prizes a set of attributes, such as the individual's creative and 'free' spirit, which can 'progressively challenge or moderate the pursuit of market values' (Banks 2007: 58). On the other hand, artistic creativity and independence are ultimately governed by and harnessed to the interests of neoliberal capitalism.

Similarly, self-branding presents a layer of instrumentalisation that is qualitatively and conceptually different from a focus on skill-development, which arguably always permeated vocational training. It is still acknowledged that training should 'provide a safe environment for actors to grow their artistic talent, expand their instrument and hone their craft' (Pinkham 2013: np), but this process becomes enfolded within a wider rhetoric and acceptance of market imperatives not only at a professional and aesthetic but also at a personal level. Even though self-branding, like other forms of entrepreneurialism, is presented as a pragmatic if not empowering choice, it requires considerable labour, has no guaranteed results, and openly marketises the actors' skills, social networks, private life and affective experience. When the actor's instrument turns into a branded product, the actor becomes instrumentalised twice: first in the service of creative expression and then in the service of neoliberal capitalism. Heidegger's fear that calculative thinking will envelope all aspects of human life and extend to the way humans view their own self appears dangerously close.

However, postphenomenology, in its insistence that Heidegger got it wrong, is not prepared to consider technologies of self-exploitation, especially those that operate within the creative industries. Such an attitude is particularly exemplified through Ihde's analysis of musical instruments. According to Idhe, the use of musical instruments is akin to the use of scientific instruments: in both cases the function of the instrument depends on a successful embodied relationship between instrument and user and discloses a particular world to them. Furthermore, and as a direct riposte to Heidegger, Ihde claims that 'the "world" created does not at all imply the same reduction to what has been claimed as the unique Western view of the domination of nature' (1990: 97). He further points out that 'the closest analogy to the notion of standing reserve […] that the musical "world" might take is the realm of all possible sound may be taken and/or transformed musically' (Ihde 1990: 96). Ihde claims, therefore, that engagement with musical instruments exemplifies a kind of tool-use that opens a realm beyond an exploitative relationship to the world. In fact, in a subsequent publication, Ihde reveals that his 'understanding of human-technology relations' emerged in an improvisation session, which revealed that musical instruments can be employed beyond pre-determined ways and be subjected to acts of imagination that open up new possibilities (2012: 171–2).

In light of the examples of practice reviewed in this chapter, Ihde's argument can easily map onto performer training. As we saw, the use of material objects in performer training also depends on a successful embodiment relationship. Equally, it could be noted that in the same way that a musician, in Ihde's argument, experiences the world as a series of possibilities for sonic exploration, a trainee involved in, say, stick work experiences the world as a series of possibilities for exploring weight, balance, movement. Yet, as we saw, the world of the creative industries extends way beyond the creative explorations made possible by instruments of expression and involves an insidious approach to the self as a resource to be 'branded' and marketed. A postphenomenological thesis that insists that relations with tools, and specifically relations with tools within a creative context, are free of calculative thinking, not only appears facile; it prevents the method from engaging with crucial questions concerning the socio-material conditions that underpin artistic practice and training. A similar concern is voiced by Pieter Lemmens who argues that 'it often seems as if postphenomenology considers technologies in complete abstraction of the politico-economic context in which they occur […] thereby lacking […] a *truly critical* ambition of engagement' (2017: 199, emphasis original).

To what extent then shall we accept the postphenomenological argument that creative practices can circumvent technological rationality, especially in light of the overarching marketisation of the self that is evident in the creative industries and has been recently identified as a valuable addition to performer training? Can these two layers of instrumentalisation, one led by creative expression, the other by economic logic, be combined within the same training curriculum, as suggested by recent scholarship? In what ways and to what extent should existing pedagogies adapt in the light of these changes? There are echoes here of the battle that the Open Theatre fought, and lost, over 40 years ago. If anything, the technologisation of the self seems to have intensified, and the ability of training to develop agency grounded in embodied praxis seems more fragile than ever.

The situation becomes further complicated by the inclusion of digital technologies. It is noteworthy that the majority of objects considered in this chapter are 'poor': affordable, mundane, accessible and with a production history that can be traced relatively easily. The development of entrepreneurial skills, as well as forms of digital training involve, however, digital technologies.[12] Can digital and non-digital technologies be examined through the same lens? Does an analytical framework that examines handheld tools apply to digital devices? Postphenomenology answers affirmatively. As we saw, Ihde's framework, especially the alterity relation, included electric as well as electronic devices. More recent publications in the field have also engaged directly with digital media. Nonetheless, it has also been acknowledged that

> the change introduced when the artefact at hand is a complex piece of technology is exponentially greater, and then greater still when considering the use of technologies that rely upon an integrated system of mutually referential technologies such as the digital matrices that surround us today.
>
> (Gunkel and Taylor 2014: 2)

There are, in other words, fundamental differences between digital and non-digital technologies, which the next chapter will seek to foreground. Can a postphenomenological framework offer an adequate degree of criticality to deal with a set of objects whose production and function are opaque, not to say exploitative and undemocratic? Can a postphenomenological framework deal with relations to digital technologies that are experienced as negative, and/or are seen to have negative effect? Taking these questions forward, the next two chapters examine the use of digital technologies in performer training.

Notes

1 Part of the quote also appears in McCormack (1958: 151).
2 Although Dewey's work forms one of the two cornerstones of postphenomenology and although it has been revisited more recently by postphenomenological scholarship, I have not encountered a discussion of this aspect of his thinking, at least within postphenomenological analyses. Hickman (2008), in an article that discusses the similarities and divergences between Dewey's thought and Ihde's postphenomenology also brings attention to this crucial aspect of Dewey's work, which has not been picked up by postphenomenology.
3 It is for this reason that in the remainder of the section I draw on Hickman's work on Dewey rather than on Dewey's own writing. Hickman admits that he 'attempted to push Dewey's insights beyond what is there on the printed page […] in order to see where they lead' in relation to philosophical examinations of technology (2008: 99).
4 In fact, as Hickman explains, Dewey 're-constructed inquiry [quotidian, creative, scientific and philosophical] as a productive skill whose artefact is knowing' (1992: xii).
5 These are long bamboo sticks, called staffs, and used as weapons in the martial art Kalarippayattu, which forms the basis of Zarrilli's training.
6 De Preester's thesis not only offers terminological clarity; it serves as a corrective to technofantasies of a seamless merging between human and machine: 'the idea that we are natural-born cyborgs should be distinguished from the idea […] that we are natural-born tool-users' (De Preester 2011: 135).
7 Margolies, for example, understands the use of sticks in Meyerhold's work as a form of 'constraint', and views them as 'something the actor must listen and respond to' with the explicit aim to develop physical skills (2016: 39–40). She views the relationship in terms of embodiment and misses the evident hermeneutic dimension, even though she quotes from Pitches' article on sticks.
8 Wilson does not explain the exact nature or provenance of the exercises but it can be assumed that he refers to exercises in stick throwing and catching in a circle or in pairs, such as those encountered in Biomechanics and David Zinder's training. It also bears noting that Wilson differentiates the use of the stick as a tool and the kind of partnership he puts forward. Although Wilson does not develop this point further, his distinction suggests a qualitative difference between a tool that is merely used and an object that is experienced as a quasi-other.
9 As mentioned already, Margolies positions stick-work in Biomechanics under the prop-as-constraint category. Although the stick may often act as a constraint, the category cannot account for the additional ways in which sticks are understood. For example, Margolies does not explain how an understanding of the stick as a friend, as Levinski suggests, may operate on a principle of constraint.
10 Many thanks to Steph Kehoe for directing me to the video.
11 Many thanks to Jonathan Pitches for alerting me to this meaning of the verb 'train'.
12 Social media in particular have been identified as a key resource for the 'entrepreneurial actor', since they provide actors the opportunity to market themselves and disseminate their work in ways that bypass established channels (see Simpson 2013).

References

Alfreds, M. 2013. *Then What Happens?* London: Nick Hern Books.

Banks, M. 2007. *The Politics of Cultural Work*. Hampshire: Palgrave Macmillan.

Brey, P. 2000a. 'Technology and Embodiment in Ihde and Merleau-Ponty'. In: *Research in Philosophy and Technology, Volume 19 Metaphysics, Epistemology, and Technology*, edited by Carl Mitcham. Amsterdam: Elsevier, pp. 45–58.

Brey, P. 2000b. 'Theories of Technology as Extension of Human Faculties'. In: *Research in Philosophy and Technology, Volume 19 Metaphysics, Epistemology, and Technology*, edited by Carl Mitcham. Amsterdam: Elsevier, pp. 59–78.

Camilleri, F. 2019. *Performer Training Reconfigured: Post-Psychophysical Perspectives for the Twenty-First Century*. London: Bloomsbury.

Carreri, R. 2014. *On Training and Performance: Traces of an Odin Teatret Actress*, edited and translated by Frank Camilleri. London: Routledge.

Crook, A., Pitches, J., McCaw, D., Furse, A., Zinder, D., Murray, S. and Wilson, T. 2015. 'Training and…Sticks', *Theatre Dance and Performance Training Journal*, 6 (3), pp. 363–5.

De Preester, H. 2012. 'Technology and the Myth of "Natural Man"', *Foundations of Science*, 17 (4), pp. 385–90.

De Preester, H. 2011. 'Technology and the Body: the (Im)possibilities of Re-embodiment', *Foundations of Science*, 16 (2–3), pp. 119–37.

De Preester, H. and Tsakiris, M. 2009. 'Body-extension versus body-incorporation: Is there a need for a body-model?', *Phenomenology and the Cognitive Sciences*, 8 (3), pp. 307–19. doi: 0.1007/s11097-009-9121-y.

Dewey, J. 1983. *The Middle Works, 1899–1924, Volume 15: 1923–1924*, edited by Jo Ann Boydston. Carbondale: Southern Illinois University Press.

Evans, M. 2009. *Movement Training for the Modern Actor*. London: Routledge.

Feenberg, A. 2005. *Heidegger and Marcuse*. New York: Routledge.

Feenberg, A. 1995. 'Subversive Rationalisation: Technology, Power and Democracy'. In: *Technology and the Politics of Knowledge*, edited by Andrew Feenberg and Alastair Hannay. Bloomington: Indiana University Press, pp. 3–22.

Garrison, J. and Watson, W. B. 2005. 'Food from Thought', *The Journal of Speculative Philosophy*, New Series, 19 (4), pp. 242–56.

Grotowski, J. 2015. 'Actor's Training and Technique'. In: *The Actor Training Reader*, edited by Mark Evans. London: Routledge, pp. 85–7.

Gunkel, J. D. and Taylor, A. P. 2014. *Heidegger and the Media*. Cambridge: Polity.

Heidegger, M. 1977. 'The Question Concerning Technology'. In: *The Question Concerning Technology and Other Essays*, translated by William Lovitt. New York: Harper, pp. 3–35.

Hesmondhalgh, D. and Baker, S. 2011. *Creative Labour: Media Work in Three Cultural Industries*. Oxon: Routledge.

Hickman, A. L. 2008. 'Postphenomenology and Pragmatism: Closer Than You Might Think?', *Techné: Research in Philosophy and Technology*, 12 (2), pp. 99–104.

Hickman, A. L. 1992. *John Dewey's Pragmatic Technology*. Bloomington and Indianapolis: Indiana University Press.

Ihde, D. 2012. *Experimental Phenomenology: Multistabilities* (2nd edition). Albany: SUNY Press.

Ihde, D. 2010. *Heidegger's Technologies: Postphenomenological perspectives*. New York: Fordham University Press.

Ihde, D. 2009. *Postphenomenology and Technoscience: The Peking Lectures*. Albany: State University of New York.

Ihde, D. 1990. *Technology and the Lifeworld: From Garden to Earth*. Bloomington and Indianapolis: Indiana University Press.

Kehoe, S. 2015. Email communication with author, October 2015.

Kiran, H. A. 2015. 'Four Dimensions of Technological Mediation'. In: *Postphenomenological Investigations*, edited by Robert Rosenberger and Peter-Paul Verbeek. Lanham: Lexington Books, pp. 123–40.

Lecoq, J. 2002. *The Moving Body*, translated by David Bradby. London: Bloomsbury.

Lemmens, P. 2017. 'Thinking through Media: Stieglerian remarks on a possible postphenomenology of media'. In: *Postphenomenology and Media: Essays on Human-Media-World Relations*, edited by Yoni Van Den Eede, Stacey O'Neal Irwin and Galit Wellner. Lanham: Lexington, pp. 185–206.

Love, L. 2002. 'Resisting the "Organic": A feminist actor's approach'. In: *Acting (re)considered: A Theoretical and Practical Guide* (2nd edition), edited by Phillip Zarrilli. London and New York: Routledge, pp. 277–90.

Lutterbie, J. 2011. *Toward a General Theory of Acting*. New York: Palgrave.

Mann (Chapman), T. 2017. Email communication with author.

Margolies, E. 2016. *Props*. London: Palgrave Macmillan International Higher Education.

Mauss, M. 1992 [1934]. 'Techniques of the Body', reprinted in *Zone 6: Incorporations*, edited by Jonathan Crary and Sanford Kwinter. New York: Zone Books, pp. 454–79.

McCormack, D. E. 1958. *Frederick Matthias Alexander and John Dewey: A Neglected Influence*. Unpublished PhD Thesis, University of Toronto.

McRobbie, A. 2002. 'Fashion Culture: Creative Work, Female Individualization', *Feminist Review*, 71, pp. 52–62.

Merlin, B. 2007. *The Complete Stanislavsky Toolkit*. London: Nick Hern Books.

Merlin, B. 2001. *Beyond Stanislavsky: A Psycho-Physical Approach to Actor Training*. London: Nick Hern Books.

Murray, S. 2015. 'Keywords in performer training', *Theatre, Dance and Performance Training*, Vol. 6 (1), pp. 46–58.

Pinkham, B. 2013. 'To Thine Own Brand Be True: An Actor Begins his Reeducation', *American Theatre*, January 2013, pp. 000–000.

Pitches, J. 2007. 'Tracing/Training Rebellion: Object Work in Meyerhold's Biomechanics', *Performance Research*, 12 (4), pp. 97–103. doi: 10.1080/13528160701822692.

Roberts, B., Kokkali, A., Walker, L., Saner, G. and Lambert, B. 2015. 'Answer the Question: What are your/the tools of training?', *Theatre Dance and Performance Training Journal*, 6 (3), pp. 355–62.

Rosenberger, R. 2019. 'The Experiential Niche: or, on the Difference Between Smartphone and Passenger Driver Distraction', *Philosophy and Technology*, 32 (2), pp. 303–20. doi: 10.1007/s13347-017-0297-8.

Simpson, C. J. 2013. 'Open for Business: The Artist as Entrepreneur', *American Theatre*, January 2013, pp. 000–000.

Spatz, B. 2015. *What a Body Can Do*. Oxon: Routledge.

Stanislavsky, K. 2008. *An Actor's Work*, translated by J. Benedetti (1st edition). Oxon: Routledge.

Verbeek, P. 2005. *What Things Do*, translated by Robert P. Crease. Pennsylvania: The Pennsylvania State University Press.

Verbeek, P. 2001. 'Don Ihde: The Technological Lifeworld'. In: *American Philosophy of Technology*, edited by Hans Achterhuis. Bloomington and Indianapolis: Indian University Press, pp. 119–46.

Whitmer, M. J. 2019. 'You are your brand: Self-branding and the marketization of self', *Sociology Compass*, 19 (3), pp. 1–10. https://doi.org/10.1111/soc4.12662.

Wrathall, M. 2019. 'The task of thinking in a technological age'. In: *Heidegger on Technology*, edited by Aaron James Wendland, Christopher Merwin, and Christos Hadjioannou. London: Routledge, pp. 13–38.

Zarrilli, P. 2014. 'Toward an Intersubjective Ethics of Acting and Actor Training'. In: *Ethics and the Arts*, edited by Paul MacNeill, Dordrecht: Springer, pp. 113–24.

Zarrilli, P. 2009. *Psychophysical Acting*. London: Routledge.

Zarrilli, P., Daboo, J. and Loukes, R. 2013. *Acting: Psychophysical Phenomenon and Process*. Hampshire: Palgrave Macmillan.

Zazzali, P. 2016. *Acting in the Academy*. London: Routledge.

5

TRAINING THE *HOMO CELLULARIS*

Attention and the mobile phone in performer training

Introduction

This chapter explores the use of mobile phones in performer training practice in relation to attention.[1] The inclusion of mobile phones in a study that deals with performer training and technology is hardly surprising. Mobile phones have penetrated the cultures of the global North to such an extent that college students have been called a 'tethered generation' (Mihailidis 2014); arguably a term that could also apply to their educators.[2] What is more, mobile phones are increasingly utilised by performance makers often as a means of mediating, or in some cases entirely hosting, the performance event. Within formal training contexts, such as Higher Education Institutions and conservatoires, the mobile phone may serve as a form of learning assistive technology, for example through applications for accessing virtual learning environments and Bluetooth Attendance Management.[3] In addition to institution-related use, the phone may also be employed directly in training for a range of activities, serving, for example, as an *aide memoire* for scripts, a recording device to document work-in-progress or verbal feedback, a writing pad to take notes and a gateway for accessing online spaces set up by the trainees. In addition, there is the emergence of innovative practice in terms of content creation and/or pedagogical appropriation (Crews and Papagiannouli 2019; Zanotti 2014). In short, the inclusion of mobile phones in the present study could be justified on grounds of their ubiquity in learning environments, including performer training, and performance events. Accordingly, the examination could address the ways in which they are used with an emphasis on novel methods of training and performance-making. Although these interests are not precluded from this chapter, the focus is slightly different.

As explained in the Introduction, one of the chief aims of this book is to test whether performer training can serve as a site for preparing and rehearsing a response to the issues that emerge from insidious technologisation. This chapter is aligned with this wider aspiration by addressing the question of attention. As I will explain, attention has (re)surfaced as a key theme specifically in relation to digital culture: how we 'pay' it, how 'much' of it we have; what is the best way to 'manage' it, are all questions that occur time and again in popular and scholarly debates. Attention is also a key aspect of any student's, including the student performer's, process. The aim of this chapter then is twofold: to position the use of the mobile phone in performer training within a wider critique of its function as a digital artefact, and concomitantly to explore how the new attentional regimes produced by the phone, and digital culture in general, may trouble existing assumptions of performer training practice, and especially a preference for 'deep', 'heightened' or 'concentrated' attention. Can performer training offer the space for experimenting with new configurations of attention and what role might the mobile phone have in such an exploration? Or, reversely, in what ways may mobile phones and their attendant cultures of use upset established practices of performer training?

In addition to attention, this chapter will explore the use of the mobile phone in relation to the studio space within which training often takes place. Ihde identified a category of technological artefacts 'designed to function in the background' (1990: 108–9). When functioning correctly, 'background technologies' withdraw from awareness and may go unnoticed in daily life. I would argue that studio space constitutes a background technology; on the one hand, and as I will demonstrate in the penultimate section of this chapter, the studio space is operative in the way the trainees' attention becomes orchestrated.[4] On the other, its function is hardly noticeable. In exploring the use of a digital device in relation to these two key aspects of training practice, this chapter follows the trajectory of the previous one. As argued in the previous chapter, material tools are neither auxiliary nor external to embodied performer training practice; rather they are constitutive of somatic and intersubjective experience and integral to the development of organic tools. I reviewed, for example, the way a partner exercise utilising sticks (material tool) leads to the development of a form of spatial awareness (organic tool) which is then utilised in performance without the material object. Although the mobile phone may be seen as a tool in the manner described above, two important caveats need to be added to the mix.

The first caveat is that mobile phones are not sticks. This is hardly a noteworthy observation, yet it is one that has important methodological ramifications. As implied already, the penetration of mobile phones in daily life entails that they have already influenced the way trainers and trainees relate to the world long before phones are employed in training. Due to their ubiquity, mobile phones are bound to be present in a learning environment; perhaps lying inconspicuously in silent mode or being actively used, for purposes that may be relevant or irrelevant to the learning context. Furthermore, and unlike sticks, the use of mobile phones is often a cause of concern. Popular discussions in the press as well as scholarly publications revolve around health-related risks, for example, in terms of exposure to radiation or sleep disruption, as well as the intensification of surveillance and alienation. David Berry highlights the consequences of the phone's additional functionalities:

> Our phones become smart phones, and as such become media devices that can also be used to identify, monitor and control our actions and behaviour through anticipatory computing. While seemingly freeing us from the constraints of the old wired-line world of the immobile telephone, we are also increasingly enclosed within an algorithmic cage that attempts to surround us with contextual advertising and behavioural nudges.
>
> (2014: 6)

A chief manifestation of ubiquitous computing, the smartphone becomes a surveillance mechanism that accesses and converges an unprecedented range of data: internet searches, social media accounts, personal information, geographical location and locomotion. Although it is still unclear to what extent these modes of digital surveillance impact upon political freedom and citizenship, there emerges an empirical sense of the way they affect the micropolitics of daily life. According to Anna Kouppanou:

> The data gathered are then translated into metadata and offered to consumers in the guise of personalisation. In this way, consumers end up repeating their past choices that prevent them from envisioning a different individual self or collective *we*.
>
> (2015: 1116, emphasis original)

Digital technologies, in other words, administer a loop, managed through opaque operations and perpetuated for economic gain, which narrows and homogenises the horizon of possibilities that is available to subjects, individually and collectively. Accordingly, the mobile phone has intensified a situation whereby 'no moment, place or situation now exists in which one can *not* shop, consume, or exploit networked resources' (Crary 2013: 30, emphasis original).

In addition to the above, the close fit between the mobile phone and the human body, especially between hand and device, face and screen, has produced distinct regimes of embodiment. Ingrid Richardson argues that 'mobile device usage' needs to be understood as a 'mode of embodiment, a way of having a body' (2005: np), since the body is rendered into a 'mobile-specific *mediatrope* – inclined metaphorically, corporeally, communicatively and gesturally towards the mobile media device' (2005: np, emphasis original). Mediatropic embodiment, therefore, operates simultaneously on an individual level, as a series of kinetic organisations and habits, as well as on a social level, as a set of gestures that have communicative and affective potential in and of themselves (Nakamura 2015). In a more critical vein, Berry identifies in mobile phone use 'new forms of rationalised communication of estrangement and alienation', which, whilst providing access and eliminating distance, also 'raise important questions about our being-in-the-world when we are constantly pulled out of the world' (2014: 171). Like any tool, therefore, the mobile phone is constitutive of its user. However, as the *homo faber* becomes superseded by the '*homo cellularis*' (Eco 2014: viii), there is increasing concern about the effects of *this* instance of tool-human co-constitution. The question that emerges therefore is whether an attempt to use mobile phones within a performer training context can maintain an adequate level of criticality and, if so, how.

As explained in the previous chapter, postphenomenology examines technology by focusing on the cultural and embodied specificities of the relations between arte-facts and users. In this way, the method sets out to provide a more nuanced under-standing of technology than the one offered by a determinist view. As a result, however, postphenomenology has refrained from engaging with thorny issues. According to Pieter Lemmens:

> There seems to be an almost methodical aversion among postphenomenolo-gists for everything that even resembles alienation critique of technology. After having once and for all disqualified Heidegger's supposedly 'mono-lithic, abstract, and nostalgic' philosophy of technology deemed 'inadequate' (Verbeek 2006: 60) – a critique also levelled against Ellul, Jaspers and Marcuse – and after having rejected wholesale the 'excessively gloomy picture' (ibid. 4) of technology supposedly maintained by those authors, postphenomenol-ogy has lost sight of the *systemic* and *systematically conditioning* nature of tech-nology, in particular contemporary media.
>
> (2017: 199, all emphases original)

Recent work in postphenomenology has engaged with contemporary media, and studies focus not only on mobile phones (Wellner 2015), but also their detrimental effect (Aagaard 2016; Rosenberger 2019). In this respect, Ihde's thinking has been extended in helpful ways. However, even in recent works that may be critical of a certain technology and/or kind of use, the methodological preference of postphe-nomenology to reveal positive relations to technology remains unaddressed.

The mobile phone, specifically, both exemplifies the prescience of Ihde's formu-lation of the alterity relationship and exposes the persistence of the postphenome-nological method to foreground positive experiences. As we saw in the previous chapter, the key thrust of Ihde's argument is that in alterity relations, the technolo-gical artefact is experienced by the user as a quasi-other in a positive manner. Accordingly, the chapter discussed instances of performer training where the signifi-cance bestowed on the technological artefact was linked to intentional pedagogical outcomes, whereby, for example, the artefact is approached as a source of know-ledge (teacher); as a reference point that might spark new ideas or enable the per-former to deal with difficult given circumstances (partner); or even as a saviour, when the actor struggles to concentrate. However, and as we have seen already, there is mounting concern about the negative impact of the mobile phone and, here, I do not mean that the mobile phone might have unintended consequences, as indeed any technology might. I specifically refer to negative experiences result-ing from the alterity relationship.

As we saw, the definitional operation of the alterity relation is premised on the user's attention, which is directed towards the artefact, whilst the 'world [...] may remain context and background' (Ihde 1990: 107). The mobile phone, specifically, has been identified both as a technology that structures the way in which attention functions (or mal-functions according to some commentators) and determines the object on which attention is focused. As noted already, Richardson understands the mobile phone as a key factor in organising the person's kinesphere and perceptual field, since it 'modifies what we pay attention to, what we "turn to" and face (and turn away from) in the everyday lifeworld, and the modalities and *durée* of that attentiveness' (2005: np). The mobile phone then both shapes and becomes the object of the user's attention, and this is, indeed, the hallmark of its function as a quasi-other.

Of course, an interplay between being 'in' and being pulled 'out' of the world – as Berry puts it – may occur independently of technological mediation; for example, in daydreaming or reverie. However, in information-saturated cultures, and especially when the object 'receive[ing] the multiple attentions humans give the different forms of the other' (Ihde 1990: 107) is the mobile phone, such interplay turns into an acute tension. Indeed, the direction of the user's attention away from face-to-face interactions and towards the mediated ones made possible by the phone, is a recurring theme with reference to a wide range of social contexts and daily activities, such as driving (Rosenberger 2019); socialising (Aagaard 2016); learning (Lepp et al. 2015); and theatre environments (Gardner 2012; Nedelkopoulou 2017; Richardson 2014). Aiming to dispel dystopian evaluations of technology, Wellner argues that 'technologies that maintain alterity relations with their users do not fully replace humans nor are they an identical substitute' (2015: 118). Specifically in relation to the mobile phone, she contends that users are able to distinguish between mediated and unmediated interactions.

The relationship between the two, however, is more complicated. As Aagaard (2016) explains, when using a mobile phone whilst in the process of face-to-face social encounters, a person assumes a closed physical position, acquires a different rhythm and ceases to emit signs that inform the moment-to-moment unfolding of communication. As a result, an *'unintentional misattunement'* sets between interlocutors (Aagaard 2016: 229, emphasis original). If we add to this mix nomophobia, a condition related to the fear of not having one's phone, it could be argued that the mobile phone pushes the alterity relation to its extreme: it is experienced as a quasi-other that users can no longer do without and often seem to prefer over 'real' others, whether such others are friends, teachers or performers. However, since Ihde's formation of the alterity relationship is fundamentally a positive one, then the question arises of whether it is adequate to address the multiple dimensions and often negative experiences associated with mobile phone use.

The second caveat concerns the notion of attention. As we saw in the previous chapter, attention has been identified as a key 'tool' for actors (Lutterbie 2011; Merlin 2007) and is one of the prime organic resources that training is expected to cultivate. As Soto-Morettini observes, 'in nearly every acting book you will ever pick up, you will generally find great emphasis on the importance of the actor's ability to concentrate' (2010: 66). Attention, then, becomes the *object* of training but it is also the very *medium* through which training takes place. In Zarrilli's words, 'actor training might be productively viewed as a specific form of "perceptual apprenticeship"' (2015: 83). Performer training, then, is not only aimed at training the actor's ability to be attentive; like any other form of education it engenders the modality by means of which one is expected to attend and learn. It is precisely this operation that actualises the possibility of training to serve both as a form of inscription and empowerment. As Jonathan Crary observes, 'attention is the means by which an individual observer can transcend those subjective limitations and make perception *its own*, and attention is at the same time a means by which a perceiver becomes open to control and annexation by external agencies' (2000: 5, emphasis original). Attention, therefore, is a skill to be trained with the aim to enable the performer to make sense and create meaning out of the plethora of stimuli that comprise rehearsal and performance processes. It is also the mode through which training takes place, disciplining the trainee in a particular perceptual state that can make them receptive to tuition.

Matters become further complicated by the fact that attention constitutes a complex process of embodiment and enculturation. Unlike other aspects of the performer's work, attention is not a self-standing entity, nor can it be located in a specific part of the body. Attention is a state rather than a thing and it is a state that can only be defined/identified in terms of a relationship between subject and the world. 'All societies' writes Bernard Stiegler,

> are characterised by types of attention: types of attentional forms and knowledges that are also types of concern, systems of care, of techniques for care of the self and of others, together constituting ways of life that characterise cultures and civilisations.
>
> (2012: 3)

According to Stiegler then, in the way it is conceptualised, practised and lived, attention forms part of the '*already there* [that] precedes the experience that it renders possible' (2012: 10, emphasis original). Attention, therefore, is inherently relational and, as I will demonstrate in the next section, its understanding and conceptualisation is linked with historical, social, cultural, material and economic exigencies. Here are, then, the two caveats this chapter needs to address: the use of the mobile phone in performer training is in danger of uncritically replicating existing cultures of use and thus reinforcing a host of attitudes that, despite being naturalised, are problematic. More specifically, the mobile phone, in its various entanglements with the user's daily life and focus, messes with, and arguably up, the most valued aspect of the trainee's involvement. Yet, attention as a mode of engaging with the world is not a pre-given faculty but rather becomes constituted through our interactions with the world, including our interactions with technologies. As a result, this chapter needs to advance a kind of bi-focal analysis: one that can both elucidate the possible pedagogical contribution that the mobile phone can make to performer training practice *and* maintain a critical distance from a technology that is deeply implicated in the way trainees and trainers engage with the world.

Towards achieving this end, this chapter turns to the concept of *pharmakon*. Denoting both poison and cure, the *pharmakon* appears in Plato's dialogue *Phaedrus*, in a discussion on the effects of writing for knowledge production. Since then, it has been employed in examinations of technology, especially in the work of Bernard Stiegler, as a way of capturing the enabling, or remedial, as well as toxic effects of technology. As we saw, for Stiegler, the formation and practice of attention is a significant factor for social cohesion, knowledge production and consequently power. According to Stiegler, technology is a prime means through which modes of attention become communicated and passed down, since 'culture is the inter-generational transmission of attentional forms invented in the course of individual experience which becomes collective because psychosocial memory is technically exteriorised and supported' (Stiegler 2012: 4). Technological artefacts, in other words, operate as a means of socialising knowledge and activating memory. In this process, localised insights or skills become collectively shared and, as such, techno-logy can have positive effects. But for the very same reason, it can also lead to modes of knowledge production that are problematic. Stiegler explains: 'what Soc-rates describes in *Phaedrus*, namely that the *exteriorization of memory* [through writing] *is a loss of memory and knowledge,* has today become the stuff of everyday experience in *all* aspects of our existence' (2010a: 29, all emphases original). Stiegler diagnoses a situation whereby the new modes of cognition and embodiment emerging from digital technologies engender modes of attention that are not conducive to demo-cratic, empathetic and egalitarian ways of life. According to Stiegler, then, techno-logy as *pharmakon* 'is at once what *enables* care to be taken and that *of which* care must be taken – in the sense that it is necessary *to pay attention*: its power is curative to the immeasurable extent [...] that it is also *destructive*' (2013: 4, all emphases original).

Within this formulation, the distinction between practice and use is paramount. As Lemmens explains in relation to Stiegler's pharmacological approach, '"use" represents sheer *adaptation* to the marketized media commodities', whereas practice suggests a process of '*therapeutic adoption*', foregrounding the remedial potential of a specific digital technology-as-*pharmakon* and bringing forward 'new ways of living' (2017: 200–2, all emphases original). The notion of *pharmakon*, therefore, suggests the possibility of appropriation, tinkering and repurposing. As such, it echoes with the postphenomenological thesis that relations to technology are not pre-determined but can and do evolve in conjunction with embodied and cultural practices. The *pharmakon*, however, also serves as a constant reminder of those aspects of techno-logy 'of which' care should be taken. In terms of the mobile phone these are: the gestures, and possibly risks, associated with its daily use, as well as the ethics of its production and the politics of its operation.

The *pharmakon* also invites a consideration of the relationship between (estab-lished) use and (novel) practice. As noted already, the cultivation of new practices relies on fundamental processes of embodiment and perception; indeed, as we saw in the quote above, for Stiegler the operation of technology as *pharmakon* necessitates that we *pay attention*. However, attention, as a key modality through which the user relates to the world is caught up – or, as some commentators would have it, becomes modified – by the mobile phone. How are we then to configure new practices, if the modality that can enable us to do so is affected by the very technology we are aspiring to rethink? Indeed, this is an impasse that underlies Stiegler's overall critique of technology. As Kouppanou explains, Stiegler's thesis

> suggests that the human being, which is displaced by technology and by a relation that is no longer compositional, is to reclaim its position in terms of deciphering what needs to be maintained as human and indeed insert itself back in the relationship. This, however, presupposes a type of knowledge concerning the way this relationship works and might work in the future that I am not certain we can pinpoint.
>
> (2015: 1117)

Within the pharmacological approach, in other words, there is an inherent contradiction: if an ability to develop new practices is premised on 'paying attention', how can relational, caring, empathetic ways of being in the world emerge in and through relation to technologies, when these very technologies foster a way of being in the world that 'pulls' us out of it? It is instructive, at this point, to review how this tension manifests in an instance of performer training practice.

In 2012, Marisa Zanotti at the University of Chichester launched an application for choreography co-created with dance company bgroup. Based on a piece for screen-dance, *Passing Strange and Wonderful*, which Zanotti and bgroup developed together, the phone was employed as a one-stop terminus where course material could be gathered, including footage of the piece, exercises for developing choreographic scores and links to further research. Zanotti emphasised that the project was developed specifically for mobile media, not only because of their ubiquity in training studios, but also because she wanted to draw links between the kinetic repertoire of the choreography and the actions of the user. For example, progression through the content of the app was achieved through a sweeping motion of the hand, which resonated with the lateral movement that was explored in the choreography (Zanotti 2018, interview with author).

Zanotti's project demonstrates the emergence of a new form of practice that not only utilises the mobile phone as a pedagogical compendium for bespoke content; by appropriating existing functionalities and cultures of use, it foregrounds their creative and artistic potential. Nonetheless, even well-thought and deliberate practices that adopt and appropriate the existing use are not immune to the 'toxic' dimension of the *pharmakon*. Proving the simultaneous presence of poison and cure, the phone also offered access to activities that were not relevant to the training/learning situation. It bears noting, in this respect, that Zanotti not only developed a bespoke application that necessitates the presence of the phone in the studio; she also introduced a code of practice explicitly stipulating that phone use should be limited to class-related activities only (Zanotti 2018, interview with author). Even when it is harnessed for artistic-pedagogical ends, the mobile phone, like any other technological artefact, produces what Stiegler calls an 'already there', a pre-existing context in which a new form of practice is due to emerge. This might not pose a problem, and Zanotti attested that the students were able to discriminate between the new practice introduced by the app and existing cultures of use, which could arguably undermine the pedagogical potential of the new practice. However, it also becomes clear that when a pharmacological approach is tested on the ground, so to speak, the demarcations between existing use and novel practice might not be easily maintained. Specifically in relation to mobile phones, an aspiration to develop novel practices is concomitant with a need, at least within a training context, to circumscribe, or indeed alter, existing use. This can take the form of an etiquette put forward by the educator, as Zanotti did, or the trainees. If, however, such etiquette fails, phone use can be experienced as a source of distraction, especially when it takes place in situations in which 'paying attention' is the normative and expected behaviour.

The question, therefore, is not only whether the mobile phone can be used towards the development of novel pedagogical practices – it clearly can. What we also ought to ask is whether new pedagogical practices that employ the mobile phone can engender modes of attention that can be conducive to the learning situation. To put it another way: if the mobile phone shapes regimes of attention, which may be inappropriate or undesirable (poison) for performer training purposes, may its use in performer training also make possible different ways of paying attention (cure)? Can the mobile phone in a performer training context ever serve as a medium through which the *homo cellularis* may become 'care'-fully attentive towards the world and others? What might such attention look like and what kind of relationship to the world might it enable? Addressing these questions necessitates therefore not only practical experimentation but also a rethinking of what attention is and how it is configured in performer training practice, including the confines of the studio space. In the remainder of this chapter, I will review recent debates on attention as well as the way attention is assumed and practised within dominant performer training regimes and spaces. Against this background, I will present an exercise, developed within a higher education context, that utilises the mobile phone, and explores the possibility of engendering a form of attention that seeks to go beyond a distinction between the kind of 'deep attention' favoured by Stiegler, as well as performer training practice, and the kind of fragmented or 'hyper' attention arguably produced by the phone.

Training attention

In his seminal *Suspensions of Perception* (2000), Jonathan Crary examines the way attention has been theorised and understood from the nineteenth century onwards. Crary observes that during this period attention surfaces as a problem, which coincides with an increase in the quantity and intensity of sensory stimuli as well as with a radical shift in the way the human subject is conceptualised. As a result, he traces the co-emergence of 'an imperative of a concentrated attentiveness within the disciplinary organisation of labor, education and mass consumption' as well as 'an ideal of sustained attentiveness as a constitutive element of a creative and free subjectivity' (2000: 1–2). Attention-as-problem, therefore, appears during the nineteenth century within a paradoxical situation: on the one hand, modern capitalist living and labour conditions increase the range of stimuli that pervade daily life, posing thus the 'danger of inattention'; on the other hand, an imperative for economic profit depended on the subject's ability to manage the sensory overload and concentrate (Crary 2000: 13–14). Attention then becomes equated with 'the relative capacity of a subject to selectively isolate certain contents of a sensory field at the expense of others in the interests of maintaining an orderly and productive world' (Crary 2000: 17). Crary's study, therefore, approaches attention not as a neurological function, but as a set of practices and explanations, which, albeit at times contradictory, aimed to institute a normative position. This could serve, amidst technological, economic and social change, both as a definition of modern and, as we shall see, adult subjectivity, as well as the desired mode of being in the world.

Attention then is understood in a dialectical fashion, involving internal moderation, which is contingent upon external stimuli. Consequently, attention becomes equated with a process of selecting, ordering and isolating focal points and, at the same time, becomes differentiated from states of distraction, which threaten to disrupt the subject's capacity to create a unified world. Accordingly, the imperative to pay attention, as an essential aspect of constituting a coherent reality, both signals the subject's 'precariousness, contingency and insubstantiality' and serves as proof of the 'subject's self-possession as potential master and conscious organiser of that perceptible world' (Crary 2000: 45). The constitution of a coherent reality was predicated, in other words, upon the subject's ability to select appropriate stimuli and control such processes. In this manner, attention becomes an exercise of will and an object of training.[5]

As Crary notes, a key thinker in configuring attention as a force for organising consciousness, which would otherwise remain chaotic, was William James (2000: 61). In the chapter 'Attention' in his celebrated *Principles of Psychology*, James defines attention as a selective, focalised and concentrated activity which 'implies withdrawal from some things' and is further contrasted with 'the confused, dazed, scatter-brained state [...] called distraction' (1950 [1918]: 403). Although James acknowledges a continuum between attention and distraction, attention is ultimately defined as 'concentration upon one single object with exclusion of aught besides' (James, 1950 [1918]: 405). Correspondingly, a state of mind that darts from one interest to another is, according to James, a characteristic of children and should be tamed through education (James 1950 [1918]: 417). James' work contributed to the establishment of two important tropes, which had a significant impact on performer training and still have valence today: an understanding of attention as the opposite of distraction and as a voluntary act that can be trained.

As we saw in previous chapters, issues of attention and concentration were also a chief concern for Stanislavsky. Influenced by William James, Stanislavsky's work demonstrates both an appreciation of the importance of attention for the actor's work and provided an enduring understanding of what attention is and how it can be cultivated. Indeed, echoing James' conviction that attention can be trained, Stanislavsky dedicates a considerable part of his System to such training, specifically tailored for actors. As discussed in Chapters 2 and 4, in the section on 'Creative Concentration and Attention', Stanislavsky utilises the propensity of electric lights to foreground some aspects of the environment whilst leaving others in darkness. He also employed flickering lights to demonstrate distraction as a state that can neither be differentiated nor sustained. Echoing James, then, Stanislavsky also presents attention as a by-product of a process of selection and exclusion, and in opposition to distraction. Indeed, anticipating Hayles' distinction between 'deep' and 'hyper' attention, Stanislavsky expresses an explicit preference for the 'deep' kind. Tortsov reminds the students: 'concentration [...] must [...] be extremely stable in acting. We don't need the kind of concentration which superficially skims the surface' (Stanislavsky 2008: 109).

What is more, within Stanislavsky-based pedagogies an understanding of attention as a monofocal and exclusionary activity continues to prevail. For example, Zazzali notes that 'borrowing [...] from Stanislavsky, Strasberg wanted his actors to avoid external distractions [...] in favour of focusing on a particular object that would evoke the desired emotional expression in creating a character' (2016: 30). Confirming Zazzali's observation, Lauren Love identifies in her Method Acting training the institution of a perceptual dichotomy:

> I am not supposed to be distracted in any way by the conditions of production, most especially the diverse group of spectators. Should my focus on my inner truths falter, I am instructed to build a more complex inner life for my character so that it will involve my attention completely.
>
> (2002: 282)

In more recent, psychophysically informed reiterations of Stanislavsky's System, such as Merlin's work, a focus on inner emotion is substituted with a focus on external action. Yet, *concentration* of attention is still considered a key part of the actor's toolkit (Merlin 2007: 36–44).

Similarly, in approaches to psychophysical training post-Stanislavsky, attention remains a key aspect of the performer's preparation. A key exponent of the psychophysical paradigm, Phillip Zarrilli developed a form of training that combines somatic and meditative practices within a theoretical framework of 'enactive cognition'. Performers are trained in 'increasingly subtle and complex modes of directing one's attention and opening one's sensory awareness' in relation to a specific 'performance score' and 'theatrical environment' (Zarrilli 2015: 83). In comparison to Stanislavsky's formulation, Zarrilli's work on the cultivation of attention is emphatically premised on a holistic, psychophysical engagement that enables the actor to attend to different aspects of the performance activity all at once. Arguably, Zarrilli's model is a lot more encompassing of the performer's environment than Stanislavsky's 'circles of attention'. Zarrilli also stresses that 'the shape and feel of a specific training practice or of a performance score is not derived from or intrinsic to some essential "notion" of attention but rather are specific to and gained from embodied attention and specific awareness *in specific ways*' (Zarrilli 2020: 119, emphasis original). Although Zarrilli does not engage with the debates on attention reviewed here, his statement could be seen as an attempt to distance the 'perceptual apprenticeship' fostered through the training he devised from essentialised or idealised understandings of attention. Nonetheless, Zarrilli also expresses a clear preference for what he calls a 'heightened mode of attending' (2015: 88). This is conceived as a 'heightened attunement of sensory and perceptual awareness of a certain sort' that would allow the actor 'to be fully responsive to theatrical environment and dramaturgies' (Zarrilli 2020: 121). What is more, 'heightened attention' is also pitted against the 'squirrel-like "busy" mind of the actor' (Zarrilli 2015: 84).[6] As a result, training is offered as a kind of remedy, with breathing exercises serving as 'a way of "deconditioning" our busy, analytical, squirrel-like minds' (Zarrilli 2015: 86). Similarly to James and Stanislavsky, then, Zarrilli identifies distraction as a state to be remedied by education, this time through breathing.

We see, therefore, that performer training, similarly to other fields of knowledge production, '*constitute[s] an attentional form furnished with its own particular rules*' (Stiegler 2012: 6, emphasis original). Moreover, such form is communicated in terms of a 'heightened' or 'concentrated' attention and is differentiated from distraction. In this manner, performer training serves as a sophisticated means of educating attention, especially in light of the fragmentation and dispersion of attention that can be caused by digital technologies. Indeed, we could say that performer training, by having prioritised, throughout the twentieth century, the trainee's ability to direct and focus her attention in a psycho-somatic rather than purely cognitive manner, is well ahead of the curve in developments in educational practices, such as the inclusion of mindfulness in school curricula (O'Donnell 2015). Nonetheless, as noted already, ideas and practices of attention are also historically contingent and specific understandings may be prioritised over others.

As a result, attention may emerge as an ideal and an inability to pay attention in the expected 'concentrated' or 'heightened' manner can become pathologised or seen as a failure of the will. The situation can become further complicated if the educational context involves technology. Reviewing literature on educational technology, Jasper Aagaard, for example, notes that

> unintended consequences such as distraction in the classroom are ascribed to internal psychological shortcomings such as deficient self-regulation […], low abstract reasoning […], or lack of academic engagement […] on behalf of the students.
>
> (2017: 1128–9)

A similar position is repeated within theatre education. In their article, 'Toward Revising Undergraduate Theatre Education', Peter Zazzali and Jeanne Klein suggest a cause-and-effect relationship between the use of social media and decline in academic performance. They make the explicit claim that 'multitasking with social media […] further harms the ongoing physical maturation of their [the students'] brains' (Zazzali and Klein 2015: 262). Later in the article, they repeat Mark Bauerlein's assertion that current college students are '"the dumbest generation" while depicting troubling declines in their skills relative to what employers require' (Zazzali and Klein 2015: 263). Zazzali and Klein, in other words, are concerned with the long-term effects of technologies on academic performance and employment. Within such a configuration, however, the student has already been positioned as ailing, or even damaged, from daily interactions with technology.

The conceptualisation of attention as a problem endures and, in fact, has become intensified in the context of daily and learning environments pervaded by technologies. It can be further observed that even in instances where the technology is deliberately employed for pedagogical purposes, a preference towards a concentrated form of attention remains. Yet, it could be assumed that within such contexts the contemporary 'mediatropic' body would have no productive value and would, instead, be expected to be managed or rectified. The paradox noted by Crary with regard to the nineteenth century continues to be operative: whilst digital technologies are assumed to have an adverse effect on the subject's attentive capacities, the ability to master one's attention is all the more valued.

Attention beyond distraction

In tandem with a contextualisation of attention in relation to specific historical and economic circumstances, value-laden distinctions between attention and distraction have also been challenged, specifically by Katherine Hayles. Echoing Stiegler, Hayles contends that 'whenever dramatic and deep changes occur in the environment, attention begins to operate in new ways' (2012: 98). Unlike Stiegler, however, who argues that a continuation of deep modes of attention are needed in response to the social and political crises caused by and within digital culture, Hayles seeks to articulate different kinds of attention and accordingly examine whether they might have pedagogical value.[7] The first step in Hayles' argument involves a recasting of the opposition between attention and distraction in terms of 'deep' and 'hyper' attention:

> Deep attention, […] is characterised by concentrating on a single object for long periods […] ignoring outside stimuli while so engaged, preferring a single information stream, and having high tolerance for long focus times. Hyper attention […] is characterised by switching focus rapidly between different tasks, preferring multiple information streams, seeking a high level of stimulation, and having a low tolerance for boredom.
>
> (Hayles 2007:187)

Hayles (2007; 2012) notes that these two kinds of attention mark a generational divide, with young people having a strong preference for the hyper mode. She further observes that deep attention is the normative cognitive quality expected in humanities, whilst 'hyper attention [is] regarded as defective behaviour that scarcely qualifies as a cognitive mode at all' (Hayles 2007: 188). The main contribution of Hayles' work, therefore, has been the contention that distraction is a mode of attention and that different modes of attention may enable different kinds of engagement, depending on the context:

> Deep attention is essential for coping with complex phenomena such as mathematical theorems, challenging literary works, and complex musical composition; hyper attention is useful for its flexibility in switching between different information streams, its quick grasp of the gist of material and its ability to move rapidly among and between different kinds of texts.
>
> (Hayles 2012: 69)

In this manner, Hayles' work challenges hierarchical divisions between attention and distraction and exposes them as results of convention as well as part of a disciplinary mechanism. Instead of talking of attention and its 'opposite', Hayles proposes two different modalities and accordingly asks whether they might have pedagogical potential. She further calls for 'pedagogical strategies that recognise the strengths and limitations of each cognitive mode' and stresses the 'necessity of building bridges between them' (Hayles 2012: 12). In a certain respect, Hayles' work can be seen as a continuation of Crary's project: not only is the distinction between attention and distraction challenged; Hayles also sets out to demonstrate that humanities, as a field synonymous with practices of deep attention, can be productively reconfigured and include additional modes of knowledge production.

However, Hayles' work does not address the central concern that underpins Crary's and Stiegler's concerns, respectively. Against Hayles' thesis, Stiegler argues that, on the one hand, what may be called deep attention has been appropriated by media technologies. Whereas a practice of deep attention in a different context may be a source of critical reflection, the fixation of attention underpinning popular technologies of 'capture', such as video games and internet surfing, now causes isolation. Similarly, Stiegler disputes that hyper attention can have any political or pedagogical potential. He argues that hyper attention, as a social phenomenon localised within specific practices, is unable to engender the ability to critically scrutinise the operation and effects of technology, especially during a period when such scrutiny is badly needed (Stiegler 2010b: 72–93).

On the other hand, Crary shares some of Hayles' conclusions but also the concerns voiced by Stiegler. Echoing Hayles and departing from Stiegler, Crary sees in the recent crisis of attention a fabrication of distraction as a pathology, which is, furthermore, exploited for economic profit (2013: 55). However, unlike Hayles who wishes to 'rehabilitate' distraction in the form of a potentially valuable 'hyper attention', Crary's conclusion gives little cause for optimism:

> Most important now is not the capture of attentiveness by a delimited object […], but rather the remaking of attention into repetitive operations and

responses that always overlap with acts of looking or listening. It is less the homogeneity of media products that perpetuates the separation, isolation, and neutralisation of individuals than the larger and compulsory arrangements within which these elements, and many others, are consumed.

(2013: 52)

Similarly to his previous work that argued that regimes of attention in the nineteenth century were directly linked with the establishment of capitalism, in his latest study Crary understands current regimes of attention as part and parcel of a globalised technocratic hegemony. What is at stake, in other words, is not whether deep attention is waning and whether hyper attention can be a productive mode for knowing; rather, the question is how regimes of attention perpetuate hegemonic interests. And again, we reach the same impasse: how can these new forms of attention be politically and pedagogically productive when they have been naturalised as part of a prevailing technocracy? Yet, as Stiegler insists: 'it is only as a result of such psychotechnologies [...], that one *must* think (and that it is *possible* to think) the future of teaching' (Stiegler 2010b: 73, all emphases original). We can neither escape nor occupy a space outside our entanglement with technologies; like the family going on a bear hunt: 'we can't go under it, we can't go over it, we have to go *through* it' (Rosen and Oxenbury 1993, emphasis added). In order to do so, however, the very practice of education needs to be reconfigured.

Despite his pharmacological proposition to deal with technology through technology and his emphasis that such a task needs to be undertaken by education, Stiegler's argument does not allow for change in the way education is thought and delivered. As Joris Vlieghe argues, 'Stiegler remains stuck in a traditional and nonproductive definition of education' (2014: 534), and, as a result, 'precludes the possibility to rethink the whole idea of education in view of fundamental changes in societal and cultural conditions' (2014: 535). Against this background, I would contend with Hayles, that it makes pedagogical, and possibly political, sense to substitute dichotomies between attention and distraction with a broader notion of what attention is and could be. However, keeping in line with Stiegler and Crary, I would also argue that Hayles' formulation downplays the economic imperatives and hegemonic interests that underpin the cultures of use that foster hyper attention. Moreover, I would also posit that from a pedagogical point of view, Hayles' solution to keep deep attention intact and assign different tasks to different modes, does not go far enough in exploring new possibilities.

With specific reference to performer training, my proposition would be that instead of recasting a dichotomy between attention and distraction into a distinction between deep and hyper attention, we move away from assigning different kinds of attention to different tasks. An exploration can thus focus on how different modes of embodied perception and engagement with the world can be productively combined within a single, but differentiated, matrix of a given situation. Following Timothy Campbell's call for a practice of creative attention, I also propose to favour a mode of 'attention that holds together elements in a kind of compositional space [and] does not posit a division between proper and improper but notes why they are located in the space' (Campbell 2011: 147). To support this proposition, I will draw on the concept of 'polyattentiveness'.

Encountered in John Cage's work (Copeland 1983: 321), polyattentiveness has been defined as 'a quality of picking up and according recognition to events in the environment, acknowledging other claims to selfhood while simultaneously making one's own' (Belgrad 2016: 293). The term has recently resurfaced in discussions on interactive environments (Hawksley 2016), dance training (Hawksley 2012) and literary practices involving mobile phones (Raley 2009). In line with this background, I propose polyattentiveness as a relational and embodied process of composition that can contain both the multitude of stimuli that inhere in hyper attention as well as the sense of organisation and immersion that underpins deep attention. In this respect, polyattentiveness has close affinities with the kind of heightened attention favoured in psychophysical regimes. Indeed, if we think back to Loukes' work with the stick examined in Chapter 3, it could be argued that by engaging with the space, the stick, the partner, and her movement, including her breath, Loukes is paying attention to several aspects of her environment at once and synthesises them in a meaningful whole. Psychophysical training is underpinned by and cultivates the plurality that marks polyattentiveness. The difference is that, unlike the psychophysical paradigm that valorises heightened attention over and against a distracted and unfocused state, polyattentiveness allows, indeed counts on, the subject's attentive focus to pass through different states of concentration. As Raley observes in relation to a similar preference for deep attention in reading practices, 'polyattentiveness ups the ante on "reception in a state of distraction"' (2009: 4). By extending the metaphor of pharmacology, I propose to consider polyattentiveness as immunity, a form of engagement that is not threatened by distraction, precisely because it does not try to master attention.

Below I present an exercise as an example of the way such an approach may be fleshed out within a specific performer training context. First, I will explain the exercise, then outline the way in which it departs from key performer training conventions related to the use of space. Finally, I will discuss the relations it produces in terms of the trainees' and the trainer's involvement; the operation of the artefact; and the overall constitution of the training event. It needs to be stressed that the exercise is not positioned by any means as a model or 'solution' to the crisis of attention that education is called to resolve. Rather it is offered as an instantiation of a pharmacological attempt within a specific context and in relation to a specific artefact. Such an attempt seeks to examine the way the mobile phone could be utilised within performer training in a way that productively unsettles both existing cultures of mobile phone use as well as performer training practice.

Feel/Hear/See/Do: towards a practice of polyattentiveness

Feel/Hear/See/Do developed out of an experimentation I undertook as part of my teaching on a second-year module of the Theatre and Performance BA at the

University of Leeds. It forms part of a larger project interrogating mobile phones as a means for creativity and has since been used in several training situations, including preparation for the development of material for an interactive peripatetic performance.[8] The exercise involves the use of a messaging service and takes place outside. It is inspired by *IntuiTweet*, a project developed by choreographer Susan Kozel with Mia Keinanen and Leena Rouhiainen. Kozel and her partners, located in different geographical places, exchanged messages on Twitter describing movements or kinaesthetic sensations they experienced throughout the day. In response to a message from one member of the group, the other two would improvise and send a message back (Kozel 2014).

Feel/Hear/See/Do utilised text messaging and was done in pairs. Each partner was positioned at a different place on the university campus. In response to a kinaesthetic sensation or event in the space in which they found themselves, they had to compose a text and send it to their partner. The partner had to then undertake the task suggested in the text message and, out of this experience, compose a new text to send back. For example, Partner A invited Partner B to look at the trail of airplane fumes in the sky. As Partner B engaged with the task, their movement changed: B looked upwards and began walking backwards following the line the airplane left behind. The new movement formed the basis of the next instruction B sent to A: 'Walk backwards until you find an obstacle'. The exercise thus aimed to establish a feedback loop between sensation–experience–action, which involved the two partners and the surrounding space, and was mediated by the messaging service.

After initial free play, the exercise was structured around the senses, following a progression from sensing to doing, reflected in the title. This served two aims. The first aim was to ensure that any action the trainees might invite or engage with in the 'doing' part of the exercise would be a result of and/or in tune with an enhanced sensory perception that included the person doing the exercise, the absent partner, other people that happened to be physically present, and the surrounding environment. This progression also marked a trajectory from instructions that could be considered 'safer' – since engagement with the initial invitations to 'Feel' and 'Hear' would not draw attention to the doer – towards instructions that could entail visible movement. The intention was that by the time the trainees were invited to perform an action, they would have been already involved in a sensory trajectory that progressed from sensing, which remained fairly internal and invisible to an external observer, towards doing that was visible and could attract attention. The exercise therefore relies on the following three premises: it takes place outside; the communication between the partners is enabled by text messages; and the trainees need to have a working phone with them.

As such, the requirements of the exercise begin to upset one of the most established aspects of performer training. Training, in formal university and conservatoire settings, most often takes place inside, usually in a studio space. Being a technology in and of itself, the studio space is also conducive to the kind of deep attention that is expected in a training situation. As Robert Rosenberger argues:

particular spaces modify our cognitive capacities, but also [...] influence the characteristics of our lived experience, activating learned perceptual habits, inclining certain organizations of awareness, and inciting some things to be encountered as meaningfully present and others to drop back with less meaning and relevance.

(2019: 317)

Accordingly, Rosenberger puts forward the notion of the field of awareness, which encompasses 'the totality of what a user is aware of in any given moment' (2017: 152). It includes:

What stands forward within one's awareness, what stands back, how these things are arranged among one another, how deeply set these things may be within our habits of perception, and then also how these things can change, or become 'reorganised', as one's technology usage changes.

(Rosenberger 2017: 152)

An examination of the trainee's field of awareness within the paradigmatic space of the training studio would reveal that 'what stands forward' is the training situation, and 'what stands back' is the everyday; in the form of belongings, such as bags, shoes and, indeed, phones; surrounding objects, such as chairs and walls; and behaviours, such as small talk, giggling and swearing. The studio, in other words, renders certain aspects of daily life irrelevant to the training by a literal and metaphorical positioning of the everyday to the margins of the room and the periphery of one's awareness. Accordingly, it establishes what the trainee should pay attention to, what should be encountered as 'meaningfully present' by offering, again, both spatially and cognitively, a 'centre'. In this manner, spatial configuration structures tacitly a series of attitudes; for example, which way the trainees will face, where they are meant to leave personal belongings, and what kind of postures will be available to them. It also institutes a clear distinction between background (things that are not meant to draw attention) and foreground (things that are expected to engage the trainees). The space, therefore, suggests a set of focal points and accordingly reinforces the operation of training as 'perceptual apprenticeship'.[9]

However, in Feel/Hear/See/Do trainees are working outside. As a result, they have to make a set of decisions, which, in an interior space, would be automatically made for them by dint of the spatial configuration. Where trainees usually work within a bound space, now they are free to choose, and indeed are responsible for choosing, the place in which they are going to work; where trainees usually work in monochrome and sparse studios, and the stimuli they are expected to respond to are most often chosen in advance (for example, a piece of music or text) now they are expected to work in the midst of a plethora of events – colours, shapes, sounds, textures, changes in temperature and light – which are not and cannot be (pre)controlled; where trainer and trainees are usually the only ones present, they are now surrounded by other people who have nothing to do with the training;

where trainees are potentially visible at all times to the trainer and the trainer can be visible at all times to the trainees, they are not able to see each other. In short, working outside entails that the function of the space in regulating, and considerably reducing, the amount and type of sensory information that may be available within a training situation is now suspended.

Of course, public spaces are not free of determination; especially on a university campus, flows and activities are governed by architecture, landscaping, custom, as well as explicit or tacit rules. My point, however, is that the amount and type of information outside is far greater than it is inside. As a result, the counter-intuitive move to place an instance of performer training into a context that is not solely dedicated to it means that the trainee's process is situated in the midst of events that are neither expected nor designed to foster one's learning (as a well-designed and carefully managed studio space might do). By taking place outside, in other words, the exercise presents the trainee with a host of decisions that would not have been necessary, or at least not so acutely necessary, in a studio space. In this manner, this set of decisions comes into relief and with it the constitutive aspects of training itself.

The objection could be raised here that working outdoors is included as part of existing regimes and is the default configuration of others (see for example Quigley 2018). We need to bear in mind, however, that despite its influence on structuring a 'field of awareness', the studio space is not the sole factor in fostering an attentional quality. In the previous section, I demonstrated that performer training practice has been historically underpinned by a preference for a heightened or concentrated mode of attention. I would further argue that such preference may well be operative even when working outside (for example, through the language in which an exercise is explained, or the choice of a specific space). Outdoors space, therefore, is not enough to unsettle deeply established assumptions about the way attention is expected to operate. In this respect, the inclusion of the mobile phone in the exercise is crucial. In tandem with the movement from an interior to an exterior space, it enabled the development of a framework that both necessitated the focalisation of attention on a particular stimulus or stream of information and legitimised the interruption of such a process. In order to explore further the role of the phone in the exercise and the attentive mode the exercise sought to engender, I will consider the interactions between trainees/trainers, the device and the training context in terms of Ihde's three relational frameworks (embodiment, hermeneutic, alterity) introduced in the previous chapter.

As we saw, the embodiment relationship in instances of performer training that involve artefacts is premised on an ability to handle the artefact in ways stipulated by the exercise or the trainer. The process is aimed at the development of specific skills, such as balance, strength and spatial awareness. In Feel/Hear/See/Do, however, the aim was not to develop a new skill in the way the mobile phone was handled; rather the exercise aimed to both exploit and disrupt the sedimented embodiment of phone use. As such, the exercise is situated within the mundane kinetic repertoires of the 'mediatropic' body, but instead of wanting to suspend or correct them, these repertoires become a constitutive part of the exercise.

Specifically, the exercise was premised on an interplay between key characteristics of mediatropic embodiment specifically related to texting – closed body shape, narrowing of eye focus, proximity between hand and face – and a set of bodily attitudes that belong to the psychophysical paradigm – heightened spatial and auditory awareness, peripheral vision, wide range of motion.[10] In this manner, trainees were required to switch between very different focal qualities: staring at one's phone was alternated with a sense of 'open' viewing and sensing of one's environment, which again could be interrupted at any point by an incoming message. None of these modes was prioritised; rather what was exercised was an ability to move between them.

In this manner, the exercise exploited the trainees' existing competencies as mobile phone users but also sought to set these competencies into a dialogue with forms of embodiment that transcended quotidian registers. For example, the exercise substituted an instrumental relationship to space with an attitude of playfulness and discovery. As the trainees who took part in the exercise observed, campus pathways are treated routinely: as routes from one space to another and as an insignificant aspect of one's daily routine. By contrast, in this exercise, trainees were encouraged to take notice, find out details, and embody kinetic relations beyond the usual ones, experiencing, along the way, their surroundings in a personal and fairly intimate manner.

Similarly, the exercise put forward a different relation between training and texting: instead of text messaging being considered an event external to the training, as would happen for example in a typical training environment, the training activity 'in-corporated' the function of the mobile phone. In fact, the content of the text messages served as a means of enhancing awareness and kinaesthetic experience, whilst somatic exploration became communicated in a text message, extending, in this way, the language and intention that is often associated with this medium. As a result, a set of gestures that comprise mediatropic embodiment acquired a novel experiential potential and made up the very activity of the training. Text messaging, therefore, was utilised as a way to both affirm and estrange the habitual repertoires associated with this function and in the process mediatropic embodiment was both accepted and enlarged by additional kinetic registers.

In addition to the effect it had on the constitution of the embodiment relation, texting also complicated the hermeneutic dimension of the exercise. Evidently, text messages involved an active process of selection and composition on behalf of the sender accompanied by an equally active process of receiving, interpreting and responding on behalf of the receiver. Activities of reading and writing, however, not only served as means for the communication of content; they had important repercussions for the pedagogy underpinning the exercise. As Mark Evans observes, the relationship between writing and movement-training practices has been a fraught one. Movement training is by default contingent, as it unfolds in the here and now of specific bodies in a specific environment. Therefore, its documentation in writing, or indeed other forms, is bound not only to be incomplete and selective, but possibly misleading.

Evans draws on *Phaedrus*, where, as noted already, Socrates doubts the efficacy of writing and is concerned that written text could be mistaken as a valid mode of knowledge transmission. 'Writing on movement training', observes Evans, 'struggles with the difficulty of communicating the lived experience of the exercise and the process of its integration into the student's nervous system, into their very way of learning' (2009: 12). Confirming Socrates' apprehension, writing seems inadequate to communicate the knowledge produced through movement training and can even lead to misconceptions. As a result of the difficulties of capturing lived process into fixed language, during the twentieth century some movement trainers resisted the written documentation of their work (see Loukes forthcoming); others explored alternative writing registers as well as imagery with the aim to convey the gist of a pedagogy (Evans 2009: 13; Paterson and McCaw 2016). In all these cases, however, the assumption has been that the act and content of writing will be temporally distanced from the act and content of the lived experience. Indeed, this temporal difference between a live audience and a piece of text, written before and elsewhere, is a key aspect of Socrates' arguments about the inefficiency of writing to produce knowledge (Plato 2001: 395–7).

In Feel/Hear/See/Do, however, the temporal lag between experience and writing, reading and following instructions is minimal. Writing takes place right after an event has been identified and possibly still within its midst (the fumes of the airplane were still visible after they were recorded in the text message; indeed, the message would not make sense otherwise). Similarly, the reading of the text message, which is effectively a set of instructions for embodied exploration, is followed straight away by action. More importantly, the writer and reader of the text occupy the same environment; even if they feel, hear, see and do different things, they are still susceptible to the same time, weather, temperature and light. In this manner, the functionalities of the mobile phone rendered possible the inclusion of a textual practice that was synchronous with the action and the surroundings. What the digital device affords, in other words, is the closing, but not the elimination, of the temporal gap between experiencing and writing. Language in this way becomes a structuring device of the experience; in order to write down a set of instructions that relate to one's environment, the writer had to engage in an act of ecological and linguistic process of noticing, selecting and noting. Equally, interpreting the written text into action, entailed that the reader had to test these instructions against the environment they found themselves in (for example, fulfilling the instruction to walk backwards presupposes a kind of reality check; does the space allow such movement or does it require some form of adjustment?). With the performer trainer unable to oversee each and every interaction, the responsibility for these processes lay with the trainees.

As I argued in the previous chapter, a key aspect of the learning process is a state of care-ful being-with, whereby the trainer picks up a range of clues emanating from the trainee's embodiment and interprets them according to a set of criteria underpinning any particular regime; for example, the way a trainee walks can offer information about levels of energy, tension and spatial awareness. Feel/Hear/See/

Do suspends this relationship, as the trainer cannot see the trainees, nor can the trainees see the trainer or each other. Rather, the hermeneutic function produced through acts of looking and sensing that take place in a shared physical space is now substituted with acts of reading and writing that are facilitated by a technological device. The hermeneutic relation becomes (re)mediated. As a result, the fundamental process of caring that is involved in the hermeneutic act of looking–sensing between trainer and trainee becomes spread amongst the assemblage of the two partners and the mobile phone. In other words, an evaluation of the exercise, for example whether it fulfilled its aim in developing a state of polyattentiveness or a non-quotidian relationship with the space, cannot be achieved through observing the students' work; rather an evaluation can only take place afterwards and with reference to the text messages and the responses they generated. Accordingly, further practice in the exercise increases the trainees' awareness of the kind of events and language that are more likely to instil an exploratory and polyattentive attitude in their partner.

What is then the phone's function as a quasi-other in the specific exercise? As I mentioned in the introduction, the phone not only exemplifies Ihde's alterity relation; it pushes alterity to an extreme and produces in the process a wide range of social and communicative effects. Clearly, in this exercise the phone continued to operate as a quasi-other, indeed we could say that in being an integral part of the exercise, the phone was a quasi-partner. As noted already, the trainer's privilege and responsibility to maintain an overview of an exercise is suspended, and no single person can keep track of what is going on. Similarly to Merce Cunningham's choreographies that required from dancers and audiences alike a state of polyattentiveness (Copeland 1983: 323), in Feel/Hear/See/Do there is no centre, no privileged point of view from which the training situation can be observed and made sense of. In this respect, the exercise institutes a degree of alienation; trainees are literally and deliberately distanced, and their communication is entirely dependent on the function of the device. At the same time, though, the exercise can foster new and intimate experiences to one's surroundings, as well as between the partners. Indeed, the partners extrapolate text, movement, imagery *out* of their physical surroundings, communicate these extrapolations *through* a shared virtual space, and then undertake a new set of actions, which are 'discharged' back *into* the physical space. The virtual then operates in both senses of the world: in the way in common parlance it designates online spaces that are not 'real', as well as in the way in philosophical discourse it designates the possible. In the exercise, text messaging is foundational of a non-physical space, which exists exclusively on a digital medium. At the same time, it 'potentialises' one's relation to the surrounding environment by offering new possibilities for exploration, that is new relations with the real. In this manner, the exercise simultaneously 'pulls' trainees out of the world, as Berry puts it, but also 'emplaces' them, as Pink and Hjorth (2012) put it. In this manner, the exercise has the potential to produce what Kozel calls with regard to her own project, 'gift[s] of motion' (2014: 91), invitations for sensing, interacting or acting upon the environment that move beyond familiar and often narrow kinetic repertoires associated with mobile phone use and behaviour in public spaces.

The way the exercise appropriated a specific, and deeply acculturated, function of the mobile phone required several modes of attention. In the terms I have already reviewed in this chapter, it could be argued that the exercise combined: a 'heightened' ecological mode, which invited the trainees to engage with but also to explore new aspects of their environment; a 'hyper' mode, which invited trainees to remain exposed to and 'skim' over several stimuli at once; and instances of distraction, which could be caused by an incoming text message or indeed by any other event in the space. Of course, each trainee's engagement with and commitment to the exercise might be radically different. Crucially, however, the exercise does not valorise one mode of attention over another. Nor does it rest on a pre-conceived assumption with regard to what needs to be selected and what needs to be excluded from the trainee's field of awareness.[11] In this manner, the exercise moved away from an assumption that attention is an act of will that the trainee has to master. In a state of polyattentiveness, trainees are tasked with the responsibility to synthesise their own field of awareness and share aspects of it with their partner: the 'circle of attention' becomes the world.

Conclusion: performer training as a practice of immunity?

Continuing with an examination of the use of material objects as tools for performer training purposes, this chapter examined the use of mobile phones, a device that has fully penetrated daily lives, yet is all the more remarkable because of it. As I explained, mobile phone use is inextricably intertwined with the practice of attention, and attention has (re)emerged as an acute problem in relation to digital culture. This chapter employed a pharmacological approach, accepting that alternative relations to technology can be negotiated through encounters with technology and that education can offer such space. However, technologies can serve as *pharmaka* only when they are lived, that is only when their function is examined, pushed around, and reimagined through practice, and ideally through a form of practice that is sensitive to the embodied dimensions of our encounters with the world.

It is this sensitivity that performer training can arguably offer in abundance. The promise of performer training lies in the plethora of practices, lineages and pedagogies it involves that can sensitise us to the world. At the same time, though, the attentional regimes of digital culture, as well as the cultures of use of mobile telephony specifically, bring into sharp relief the deep-rooted assumptions and limitations of performer training, especially its dominant preference for heightened attention. This chapter argued, therefore, that the promise of performer training can be operational only if such sensitivity is robust enough to include and work from and with the modes of subjectivity we currently occupy. Once contemporary subjects of digital culture are positioned as distracted, the psychophysical paradigm, with its commitment to a heightened form of attention, appears out of kilter: it would either be written off as inadequate for our times or celebrated as a remedy, as is indeed the case with the wide spread tendency of 'prescribed' mindfulness. In order for performer training to fulfil its considerable potential to serve as a space for rehearsing a different relationship to technology, a readiness to doubt, suspend and alter the most foundational assumptions and conventions that make up its practices is needed. Therefore, instead of positioning psychophysical training as a corrective mechanism that promises to reach an ideal, yet ideologically informed, notion of attention, I proposed to explore the possibilities it offers for working with *this* subjectivity, the one, allegedly, prone to distraction and fragmentation. The aim is not to valorise distraction as a necessary evil, but rather to explore whether it is possible to cultivate a state of embodiment and a pedagogical framework that can be sensitively responsive and responsible to the world, including its technologies, without being threatened by their possible input. Instead of curing a pathology, I propose that we look for immunity. The next and final chapter tests the promise of performer training further; it examines a technology that is owned neither by trainer nor trainees in relation to institutional settings and professional contexts.

Notes

1 An earlier version of this chapter has appeared under the same title in the 'Digital Training' special issue of the *Theatre Dance and Performance Training Journal*. The discussion and work presented in this article has been made possible by a year-long fellowship on Mobile Phones and Digital Creativity awarded by the Leeds Institute for Teaching Excellence. For more information, see https://signalspace.leeds.ac.uk [accessed 5 April 2019].

2 Data suggest that in many countries the number of mobile phone subscriptions exceeds the total population (https://en.wikipedia.org/wiki/List_of_countries_by_number_of_mobile_phones_in_use [accessed 29 June 2018]). Goggin and Hjorth similarly predicted that by 2014 'mobile phone subscriptions will have exceeded seven billion' (2014: 1).

3 Bluetooth attendance management systems enable students to register for class through the signal emitting from their phone.

4 For a discussion on the way studio space organises training also see Camilleri (2019).

5 As Crary demonstrates there were other conceptualisations, including understandings of attention as a reflex as well as an automatic process (2000: 42). I focus on explanations of attention as a willed response, because of the endurance and relevance of this understanding specifically to learning environments.

6 Zarrilli borrows the metaphor from Zeami, a fourteenth-century Japanese Noh Master.

7 For details on the debate see Stiegler (2010b: 72–93) and Hayles (2012: 250–1).

8 For more information, see https://signalspace.leeds.ac.uk

9 A similar argument has been developed by Claire Bishop in relation to performance spaces. Bishop argues that the emergence of the 'black box' in the 1960s as a paradigmatic performance space was not only a result of theatre aesthetics; it 'steer[s] and hierarchise[s] attention and thus construct[s] viewing subjects' (2018: 30).

10 The exercise is preceded by at least four or five sessions, during which the students become familiarised with different kinds of attentional foci and exercises for spatial awareness.

11 In some cases, onlookers began to watch or even film the exercise on their own phones. This blurred the boundary between training and performance and raised questions about the politics of public spaces as well as the ethics of the exercise. Students are pre-warned that their work may attract attention and are given permission to abandon the exercise if they feel uncomfortable.

References

Aagaard, J. 2017. 'Breaking down barriers: The ambivalent nature of technologies in the classroom', *New Media and Society*, 19 (7), pp. 1127–43. doi.org/10.1177/1461444 816631505.

Aagaard, J. 2016. 'Mobile Devices, Interaction, and Distraction: a qualitative exploration of absent presence', *A I & Society*, 31 (2), pp. 223–31. doi.org/10.1007/s00146-015-0638.

Belgrad, D. 2016. 'Improvisation, Democracy and Feedback'. In: *The Oxford Handbook of Critical Improvisation Studies, Volume 1*, edited by George Lewis and Benjamin Piekut. Oxford: Oxford University Press, pp. 289–306.

Berry, M. D. 2014. *Critical Theory and the Digital*. New York: Bloomsbury.

Bishop, C. 2018. 'Black Box, White Cube, Grey Zone: Dance Exhibitions and Audience Attention', *The Drama Review*, 62 (2), pp. 22–42. doi.org/10.1162/DRAM_a_00746.

Campbell, C. T. 2011. *Improper Life*. Minneapolis: University of Minnesota Press.

Copeland, R. 1983. 'Merce Cunningham and the Politics of Perception'. In: *What is Dance?* edited by Roger Copeland and Marshall Cohen. Oxford: Oxford University Press, pp. 307–24.

Crary, J. 2013. *24/7 Late Capitalism and the End of Sleep*. London: Verso.

Crary, J. 2000. *Suspensions of Perception* (2nd edition). Cambridge, Massachusetts: MIT.

Crews, S. and Papagiannouli, C. 2019. 'InstaStan – FaceBrook – Brecht+: a performer training methodology for the age of the internet', *Theatre Dance and Performance Training Journal*, Special Issue Digital Training, 10 (2), pp. 187–204. doi.org/10.1080/19443927. 2019.1613260.

Eco, U. 2014 [2005]. 'Foreword: Truth and the Mobile Phone'. In: *Where Are You? An Ontology of the Cell Phone*, M. Ferraris, translated by Sarah de Sanctis. New York: Fordham University Press, pp. vii–ix.

Evans, M. 2009. *Movement Training for the Modern Actor*. London: Routledge.

Gardner, L. 2012. 'Switch on your Phones: theatre must embrace the interactive age'. *Guardian*. www.theguardian.com/stage/theatreblog/2012/apr/25/phones-theatre-interactive-audiences [accessed 29 June 2018].

Goggin, G. and Hjorth, L. 2014. 'Introduction'. In: *The Routledge Companion to Mobile Media*. New York: Routledge, pp. 1–8.

Hawksley, S. 2016. 'Coping with the (Interactive) Environment: The performative potential of interactivity', *Journal of Dance & Somatic Practices*, 8 (1), pp. 43–56. doi.org/10.1386/ jdsp.8.1.43_1.

Hawksley, S. 2012. 'Choreographic and somatic strategies for navigating bodyscapes and tensegrity schemata', *Journal of Dance & Somatic Practices*, 3 (1–2), pp. 101–10. doi. org/10.1386/jdsp.3.1-2.101_1.

Hayles, K. 2012. *How We Think: Digital Media and Contemporary Technogenesis*. Chicago: University of Chicago Press.

Hayles, K. 2007. 'Hyper and Deep Attention: the generational divide in cognitive modes', *Profession*, 13, pp. 187–99.

Ihde, D. 1990. *Technology and the Lifeworld: From Garden to Earth*. Bloomington and Indianapolis: Indiana University Press.

James, W. 1950 [1918]. *The Principles of Psychology*. New York: Dover Editions.

Kouppanou, A. 2015. 'Bernard Stiegler's Philosophy of Technology: invention, decision, and education in times of digitization', *Educational Philosophy and Theory*, 47 (10), pp. 1110–23. doi.org/10.1080/00131857.2015.1045819.

Kozel, S. 2014. 'Dancing with Twitter: Mobile Narratives become physical scores'. In: *The Mobile Story*, edited by Jason Farman. New York: Routledge, pp. 79–94.

Lemmens, P. 2017. 'Thinking through Media: Stieglerian remarks on a possible postphe-nomenology of media'. In: *Postphenomenology and Media: Essays on Human-Media-World Relations*, edited by Yoni Van Den Eede, Stacey O'Neal Irwin and Galit Wellner. Lanham: Lexington, pp. 185–206.

Lepp, A., Barkley, J. E. and Karpinski, A. C. 2015. 'The Relationship between cell phone use and academic performance in a sample of U.S. College students', *Sage Open*, January–March, pp. 1–9. doi.org/10.1177/2158244015573169.

Loukes, R. (forthcoming) *Embodied Translation*. Oxon: Routledge.

Love, L. 2002. 'Resisting the "Organic": A feminist actor's approach'. In: *Acting (re)con-sidered: A Theoretical and Practical Guide* (2nd edition), edited by Phillip Zarrilli. London and New York: Routledge, pp. 277–90.

Lutterbie, J. 2011. *Toward a General Theory of Acting*. New York: Palgrave.

Merlin, B. 2007. *The Complete Stanislavsky Toolkit*. London: Nick Hern Books.

Mihailidis, P. 2014. 'A Tethered Generation: Exploring the Role of Mobile Phones in the Daily Life of Young People', *Mobile Media and Communication*, 2, pp. 58–72. doi: 10.1177/2050157913505558.

Nakamura, T. 2015. 'The action of looking at a mobile phone display as nonverbal behav-ior/communication: a theoretical perspective', *Computers in Human Behavior*, 43, pp. 68–75. doi.org/10.1016/j.chb.2014.10.042.

Nedelkopoulou, E. 2017. 'Attention Please! Changing Modes of Engagement in Device-Enabled One-to-One Performance Encounters', *Contemporary Theatre Review*, 27 (3), pp. 353–65. doi.org/10.1080/10486801.2017.1343245.

O'Donnell, A. 2015. 'Contemplative Pedagogy and Mindfulness: Developing Creative Attention in an Age of Distraction', *Philosophy of Education*, 49 (2), pp. 187–202. doi. org/10.1111/1467-9752.12136.

Paterson, M. and McCaw, D. 2016. (eds) Special Issue 'On Showing and Writing Training', *Theatre Dance and Performance Training Journal*, 7 (2).

Pink, S. and Hjorth, L. 2012. 'Emplaced Cartographies: Reconceptualising Camera Phone Practices in an Age of Locative Media', *Media International Australia*, 145 (1), 145–55. https://doi.org/10.1177/1329878X1214500116.

Plato. 2001. *Φαίδρος*. Μελέτη, μετάφραση σχόλια, Παναγιώτης Δόικος. Θεσσαλονίκη: Ζήτρος.

Quigley, K. 2018. 'Departure Points: beginning training in site-based performance prac-tices', *Theatre Dance and Performance Training Journal*, 9 (2), pp. 251–67. doi.org/10.1080/ 19443927.2018.1450779.

Raley, Rita. 2009. 'Mobile Media Poetics', *Proceedings of the Digital Arts and Culture Confer-ence*, University of California: Irvine, pp. 1–6.

Richardson, I. 2005. 'Mobile Technosoma: some phenomenological reflections on itinerant media devices', *Fibreculture Journal*, September, 6, pp. 000–000.

Richardson, J. 2014. 'Powerful Devices: how teens' smartphones disrupt power in the theatre, classroom and beyond', *Learning, Media and Technology*, 39 (3), pp. 368–85. doi. org/10.1080/17439884.2013.867867.

Rosen, M. and Oxenbury, H. 1993. *We're Going on a Bear Hunt*. London: Walker Books.

Rosenberger, R. 2019. 'The Experiential Niche: or, on the Difference Between Smart-phone and Passenger Driver Distraction', *Philosophy and Technology*, 32 (2), pp. 303–20. doi: 10.1007/s13347-017-0297-8.

Rosenberger, R. 2017. 'On the Immersion of e-reading (or lack thereof)'. In: *Postphenome-nology and Media: Essays on Human-Media-World Relations*, edited by Yoni van den Eede, Stacey O'Neal Irwin and Galit Wellner. Lanham: Lexington, pp. 145–63.

Soto-Morettini, D. 2010. *The Philosophical Actor*. Bristol: Intellect.

Stanislavsky, K. 2008. *An Actor's Work*, translated by J. Benedetti (1st edition). Oxon: Routledge.

Stiegler, B. 2013. *What Makes Life Worth Living: On Pharmacology*, translated by Daniel Ross. Cambridge: Polity.

Stiegler, B. 2012. 'Relational Ecology and the Digital *Pharmakon*', *Culture Machine* 13, pp. 1–19.

Stiegler, B. 2010a. *For a New Critique of Political Economy*, translated by Daniel Ross. Cambridge: Polity.

Stiegler, B. 2010b. *Taking Care of Youth and the Generations*, translated by Stephen Baker. Stanford: Stanford University Press.

Vlieghe, J. 2014. 'Education in an Age of Digital Technologies', *Philosophy and Technology*, 27 (4), pp. 519–37. doi: 10.1007/s13347-013-0131-xCorpus ID: 141001240.

Wellner, G. 2015. *A Postphenomenological Inquiry of Cell Phones*. Lanham: Lexington Books.

Zanotti, M. 2018. Skype interview with author, March 2018.

Zanotti, M. 2014. App for Screen Dance, Conference Paper, TaPRA Performer Training Working Group, Royal Holloway, University of London.

Zarrilli, P. 2020. *(Toward) a Phenomenology of Acting*. Oxon: Routledge.

Zarrilli, P. 2015. 'The Actor's Work on Attention, Awareness, and Active Imagination'. In: *Performance and Phenomenology: Traditions and Transformations*, edited by Maaike Bleeker, Jon Foley Sherman and Eirini Nedelkopoulou. London: Routledge, pp. 75–96.

Zazzali, P. 2016. *Acting in the Academy*. London: Routledge.

Zazzali, P. and Klein, J. 2015. 'Toward Revising Undergraduate Theatre Education', *Theatre Topics*, 25 (3), pp. 261–76. doi: 10.1353/tt.2015.0034.

6

TRAINING TO BE CAPTURED

Introduction

This chapter deals with motion capture and examines the different kinds of training that have recently emerged as a result of the spread of the technology in several fields. Following a discussion of the mobile phone – one of the most common digital devices owned by trainers and trainees alike – this chapter examines a technology that is 'large' both in scope and size, and neither owned nor operated by either trainee or trainer. As explained in the Introduction, a key aim of this book is to interrogate both how specific artefacts are used in training as well as how performer training might change or be reconfigured in response to technology. As I will discuss, motion capture has given rise to new forms of training as well as new forms of delivering teaching material, triggering in the process important changes in the way training is understood and practised.

As the name suggests, motion capture (mocap) records in data the motion of an animate subject, which can then be rendered into a visual form through animation.[1] The current technology originates from twentieth-century animation techniques, such as rotoscoping (Delbridge 2015: 15), as well as experimentations with capturing movement, in particular the work of Etienne-Jules Marey (1830–1904) and Eadweard Muybridge (1830–1904) in chronophotography (Delbridge 2015: 13–14) and the development of kymocyclography in Soviet Russia during the 1920s (Salazar Sutil 2015). The most common set-up currently used consists of an array of cameras that emit and record light over an empty space, a body suit with reflective markers, and a processing system for the incoming data (Figure 6.1). The capturing process involves the performer in the suit moving inside the 'volume', i.e. the space covered by the cameras. The light emitted by the cameras is reflected back from the markers on the body suit and recorded by the cameras. The incoming data are calibrated through a processing

FIGURE 6.1 Motion Capture recording of Biomechanics, UCLAN

system in relation to the performer's body and its position in the space. The data can be presented from different angles, visualised in different forms and developed further through computer graphics. Unlike other recording mechanisms that install a point of view, mocap makes possible an 'omniscient frame', 'a global frame not hindered by the formally understood notion of the "window" typified by the cinematic frame' (Delbridge 2015: 43).

The technology is being used in several fields, including medical and sports sciences, the military, as well as the entertainment industry, films and video games in particular. Its employment in the latter produces 'synthespians', hybrid performers made-up by a combination of data deriving from live action and computer-generated imagery (CGI). The technology came to prominence through its use in popular movies, such as the *Lord of the Rings* trilogy, and the creation of well-known characters, such as Gollum and King Kong. It has also been employed in live performance as well as installations. Its use within the entertainment industry sparked in the last few years the initiation of new forms of training, usually offered on a workshop basis. Furthermore, its presence within academic institutions enabled theatre and dance practitioners to experiment with the technology, often with the aim to enhance the delivery of existing pedagogies. Although different forms of training and/or experimentation that involve motion capture have been discussed on their own (Cisneros et al. 2019; Delbridge 2015; Kozel 2007, 2005; Tunstall 2012; Whatley 2015a, 2015b; Wood et al. 2017), there is no account so far that puts different forms side-by-side. Accordingly, although there is considerable material on the use of motion capture in films, scholars are predominantly concerned with the end product, its reception and influence on viewing cultures. In the light of the plethora of applications, this chapter has two interrelated aims: to map as well as comparatively discuss training approaches that involve motion capture; and to examine the relations between subjects and technology that emerge through these approaches.

Towards these ends, this chapter is structured according to a propositional typology of mocap training. Here, propositional is used in two senses of the word: with reference to specific examples of contemporary practice, the typology will propose a way of mapping existing approaches and it will do so by utilising two propositions that denote the relations between the two parts of the equation: training *for* motion capture and training *with* motion capture. As such, this chapter examines training approaches that, by teaching a set of appropriate skills, claim to prepare the performer for working in the motion capture industry. It also examines instances where the technology is used as a tool for documenting, studying and disseminating a particular regime with the aim to produce further occurrences of training. In the first instance, training is geared towards employment and professionalisation, tailored to the needs of the mocap industry. In the second instance, the technology serves as an epistemic tool, as a way of revealing aspects of somatic experience of a particular form/exercise, which otherwise would remain ephemeral and/or invisible. In the first case, the performer is trained for the technology; in the second she trains with it. The differentiation between 'for' and 'with' followed in this chapter aims not to cover each and every application of motion capture technology. It rather attempts to both include and appropriately differentiate between a set of dominant approaches that underlie the way the technology is used in and positioned towards performer training practice.

An example of the need for such differentiation is presented in Mark Evans' recent discussion of motion capture. Evans (2019) considers several aspects of motion capture performance and emphasises the need to account for the cultural, social and economic stratifications underpinning movement, even if the latter is a composite digital product created out of a complex technological assemblage. As such, Evans offers an astute analysis of the tensions between the need for the social and political recognition of bodies and the erasing of bodily characteristics effected by the specific technology. This is a key point which will be examined in more detail later. What bears noting here is that in his analysis, Evans moves between two different kinds of practice without distinguishing between them. Specifically, he considers the use of mocap in the film and video games industry as well as in an instance of training utilising mocap developed by Darren Tunstall at the University of Central Lancashire. Evans' account focuses on the importance of the performer's ability to exercise control over their movement and the sense of fracture between embodied experience and digital creation (2019: 149–51). Although these threads are present both in professional environments and in Tunstall's discussion of his project, these instances of practice are fundamentally different in their aims and scope. As I will discuss in more detail, the professional contexts that Evans considers require the development of a set of skills that will enable the actor to give a performance appropriate for the technology. This is precisely the key aim that underpins instances of 'training for'. Tunstall's project, on the other hand, explored the way motion capture could serve as a means of reflection with the aim to enhance the actor's learning, not prepare her for the mocap industry. Even though the similarities that Evans highlights are present in both cases, his analysis draws on two spheres of practice that are in significant respects very different.

The aim, therefore, of the typology proposed here is to advance an inclusive yet nuanced understanding of the influence and use of motion capture in training contexts. Accordingly, the aim of the chapter is to mobilise a differentiation between 'for' and 'with' not as a neat system of classification but rather as a means for developing a dialectical relationship between different instances of and approaches towards performer training practice. As I will demonstrate throughout the chapter, instances of performer training that work 'with' or 'for' motion capture are contemporaneous, involve the same, or similar, kinds of technological apparatus and draw from the same genealogy of twentieth-century performer training pedagogies. They are also marked, however, by distinct differences in tone, language and aims, and are situated within very different socio-cultural settings. As such, a differentiation between 'training for' and 'training with' can reveal both the common ground shared by many approaches as well as their fundamental differences, especially in terms of the relationship each institute between pedagogy and technology. 'Training for' and 'training with' will serve one another as a point of reference, so that together they can advance a reconsideration of key aspects of performer training practice in terms of three axes: the presence and absence of the technology and the trainer respectively; tradition and innovation; and autonomy and heteronomy.

In this manner, the dialectical analysis proposed here enables us to return to the chief idea that has been running throughout the whole book: that it is possible to develop different relationships with technology. In Chapter 3, I presented Heidegger's argument that a 'free relationship' to technology can become realised through techne and I explored this idea in relation to the artistic practice of the 1960s avant-garde theatre and performer training practice. As we will see, this idea resurfaces in the work of contemporary practitioners working with motion capture. The aim of this chapter then is twofold: to examine how the argument for a free relationship to technology is advanced in instances of contemporary performer training practice that use motion capture; and to tease out another aspect of Heidegger's thought. Heidegger concludes 'The Question Concerning Technology' by proposing that

> We look into the danger and see the growth of the saving power. Through this we are not yet saved. But we are thereupon summoned to hope in the growing light of the saving power. How can this happen? Here and now and in little things, that we may foster the saving power in its increase. This includes holding always before our eyes the extreme danger.
>
> (1977: 33)

For Heidegger, a free relationship with technology is premised on becoming aware of the normalisation of calculative thinking and the development of a 'double vision' that perceives both the 'danger' and the 'saving power' of technology. In other words, Heidegger proposes that we need to both be alert to our susceptibility to see everything as a resource to be exploited, as well as embrace attitudes that transcend such disposition. This double operation has attracted renewed interest and been put by recent scholarship in terms of 'a gestalt switch' (Dreyfus 2002: 103; Feenberg 2015; Thomson 2009: 147). Iain Thomson explains the term by employing a bi-variational optical illusion, when, for example, a drawing can appear as a duck or a rabbit. Using this as an interpretative device, Thomson points out that in Heidegger's formulation

> the relation of the danger to the promise of technology is very much like the relation of the duck to the rabbit […]: both can be 'gestalted' otherwise; each has a second, non-simultaneous aspect, which we can learn to see in the place of the first, as replacing it, standing in its stead.
>
> (2009: 159)

According to Thomson's reading of Heidegger's thesis, then, danger and salvation both inhere in our relationships with technology *and* are mutually exclusive.[2] In other words, a free relationship to technology involves the suspension of calculative thinking (the danger), and an appreciation that

> efficiency – getting the most out of ourselves and everything else – is fine, so long as we do not think that efficiency for its own sake is the *only* end for man [sic], dictated by reality itself, to which all others must be subordinated.
>
> (Dreyfus 2002: 169, emphasis original)

Dreyfus (2002) argues that this process can be accomplished by fostering cultural practices that are pursued for their own sake, and Thomson (2005) explores in detail the role of education. But Heidegger's vision for a different relationship to technology has also been identified by scholar-practitioners that work with technology, and motion capture specifically. As I will discuss in more detail in the third section of this chapter, Susan Kozel draws a link between the response that Heidegger is inviting his reader to ponder in relation to the question of technology and the response the performer is expected to develop within interactive systems. Although Kozel's projects with motion capture were not directly concerned with issues of training, her account is relevant to this discussion because she views the dancing studio effectively as a kind of training ground for a new subjectivity: a place where a form of intersubjective and inter-species ethics can be rehearsed with the potential to reach contexts and environments beyond it. She explains:

> For a system to be responsive, there needs to be a feedback loop whereby both the system and the participants respond to each other. What this means is that we, as participants, need to allow ourselves to assimilate what we receive from the system into our bodies and thoughts; equally the system needs to be designed to generate meaningful responses.
>
> (Kozel 2005: 40)

In this process, Kozel identifies a move away from mastery, an approach which according to Heidegger is the hallmark of the 'technological', and towards a form of symbiosis that allows space for 'unpredictability' and 'otherness' (Kozel 2005: 43). Although Kozel does not specifically refer to the idea of the gestalt switch, the way she presents her praxis arguably serves as a form of embodied disposition that can, to paraphrase Thompson, 'gestalt' technology otherwise and confirm Heidegger's supposition that a free relationship to technology is possible. There is, however, another understanding of the gestalt switch, which is particularly pertinent to discussions on motion capture.

Whereas in Heideggerian thought, as well as in Kozel's account, the gestalt switch is explained in terms of an individual ability to see and reconfigure technology differently, Andrew Feenberg (2015) understands the gestalt switch as a social process pertaining to the struggles between the needs of subjects and the agendas of institutions. Drawing on both Heidegger and critical theory, Feenberg locates the problem of technology on a social level: 'technologies, bureaucracies, and markets are rational institutions that impose form on the stuff of everyday experience. They define human beings as objects in ways similar to the construction of nature by natural science' (2015: 235). For Feenberg, the solution, therefore, lies not in changing the sensorium and/or the ethical disposition of the individual, as suggested by Kozel, but rather in intervening in the way social, economic and political systems operate. Specifically, Feenberg calls for a 'dereification of technology', which entails 'a more fluid interaction between rational disciplines, systems, and artefacts and the demands of the lifeworld of concrete experience' (2015: 234).

Feenberg, in other words, wants us to remember that political and social systems are not fixed, they only appear to be so. They can and do respond to pressures from below and the responsibility of citizens is to exert such pressure. There are two ways in which the gestalt switch can be understood then: as a form of individual transformation following embodied experience and as a form of political transformation following activist interventions.

In the light of these two understandings of the gestalt switch, a dialectic between 'training for' and 'training with' can alert us not only to the interplay between subject and technology at a perceptual somatic level, which largely occupied the previous chapter, and, as we shall see in this one, can be realised in instances of practices that I group under the 'training with' heading. Precisely because the particular technology cannot be accessed individually, an examination of motion capture also reveals the institutional settings and logics that sustain different instances of practice.[3] In other words, this chapter is concerned with how the characteristics of 'training for' and 'training with' are aligned with and gain their flavour from the institutional settings in which they take place. Indeed, as we saw in Chapter 3 with regard to the work of the Open Theatre, their endeavour to develop a form of training that would enable a different form of perception (a gestalt switch at an intersubjective and somatic level) was subject to institutional support. And one of the reasons for the group's disbandment was its increasing reliance on such support. This tension between pedagogical purposes and institutional agendas becomes further accentuated when training in reperceiving involves expensive technological infrastructure, which can only be provided by institutions. Motion capture, therefore, merits our attention not only on the grounds of its recent popularisation and adoption within performer training settings. Its use in training opens a key question: what is the relationship between institutional agendas and modes of cultivating a free relationship to technology? Is change at an individual level adequate enough?

The chapter will examine 'training for' and 'training with' consecutively in two separate sections, followed by a discussion on the key points around which a dialectic between them is constituted. The analysis will draw on resources that are publicly available, interviews with practitioners, as well as my participation in introductory workshops with key providers: Mocap Vaults, an international training and production company that offers mocap training across the world; Shapes in Motion, a UK-based company specialising in movement training for actors; and Asha Jennings-Grant (2018), an emerging professional who offers ad hoc workshops.

'Training for' motion capture

The consideration of motion capture in the last chapter of this book is aligned with the ambivalent sense of both beginning and end invoked within the film/mocap industry. Renowned directors and actors, as well as actor trainers, salute the birth of a new medium and emphasise the professional and creative opportunities it could offer for performers. As Nicholas Bestor observes, Robert Zemeckis presents the use of motion capture in rather grandiose terms, as a form of technology that can 'liberate actors from certain profilmic realities' (Bestor 2016: 179). Similarly, Andy Serkis maintains that performance capture is an 'important component in the evolution of the ancient art, craft and tradition of acting' (Serkis 2010 in Bestor 2016: 183). On the other hand, critics express an anxiety about the displacement of human creatives, actors as well as animators, by a cost-effective technology. Mihaela Mihailova notes that the 'likelihood [...] of creative artists becoming auxiliary and subordinate to machines (or even unnecessary), remains a topical concern in today's efficiency-obsessed world [...]. It is an artist's nightmare born out of an artist's dream' (2013: 145). Despite their opposing message and tone, it could be argued that both celebratory and antagonistic accounts demonstrate the fundamental changes that motion capture has effected in film production as well as viewing cultures.

In terms of the performer's work, mocap consists of two main components: 'the internal knowledge, the sensory experiences, the bodily-ness, the physicalities, the lived-in-ness of the body' that comprise the movement captured by the technology and the rendition of the data of this movement into a 'visual code' (Ng 2012: 283). As many commentators, including Ng, emphasise, the peculiarity of motion capture lies precisely in recording the performer's movement, but doing so without recording their image. Yacov Freedman explains:

> The basic process captures live movement as digital data instead of completed images, providing a three-dimensional rendering of the action. The rendering can then be easily inserted into any digital environment, freeing a performance from the constraints of a static setting. The downside, however, is that motion capture provides much less immediate detail than is available in a photograph or reel of film [...].[...] An image is being recorded, to be sure, but in practical terms, the data are impossible to view—let alone exhibit— until they have gone through multiple layers of digital modifications.
>
> (2012: 39)

Although any performance features a dialectic between a physical score and a set of meanings/representations, in mocap these two levels are entirely distinct both during and post-production. In this manner, mocap drives a wedge between the performer's embodied practice that will produce the movement and the inscription practices that will eventually make the movement visible.[4] In this manner, as Drew Ayers notes, motion capture consists of a human–technology assemblage that engenders a 'multilocal self' (2014), a mode of subjectivity that has a physical manifestation but also becomes constituted through the technological system. Accordingly, 'training for' motion capture offers a space for professionalisation that aims to harness existing understandings and skills of acting/movement towards the specificities of the new medium. Introductory workshops, including the ones I attended, are advertised on public fora, incur a one-off fee, and are open to all levels of experience. They tend to attract emerging as well as consummate performers with an existing expertise in drama, voice work, and/or movement disciplines, such as martial arts, stage combat, and stunt work, as well as a passion for video games.

Introductory trainings do not involve the technology at all. This is justified both in economic and pedagogical terms. In his welcome email to the participants of the introductory workshop offered by the Mocap Vaults, co-founder Oliver Hollis-Leick specified that 'this class is not held in a mocap studio as that simply serves as an expensive distraction at this stage. Here, we focus on the core essentials: body and imagination' (Hollis-Leick 2019 email communication with author). Hollis-Leick's assertion, which was repeated by Jennings-Grant during her workshop, also chimes with the experience of other practitioners. For example, Steph Hutchison, a performer who has worked with motion capture in performance and artistic research environments attests that, regardless of her longstanding experience with mocap, 'seeing yourself as a cloud of markers when you first walk into a motion capture volume is always strangely exhilarating and exciting, but also an experience of vulnerability' (Hutchison and Vincs 2013: 1).[5] Similarly, John Dower, the other co-founder of Mocap Vaults, draws attention to the revealing nature of the body suit and the possibility of causing the actor to feel self-conscious (in Pizzo 2016: 7). It can be assumed then that for someone with no prior experience, the presence of the technology at the beginning of the training might have an adverse effect.

At the same time, it can also be argued that right from the start 'training for' institutes a split between performer and technology. As we saw, in the welcome email by the Mocap Vaults, there is an explicit distinction between the technology, presented as an 'expensive distraction' and acting, presented as an unmediated psychophysical activity consisting of 'the core essentials' of body and imagination. Similarly, in a YouTube video, Hollis-Leick asserts that mocap performance is 'pure acting'. (Hollis-Leick www.youtube.com/watch?v=A0BjMXALRqY [accessed 17 June 2020]). Such stark distinction between acting and technology might be seen as a reflection of a wide-spread discourse in the mocap industry, which 'den[ies] a break with traditions of acting and performance' (Allison 2011: 337). Yet, such a tendency, especially within a performer training context, appears entirely paradoxical: on the one hand, the overall aim of the training is to enable the trainee eventually to work with the technology. On the other hand, the technology is positioned as a source of distraction that can side-track the trainee from the training process. As a result, 'training for', institutes and must reconcile a tension between the explicit goal to prepare actors for a new medium and an understanding of acting as an unmediated activity that could be disrupted by technology.

Up to an extent this tension is resolved through the content and language 'training for' foregrounds. Introductory workshops in mocap concentrate on the specific competencies that working with motion capture in a professional environment would eventually require, such as imagination, physical accuracy, body memory, and expressivity. Such skills are often explained in terms of techniques and/or terminology drawing from existing regimes. For example, movement director and founder of Shapes in Motion, Sarah Perry draws on Laban Movement Analysis as a way to create a movement language that could both guide the performer's creation and be legible to an animator (Perry interview with author June 2018). Similarly, Dower utilises Stanislavsky-based prompts in order to enable actors to clarify the motivations of their character and work with the given circumstances of a particular scene. For example, he may guide the actor with questions, such as:

> What is your objective? Why are you there? What do you want? Where are you going next? What is your background? [..] Is the action taking place in a dragon's cave? Are you in a forest? Do you have to talk quietly?
>
> (Dower in Pizzo 2016: 3)

In some significant respects, then, training for mocap harks back to existing practices, both in terms of a wider understanding of what acting is as well as in terms of training techniques. Nonetheless, as Jennings-Grant attests, the training involves an enhancing and repurposing of existing skills.

To begin with, in a professional shooting the performer will have none of the physical infrastructure that can be found on a film set and would make up the world of a scene. As a result, the performer needs a vivid imagination in order to develop movement consistent with the character specification and the given circumstances the character will eventually inhabit. As the character specification may amount to no more than a couple of sketches and/or brief descriptions given on the day of shooting, the performer will have to be able to identify those aspects of her movement skills that can yield the appropriate characterisation, often second guessing what the final result is expected to look like. As Hollis-Leick attests, a fundamental part of the trainer's work, then, is to 'take people back to the most basic form of imaginative work' (www.youtube.com/watch?v=A0BjMXALRqY 15:50 [accessed 17 June 2020]) and accordingly Dower's prompts may be seen to serve this wider objective.

In addition to a vivid imagination, a considerable amount of physical dexterity is also required. Since the performer's movement serves as the basis for the animation, it needs to be precise so that the motion capture data can be easily aligned with the computer graphics. For example, as explained in the workshop with Mocap Vaults, in video games production, the actor may be asked to develop a series of gestures that can be utilised for the character at different moments in the game. Depending on the character's role within the game, these gestures can amount to 2,000 movements, recorded separately but grafted onto a basic position, which the character acquires when she is not active in the game. As a result, for the recording of each of these gestures, the actor would need to repeat with painstaking precision the initial position. As an experienced mocap artist attests, in professional shootings:

> You will have few days where they will basically just want you to bash out every single move that those characters in the games are going to make, what the controller can make them do as a player. It is extremely repetitive [...]

because everything you do you have to do straight on, forty-five, ninety degrees, one hundred and eighty, and three hundred and sixty, both ways'

(Taylor 2015 cited in Evans 2019: 162)

The level of precision and accuracy entails considerable proficiency in terms of strength, endurance and body memory, which require ongoing training. Introductory workshops, therefore, do not aim to directly train these skills, since it is presumed either that the participants have already received prior training or that they will seek to engage with available techniques. In other words, introductory workshops aim to foreground the skills that will be needed and explain what makes these skills necessary, rather than train these skills from scratch. As such, a key component of the training is to introduce participants to the particularities of both the mocap industry and the technology.

As noted already, what the motion capture system records is not the image of a movement but rather the traces produced from the reflective markers. Ng argues that unlike conventional cameras, in motion capture 'the human actors are not seen through the camera, only sensed' (2012: 277). Following Ihde's analysis of technological equipment presented in Chapter 4, we might say that the intentionality between filmic cameras and mocap systems is very different and, accordingly, part of the training is to enable the trainee to align her intentionality (the 'ofs' and 'abouts' that constitute her moment-to-moment awareness) with the intentionality of the technology. For example, in the introductory workshops I attended, participants were made aware of the eventuality of 'marker occlusion': instances 'when the infrared cameras lose their stable connections with one of the optical markers on the suit' resulting in '"data gaps", which may be difficult or impossible to repair in "data processing"' (Karreman 2015: 19). As such, participants were alerted to movements that can cause marker occlusion, such as moving too close to another body, bending and rolling on the floor.

It can be argued, therefore, that an accomplished mocap artist is not only physically and imaginatively nimble; she has a good understanding of what the technology can and cannot do and which aspects of her movement would lend themselves to the medium. As Allison notes, in relation to Andy Serkis' performance in King Kong, 'Serkis [...] had to learn not only how to move his face like a gorilla, but to move his face in such a way as to make a computer recognise it as a particular gorilla expression' (2011: 329). In this respect, mocap training involves the kind of proprioceptive and kinaesthetic education common in tool-use. Indeed, Serkis' assertion that 'just as Ancient Greeks wore masks [...] so Zoe Saldana dons a motion-capture suit with markers' (Serkis 2010 cited in Bestor 2016: 185) points towards the embodiment relation that is at play and the somatic and kinaesthetic adjustments that underlie any tool-use.

Serkis' assertion, however, erases the many other aspects that comprise motion capture. It is noteworthy that, according to the embodiment relation between user and tool, put forward by Ihde, the technological equipment is expected to be in contact with the user's body, most likely with the user's hand(s). Accordingly, the two previous chapters explored the embodiment relation with reference to tools that were proportionate to the body and could be handled, such as sticks and mobile phones. Similarly to these instances of practice, training for mocap also aims to cultivate a seamless embodied relation between trainee and technology, manifesting, for example, in an alignment between the trainee's physical and spatial awareness and the specificities of the technological system.

However, the difference in this instance is that the technology is multi-faceted and dispersed. As noted already, a motion capture system consists of several parts, each of which has a different relation to the body: the body suit covers the performer's entire body; the cameras are placed above the performer and cover the performance space; and another set of tools, in the form of prosthetics and extensions, may be attached to the performer's limbs. An additional component of the system is the screen, which the performer may or may not be able to see, and on which the live data can be visualised, in a fairly simple form, synchronously with the performer's movement. The embodiment relation in mocap environments, therefore, is bound to be far more complex: the technology is both on as well as above the performer's body and her movement can be seen live, on the screen and from any angle. As a result, the performer has to work simultaneously with several components that make up the system and manage a range of proxemic configurations. One could respond to Serkis that, unlike the Ancient Greek mask, mocap requires a kind of embodiment relation that pushes the very idea of the body as a self-contained entity to its limits. Such embodiment, to use Ayers' term, may be adequately described as 'multilocal', since it manifests in both mediated and unmediated manners; spreads across a technological assemblage, and interacts with 'the affects, intensities and foldings of an environment and its human and nonhuman inhabitants' (Ayers 2014: 217).

What is more the structure and content of the curriculum is determined by the specificities of the industry environments, and, as such, it is largely based on the type of material a mocap artist will be expected to perform in a professional shooting. In line with the subject matter of video games and films that utilise the medium, the content of training for mocap involves a range of creatures, such as goblins, gremlins, zombies, ogres and dragons, as well as intense physical activity, such as combat (Figure 6.2). Accordingly, the curriculum of Mocap Vaults is structured in four levels and progresses from an introductory workshop at Level 1, into a class on 'Heroes and Monsters' at Level 2, with optional modules on 'Action and Combat' and 'Swords, Magic and Mayhem' at Level 3. At Level 4, the training culminates with a two-day event, which is open only to those that have already attended the previous sessions and offers participants the opportunity 'to shoo[t] a dramatic scene on the stage to get the full experience of what it's like to be a pro' (www.themocapvaults.com/curriculum [accessed 17 June 2020]).

Similarly, the introductory workshop offered by Shapes in Motion is followed by the workshop 'Hitting the brief', which aims to reproduce industry conditions.[6] For example, one day before the workshop I attended, participants were emailed a sketch of the creature we would be expected to embody. The timing of the email

FIGURE 6.2   Shapes in Motion Workshop, 'Primate Performance' taught by Sarah Perry

aimed to mimic industry practices, where details on the project may be shared very close to the time of the actual shooting in order to ensure confidentiality. In this second workshop, animators were also invited, and opportunities were created for the animators to direct the participants. Following a trajectory of professionalisation, Shapes in Motion also offers workshop participants the opportunity to audition for the Mocap Troupe, a collective of mocap artists that are represented together on the company's website, and continue with the fitness and specialised training required by mocap (Perry interview with author June 2018).

In this manner, 'training for' offers an intermediary space between existing training skills, which trainees are expected to have or continue to acquire, and the specificities of mocap industry. According to Perry, workshops aim at the development of a shared language that will enable trainees to understand what animators are after, and equally enable animators to understand how actors work and what kind of information would help them to develop the desired kind of movement (Perry interview with author June 2018). The training also offers insights into the professional conditions a performer is bound to encounter in the mocap industry. If a stage actor is trained to think about the proverbial audience member sitting in the last row, or perhaps more pragmatically, about casting directors and agents, the immediate recipient of a mocap performance is the animator and the 'client', i.e. the production company that will make use of the material.

A less explicit, nonetheless important, message, conveyed during the introductory workshops I attended, concerns the performer's position within the social and economic hierarchy of professional environments. On the one hand, trainees are presented with the extent and types of negotiation that can be accommodated in an industry setting. For example, they are advised that on the day of the shooting they can ask questions or make suggestions about the character they are expected to create or about the order in which a scene or movement can be filmed. On the other hand, it is also made clear that mocap professional environments are underpinned by economic imperatives, since the accuracy of the performer's movement is proportionate to the extent of intervention or 'clean-up' that will be required at the animation stage. In other words, an alignment between the performer's embodiment and the intentionality of the technological equipment has financial implications: reductions in clean-up save money as well as time and eventually make the performer employable.

'Training for', therefore, draws on three key sources: the specificities of the technology; the 'visual codes' that circulate in the entertainment industry; and the arrangements that operate in professional environments. In this manner, however, the content of the training inadvertently complies with a set of practices or wider ideologies that may be problematic. For example, Evans notes, that in following the characters and aesthetic of action films and video games, mocap training prioritises certain kinetic registers, such as 'combat, conflict, exertion, and pursuit', over others, such as hugging and kissing (2019: 159). What is more, Jonathan Burston traces these elements in what he calls a 'military industrial media complex' (2005: 251), which emerges through conceptual as well as real convergences between mass entertainment products and military operations (2005: 251–2). Confirming Burston's argument, which was made with reference to film and video games material, the syllabus of the introductory workshop of Mocap Vaults includes an improvisation that asks trainees to enact a conflict scene in Afghanistan. In line with an overall focus on professionalisation, in the session I attended, the trainees' attention during the scene was directed towards the technicalities of their performance, specifically the ability to manage their corporeality in ways consistent both with the specificities of the technology and the given circumstances of the scene. Technical accuracy, in other words, was prioritised over questions of representation and, in such a manner, a consideration of the ethics underpinning the scene was positioned beyond the scope of the exercise.

It could be argued, however, that when training is exclusively geared towards serving the needs of the industry, there is a danger that a deeply contentious human and political affair becomes naturalised, in the process dramatically limiting, or worse still rendering irrelevant, the possibility of training to serve as a space for resistance, reflection and critique. Of course, it could be objected that there are other instances of training where technical proficiency is prioritised over engagement with social and political issues. In this case, however, this tendency becomes further exacerbated due to the ideological, historical and material links between real military operations and the industry, as well as the technology of motion capture.

I would further contend that the way in which issues of representation are (un)acknowledged and handled within the training space is directly related to the intentionality of the technology itself. As we saw earlier, Ng points out that motion capture cameras do not 'see'. Anselm Franke similarly observes that motion capture instantiates a mode of '"seeing"' that is

> detached from the labor of making a representation; it knows 'recognition' only as a technical process of identification, in stark contrast to the meaning of recognition in human affairs and in politics. It is an a-subjective recognition in the best sense of the word.
>
> (2014: np)

Motion capture does not simply require that performers learn to adapt their performances for a new medium, in the way for example that an emotionally intense moment needs to be performed differently for the camera and on the stage respectively. What is also changing here is the ontology of the terminal point of the actor's work. As we saw, the uniqueness of motion capture lies precisely in the technology's ability to separate the object of the recording from the subject of the representation. In this manner, the technology is 'intentional' in Ihde's sense of the term; that is, it has a set of propensities in relation to the surrounding environment. But this capacity is politically agnostic. As a result, the performer in a mocap environment needs only worry about the efficiency of the movement, not the politics of representation, since she is cut off from the site of representation, both in terms of the creative process (the performer's data do not have an image as such) as well as the end product (the performer might not be able to recognise her performance in the final creation). Even in introductory workshops, then, where the technology is absent, the trainee is inculcated in a specific scopic regime brought forward both by the technology's intentionality as well as the wider discourses that underlie the industry in which the technology is used.

It is noteworthy, in this respect, that current systems of mocap are linked with the development of both the 'moving image' as well as 'an emerging science of work, for the rationalization of labor on the assembly line' (Franke 2014: np). In his study on the experiments that took place in post-revolutionary Russia in the 1920s, Salazar Sutil examines the development of early technologies of motion capture as a means to analyse the labourer's movement with the aim to increase productivity. He also traces an inverse process whereby the scientific analysis of the movement was then imposed as an ideal to be realised by the worker. In the light of these experiments, Salazar Sutil argues that 'movement constitutes a prime technique for the construction and control of selfhood outside the sphere of discursive ideology' (2015: 35). Or to put it in reverse, we could say that through movement an ideology becomes lodged in the flesh. Crucially, the ideological stratum, which underpinned early experiments with motion capture, can also be traced in the actor's work long before the emergence of training regimes associated with the technology. In his historiographical overview of movement training for actors, Evans locates the development of contemporary pedagogies and training regimes within a wider discourse of efficiency. He specifically identifies Marey's work in chronophotography, a precursor of current systems of motion capture, as a key factor in developing the 'ability to disassociate elements of movement and reconstitute them at will' (Evans 2009: 19). Motion capture, in other words, both historically and in its present manifestations, is intertwined with the compartmentalisation of movement and a concomitant emergence of a subjectivity set to serve economic imperatives. Accordingly, 'training for' introduces both the range of physical skills required by the technological apparatus as well as the attitudes endorsed within professional contexts.

The distance that performers are expected to keep from their data, as well as from the content of the 'visual codes' in which their data will be eventually rendered, can also be traced in the trajectory underlining the training. As noted already, the curriculum at Mocap Vaults is structured in four levels, beginning with introductory workshops that do not involve the technology and culminating in the 'Mocap summit', a two-day event that enables participants to work with the technology and film a show reel of their work. Similarly, Shapes in Motion workshops begin with introductory sessions and progress towards opportunities for further training and representation with professional bodies. As such, training progresses from a pronounced separation between trainee and technology, since the technology is not only absent from the training space but also bracketed off as a distraction, to a culturally acclaimed form of symbiosis between human and technology, manifesting in the creation of a synthespian. The production of a show reel, offered by Mocap Vaults, serves, in this sense, both as a record of the trainee's performance as well as a certificate of accomplishment; the trainee has to 'earn' seeing, let alone owning, a visual representation of her motion-capture data, by excelling in the acquisition of the relevant skills, and, in the case of Mocap Vaults, investing considerable time and money. Training thus turns the performer into a synthespian, but such competency can only be evidenced in a product that is removed from the trainee in significant ways, since the production of the mocap reel requires specialised equipment and knowledge that lies outside the trainee's skillset.

What is more, the relationship between the trainee and her data instituted in the training phase matches the working conditions in the industry. Drawing on the movement Restore Respect, Matt Stahl notes that motion capture performance has been defined 'as a technical aspect of the piece' (restorerespect.com cited in Stahl 2011: 6), enabling in this way production companies to exclude performers from 'residuals', i.e. the profit generated from the reselling of the end product. Drawing links with the scientific management that organised factory work in the early twentieth century, Stahl calls the professional arrangements in the entertainment industry 'virtual labour':

> a dynamic *political* arrangement whereby the managerially driven concealment or displacement of creative and technical cultural workers by 'synthespians' is correlated to the intensified alienation of those workers, to the erosion of their bargaining power, to the diminution of their power to claim credit, remuneration, proprietorship, autonomy, or other forms of politico-economic agency.
>
> (Stahl 2011: 4, emphasis original)

Stahl's reference to alienation appears justified. Similarly to the twentieth-century factory labourer, the performer is trained to develop a kind of movement that fits the machine; is divorced from creative and political responsibility over the final product; and has no stakes over the profits this can generate. Unlike the de-skilled factory worker, however, the mocap artist possesses extensive creative and, in this case, embodied capital, and has no professional security. Starting from a history that rendered the factory worker anonymous, motion capture renders the performer invisible. In fact, Evans identifies an invert relationship between skill and visibility: 'the more mocap […] skills that actors learn, the less worth those skills are to them, as they are ultimately designed to make them less visible as an actor' (2019: 174). Whereas this may be welcomed, if anything it may ensure the actor's privacy, it does have several implications both in terms of the politics of representation as well as contractual arrangements.

In summary, the mocap industry appears to be opening new employment opportunities, thus addressing one of the most persistent banes of the acting profession.[7] Accordingly, it has given rise to a new form of training that is distinct in the following ways. It institutes a 'poor' aesthetic and exercises the performer's ability to work in a bare space with a renewed emphasis on imagination and physical efficiency. It establishes new modes of collaboration, since the performer is now expected to work as part of a large network of creatives and in a process that is dispersed over time and space. It ushers in a new scopic regime that is both omniperspectival (the performer can be seen from any point of view), and divorced from the performer's physical reality (the visual examination and manipulation of the performer's data will continue long after its recording). It abdicates the performer's responsibility and ownership over the creative product.

In these ways, training for mocap is not only developing the skills necessary for the representations of the posthuman in the form of synthespians; it also trains a posthuman subjectivity, by instituting a professional identity that is dispersed (across technological artefacts), fractured (between different creative and technical processes), and as such economically and professionally displaced from the centre of the creative process. By contrast, the economic and legal arrangements that underpin the production and distribution system are tightly controlled: unlike the performer's movement that becomes fragmented and dispersed, ownership of the final product remains with the production companies. Accordingly, training instructs the performer in developing a dual relationship to the end product, one that involves love for the craft as well as the ability to relinquish control over creative and professional decisions.

'Training with' motion capture

'Training with' motion capture involves those instances where the technology is used as a tool that serves the delivery and further development of existing regimes, ranging from codified forms, such as Meyerhold's Biomechanics, ballet, Greek Folk Dance, and corporeal mime, to somatic disciplines, such as Skinner Releasing

Technique, contemporary dance, and acting. Unlike instances of 'training for' that are self-funded and openly advertised, instances of 'training with' take place within discrete projects or degree programmes, are supported by institutions and/or public funding, and access to the technology is ensured through institutional investment in the equipment. The emphasis in many of these projects is on the particular aspects of the pedagogy that motion capture can reveal and the new knowledge or ways of knowing that can emerge from the trainees' engagement with the mocap material. In what follows, I discuss instances of 'training with' that involve a wide range of performer training practices that are guided by two interrelated considerations: the propagation of a certain form and the student's understanding and embodiment of a particular regime.

Like other recording technologies, motion capture is being used as a means of documentation, often with an emphasis on the form's preservation, specifically its embodiment by a master teacher. In this instance, motion capture creates material that the student can then study and/or emulate in the studio. Two projects merit specific mention here. One is the recording of 'The Slap' and 'Throwing the Stone', two etudes from Meyerhold's Biomechanics, performed by Terence Mann and four undergraduate students under the supervision of Mann and Gennady Bogdanov at the University of Central Lancashire (UCLAN) in 2017, as part of the BA in Acting. The other involves a series of adagios by mime artist Marcel Marceau recorded at the Advanced Computing Centre for the Arts and Design (ACCAD) of the Ohio State University in 2001, and used as part of the MFA in Acting workshop led by Jeanine Thompson in 2014 at the Department of Theatre at the same university. Although these projects were concerned with two different regimes and took place in different institutional settings, they share important similarities in the way they were conceived and expected to operate within the delivery of the respective programmes.

To begin with, the etudes as well as the mime adagios lend themselves to the medium of motion capture, since they consist of discrete forms. Both etudes and adagios can be broken down into smaller individual movements; have a dramaturgical through-line involving a real action that takes place within a specific duration; operate according to a specific order and rhythm; and their accomplishment relies on accuracy and precision. A recording mechanism that captures the movement of the joints in an 'omniscient frame' is, therefore, ideal to reveal the underlying principles and characteristics of these movement scores. For example, the footage of Marceau's adagio 'At the Bar' illustrates the way motion capture foregrounds certain aspects of the movement, such as, the relationships between different body parts, the angle of the joints, the dispersion and shifts of weight and the directionality in space (ACCAD OSU 2016). In this way, the mocap material reveals elements of a specific form that are key to the student's learning (Figure 6.3).

Moreover, Mann regards the particularity of motion capture to record motion without image as an additional benefit. He argues that motion capture offers students and teachers the opportunity 'to analyse movement from an objective, technical viewpoint without the distraction or pre-occupation of focusing on the

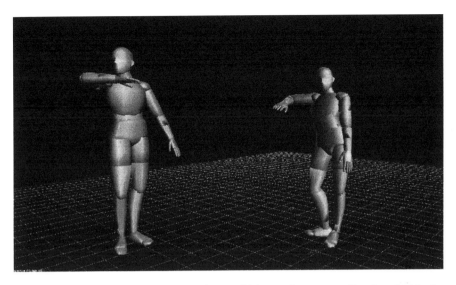

FIGURE 6.3   Patrick Wiabel's avatar and Marcel Marceau's avatar performing the 'At the
Bar' adagio

subject's external physical attributes such as body shape or the face' (Mann
[Chapman] 2018: np). Elaborating further, Mann explains that by erasing facial and
bodily characteristics, motion capture brings attention to 'the essence of an individual's movement rather than being distracted by the personality and qualities of
the external form' (Mann [Chapman] 2020 email communication with author). A
similar observation is made by Thompson in relation to her work with Marceau's
footage. As Thompson explained, she used to employ video recordings of Marceau's
work before she started working with the mocap footage. Considering the differences between the two 'instruction tools', Thompson noted that the student's
encounter 'with a set of dots demystified the [training] process' and removed it
from the authority of the master (Thompson October 2015 interview with author).
By removing the image of the specific body, with all its connotations, the students
could better concentrate on the movement. The same occurred with the recording
of the students' bodies. By using a set of identical, gender-neutral graphics to render
the motion of all the trainees involved in the learning of Marceau's adagio, the
recording, in and of itself, brings attention to the 'essence of the movement'
(Thompson October 2015 interview with author).

Within these representations, the students can still identify their own body, but
this identification operates by virtue of movement principles (for example, rhythm
and weight distribution) rather than a set of characteristics that can have a normative effect. In other words, as the students' movement in motion capture is denuded
of race, gender, age as well as other specificities with regard to the body's physical
state, the stranglehold of 'an economy of looks' (Evans 2009: 129), such as those
underpinning casting decisions, becomes loosened. We see, therefore, that whereas

the 'agnosticism' of motion capture can be an issue in instances of 'training for', in instances of 'training with', the technology liberates the form from a set of characteristics that can get in the way of the trainee's learning. Franke's observation that motion capture is blind to issues of representation can, in this instance, have a positive effect in that it democratises a physical discipline. To put it otherwise, whereas the decoupling of the movement from an image may lead to the body's disappearance, with all the implications that this may have for issues of representation, this can also work in reverse: it opens up the movement to those bodies that may have felt excluded by idealised images of the body.

Additionally, the range of 'visual codes' in which the movement may be rendered can have further pedagogical value, especially if we bear in mind that a significant part of the learning involved in any movement pedagogy is the development of the ability to recognise specific aspects of locomotion. For example, as mentioned already, in Biomechanics and mime, the training material is presented in a way that is closely aligned with the inherent emphasis of the pedagogy on the movement of the skeleton. Similarly, in the European funded project WhoLo-DancE, which explored the development of digital technologies for the learning of Ballet, contemporary dance, Flamenco and Greek Folk Dance, three avatars were developed, each having a different pedagogical aim: 'Directional guidance (The Arrowman avatar), Time-based motion volume (The Blob avatar) and Articulated visual (The Robot avatar)' (Cisneros et al. 2019: 62).[8] As the research team of the WhoLoDancE project explain, 'the more figurative avatars encourage the dancer to critically examine her movement *accuracy*, whilst the qualitative avatar encourages the dancer to engage more with her feeling state or mood' (Wood et al. 2017: 507, emphasis original). In this manner, Wood et al. (2017) identified the potential in the technology to enhance not only the skeleton-muscular understanding of a given form, but also the affective and emotional dimension of the movement. Finally, in 'Capturing Stillness', a fellowship project led by artist Ruth Gibson and examining the use of motion capture in Skinner Releasing Technique, a discipline that emphasises the function of imagery, different forms of visualisations were used. Some renditions of the captured data were presented in stick figures, whereas others 'had no overt human avatar presence but appeared to embody the dancing body in the way that they seem to breath, fold, and fly through a visual landscape, reflecting the metaphoric properties of the image action – such as "mist"' (Whatley 2015a: 200). For example, Figure 6.4 shows the rendition of the dancer's movement, who was working with the image 'axial shadow', into two pieces of cloth. Here, too, the form in which the data were presented was a key vehicle for the representation and dissemination of the pedagogy. Indeed, as Karreman argues in relation to Gibson's project, the value of the motion capture material lies in the way in which the reading of the image excites the 'kinesthetic imagination' (Karreman 2017: 215).

In view of the projects discussed thus far, it could be argued that motion capture constitutes a pedagogically sound medium not only for recording training, but crucially for providing the trainee with opportunities to engage with one's own movement. For example, Darren Tunstall's project 'Capturing the Moment' at the

FIGURE 6.4 'Falling Upwards', screenshot from Capturing Stillness Project

University of Central Lancashire, did not work with a codified movement language but aimed to explore the potential of motion capture to enable student actors to study their own movement. Furthermore, a key aspect of the projects discussed here involved the development of different mechanisms for enabling the students to work with the data. WhoLoDancE sought to create a set of digital tools for viewing and annotating the recorded material, including HoloLens, a mask that the trainee wore whilst dancing and on which they could see a synchronous rendition of their movement.[9] Figure 6.5 shows the avatar the dancer could see on the screen of the mask. Although the mask posed certain limitations in terms of the dancer's movement, it did not limit the dancer to the frontal orientation required by screens, thus enabling the synchronous unfolding of live and rendered movement.

In her project, Thompson and her team created opportunities for the students to view their recordings in relation to Marceau's recording. This, according to Thompson, served not as a corrective mechanism, but rather as a distilling process that could enable the students to identify what made their movement unique and specific (Thompson October 2015 interview with author). Similarly, the 'Capturing the Moment' project instituted an iterative process, whereby the trainee watched the visualisations of the mocap data alongside the trainer after the capture. Tunstall explains:

> I give them [the students] space to react, to make changes in another take, to view the changes, and to carry on until they are satisfied that some aspect of their movement has improved in their own judgement. At other times, we agree in advance on an intended outcome, and we work in the same way until we agree it is arrived at, or the student thinks they have achieved it to a degree even if I don't.
>
> (2012: 10)

FIGURE 6.5 Flamenco dancer working with HoloLens in Amsterdam, Holland

Echoing Mann and Thompson, Tunstall identifies the pedagogical merit of the 'drastic reduction in visual information' (2012: 6) which enabled the students to '"see" their movement qualities and habits more clearly than with other modes of representation' (2012: 8). As many trainers attest, therefore, despite, or perhaps because, motion capture presents motion without image, the visualisations foreground the kinetic 'signature' of each mover – 'their little quirks of movement, their gait, the suggestion of their body shape, their centre of gravity' (Tunstall 2012: 9), enabling a better understanding of one's embodiment as well as valorising their 'personal movement essence' (Thompson October 2015 interview with author).

It could be argued that the preoccupation with the way trainees encounter their movement data exemplifies a considerable trend in performer training to utilise a variety of audio-visual technologies and, in the process, intensifies the hermeneutic dimension of training. As I explained in the previous two chapters, an important factor in knowledge transmission in performer training is a hermeneutic action, through which the trainer 'reads' the bodies of the trainees according to a set of criteria underpinning a particular pedagogy. The trainer's active engagement in looking and sensing the trainees' bodies sets in motion an interpretative process, which can be eventually shared by the trainees, as the latter become gradually attuned to the aspects of their work the trainer is likely to monitor or search for as evidence of progress. Audio-visual technologies intensify this process by creating a material artefact – the recording – that the trainee, and the trainer for that matter, can continue to consult outside face-to-face interactions. According to the practitioners presented in this section, mocap recordings enhance the trainee's ability to interpret their work and, in this manner, institute an additional site for learning. It is instructive, in this sense, the comparison that Karreman draws between motion capture and other systems of movement notation, in terms of their ability to reveal or capture the 'corporeal truth' of a dance form. She argues that,

> while there is no such truth to be found [...] motion capture does offer us opportunities to create new worlds through which we may start to know dance differently – artistically, by creating new phenomenal images of dance; analytically, by gaining insight in spatial and rhythmical patterns; and gesturo-haptically, by offering the radical opportunity to re-enact the movement through mapping it on to other bodies.
>
> (Karreman 2015: 41)

As motion capture produces a distance between the trainee and their recording, it also creates what is often referred to as a 'me-not-me' effect (Tunstall 2012: 9; Wood et al. 2017: 508). The researchers involved in the WhoLoDancE project, for example, note that:

> The dancer is confronted with herself and a digital identity, dealing at once with her own corporeal in-body sensation whilst viewing her own avatar: a projection of herself, divided, separated yet with the potential to be merged, thus complicating the proposition, what is me and what is not me.
>
> (Wood et al. 2017: 508)

Furthermore, the space that opens up between the subject and her visual representation is considered to have ethical and political dimensions. As noted in the introduction, in this space between movement and data, Susan Kozel identifies a new form of ethics based on a different understanding of subjectivity. Drawing on Merleau-Ponty's phenomenology and Levinas' ethics, Kozel argues that the 'me-not-me' effect underpinning the mover's experience has wider implications:

> This dimension of live experience [i.e. that the body is both subject and object in the world] is brought into sharp relief when the body of the performer is split, transformed, multiplied by motion capture systems and visualisation techniques. When I encounter my digital self I discover that it is not simply me. [...] It is me because it is animated by my movement, but it is also other because it is separated from me by the thickness of the space between us and because it moves around and looks back at me – I am the one wearing the motion capture markers, the animation is projected onto a surface next to me, we are the same but we are different in space and in dynamic form.
>
> (2007: 239)

In the constant shift between being the subject of the movement and the object of the visualisation, Kozel traces an ethical dimension, since this double experience can alert human subjects to their 'objecthood' and equally make them aware of the affective potential inherent in non-human entities. Experiences of working with motion capture visualisations have for Kozel implications for 'the notion of a being: instead of a self-contained entity or agent, beingness is a changeable, dynamic construct, chiasmically connected to other beings and to the flesh of the world' (2007: 240). For Kozel then, motion capture environments are prime spaces for 'creating the conditions for an ethics that is not a prescriptive set of rules, but a value system based on a sensibility toward the other and the wider world' (2007: 215).

Echoing Kozel, in her analysis of the way motion capture was used in the project on Skinner Releasing Technique, Sarah Whatley argues that 'motion capture is a technology that can be used by artists to reveal fresh perceptual possibilities, somatic connections and new cultural, creative expressions' (2015a: 194). As I argued already, this process might be seen as a manifestation of a gestalt switch since, 'the modern technology that Heidegger was so wary of now produces work that is far from a "standing reserve" in its generation of interstitial experiments and expressions' (Whatley 2015a: 203). In its function of capturing, 'storing', 'distributing' and 'switching about' the performer's data, motion capture emerges as a concrete manifestation of the fundamental operation of technology that Heidegger diagnosed in 'The Question Concerning Technology' (1977: 16). Confirming Heidegger's thesis that 'where danger is, grows the saving power also' (1977: 34), Kozel and Whatley assert that this very function of the technology can have artistic, aesthetic and ethical implications. The 'danger' of motion capture thus turns into a form of 'saving power', by offering an embodied and perceptual experience that enables the performer and/or trainee to enter a responsive relationship with the technology and the world.

To sum up, training with motion capture both offers sophisticated means for documenting and analysing movement regimes and can create novel opportunities for embodiment: by enabling imaginative visualisations of the aesthetics of a particular dance form, as in Gibson's project; by offering opportunities for the same movement to be studied from different angles and across different bodies, as in Thompson's project; and by creating a sense of 'double' embodiment, with the physical body being grounded in sensation whilst an-other body emerges from the subject's identification with the data, enabling thus 'the dancer to exist within two realities' (Wood et al. 2017: 508).

'Training for' – 'Training with': a dialectic

In view of the examples of practice reviewed thus far, it could be argued that 'training for' and 'training with' encapsulate approaches to motion capture that are fundamentally different in key respects. In order to reveal these differences, this section discusses 'training for' and 'training with' in relation to three aspects of performer training practice: the components that comprise the training moment, i.e. who or what is present in the moment of training and where does this moment take place; the relationship between emerging and established pedagogies; and the relationship between training practices and wider contexts. The analysis that follows is accompanied by three graphs. In each graph 'training for' and 'training with' are positioned on a horizontal axis, which is traversed by a vertical axis. Each vertical axis represents one of the three aspects in terms of an interplay or tension of opposites: presence – absence (Figure 6.6); tradition – innovation (Figure 6.7); heteronomy – autonomy (Figure 6.8). Each graph, as well as the discussion that follows, aims to foreground a dialectic between 'training for' and 'training with'.

The first axis involves an interplay between absence and presence. As we saw, in introductory workshops that aim to prepare performers to work in the mocap industry (training for), the technology is absent, but will become present should the performer enter the professional field. By contrast, in workshops that use the technology with the aim to enrich the teaching/understanding of existing pedagogies (training with), the technology is present, but presumably it will be absent in the professional contexts in which the trainees might be employed. Furthermore, the presence–absence of the technology is in an inverse relation to the presence–absence of the trainer. As Paul Allain observes, 'since formalised or institutionalised actor training first began, it has been predicated almost exclusively on the core principle of live person-to-person coaching and guidance' (2019: 170). Introductory workshops of 'training for' are delivered through face-to-face encounters between trainer and trainees, following, in this manner, conventional configurations. By contrast, a key aspect of instances of 'training with' involves the employment of the motion capture recordings as an (additional) mechanism of knowledge production and transmission. For example, the WhoLoDancE project involved an annotation tool that allowed the students to view and annotate material they practised in the studio. Similarly, the projects on Biomechanics and mime respectively have an explicit self-directed dimension. Although, in both projects, face-to-face delivery is emphasised, in 'training with', motion capture visualisations enable learning to take place beyond the studio and in the absence of the trainer.

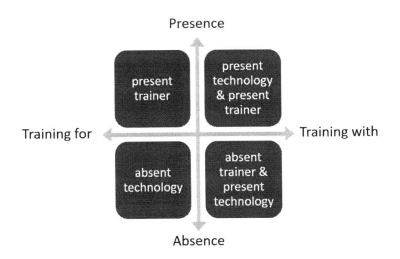

FIGURE 6.6   Presence – Absence Axis

The corollary between the presence–absence of the technology and the presence–absence of the trainer has additional pedagogical ramifications. As I demonstrated, in instances of 'training for', a considerable part of the training is aimed at familiarising the trainee with the requirements of the technology. Indeed, it could be argued that a key component of the trainer's job is to render present – through instructions, verbal description and anecdotes – the absent technology. In instances of 'training with', on the other hand, the technology is present, and as such can function as a substitute and, in a certain sense augmentation, of the teacher. Thompson's project draws on footage of a master that is no longer alive, whereas Mann's project records a form that has been developed nearly a hundred years ago. In both cases, the motion capture material is significant not only for the specific project but for the continuity and preservation of a training approach. In 'training with', in other words, the technology complements the teaching, for example by enabling the student to 'see' aspects of the training, which might be precluded in a physical demonstration. It also forms an important part of the legacy of a regime, by preserving a canonical embodiment of form-based methods, as is the case with Marceau's demonstration of adagios, and/or by offering novel visualisations of non-codified pedagogies, as is the case with Gibson's rendition of the SRT footage. It could be argued then that, even though the technology is not in the room, 'training for' is geared towards the development of the embodiment relationship between trainee and technology that will eventually allow the actor to become part of a larger equipmental context. 'Training with', on the other hand, is oriented towards enhancing the hermeneutic function, by examining how a pedagogy might be 'read' in a technologically mediated manner, for example through visualisations and annotation tools. In this process, there is a transposition of the source of knowledge, traditionally viewed to reside with the teacher, into a material artefact (Figure 6.6).

In this manner, 'training for' and 'training with' set in motion a reverse interplay between tradition and innovation. In some key respects, 'training for' can be seen as a new form of training: it involves a discrete curriculum, it is geared towards a specific medium and it is in the process of producing a new language that could be shared amongst the creatives that are involved in mocap production. Nonetheless, as it takes place through workshops, 'training for' follows a conventional route of dissemination. Although novel practices such as the Mocap Summit point towards the emergence of new sites of training, it can be assumed that until the technology becomes more affordable and accessible, the workshop model will continue to the be the most direct way for trainees to access instances of 'training for'.

By comparison, 'training with' can be seen as 'conservative', in the sense that one of its aims is to conserve a training regime rather than develop a brand new one. Indeed, as Thompson observes, the guiding rationale for capturing Marceau's movement was to 'preserve his technique for future generations' (Thompson October 2015 interview with author). It also bears noting that although Marceau had refused to have his work recorded in two-dimensional systems of notation, he agreed to being 'captured' by mocap (Thompson October 2015 interview with author). It seems therefore that motion capture can go some way towards addressing the

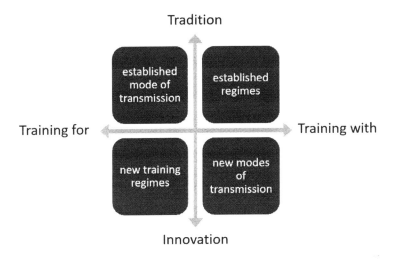

FIGURE 6.7   Tradition – Innovation Axis

longstanding suspicion that movement practitioners have towards documenting their work. And the reason for this might be precisely that, in comparison with other media, motion capture produces data that are less fixed and can reveal the 'subtlety and intention of the movement' in three dimensions (Thompson October 2015 interview with author). Accordingly, the use of mocap recordings in a teaching context can engender innovative modes for knowledge production and transmission. Within these modes, learning is assumed and constructed within a wider assemblage that combines face-to-face interactions between the trainer and the trainee, as well as mediated interactions between the trainee and the trainer's recording and/or between the trainee and their data (Figure 6.7).

The last node involves an interplay between autonomy and heteronomy. As we saw, 'training for' is self-funded and open to a wide audience, at least in the case of the introductory workshops. On the other hand, 'training with' tends to be project-based and participation is delimited to invited artists and/or students that undertake a degree programme. What is more, the different curricula that respectively comprise 'training for' and 'training with' belong to different cultural matrices. As noted, the syllabus of 'training for' draws on the 'visual codes' of popular culture, and existing pedagogies are utilised to enable the trainee to create material that is consistent with these codes. By contrast, the content of 'training with' is concerned with the pedagogies in and of themselves. Whereas in 'training for', technical accomplishment aims at enabling the trainee to develop accurate embodiments of combat and otherworldly creatures, in instances of 'training with', technical accomplishment is only relevant to the language and aesthetic of a particular regime. In this manner, 'training for' prioritises a set of heteronomous demands, originating from contexts outside the training, whereas 'training with' serves the needs that are intrinsic to a specific pedagogy and/or the trainee's movement.

This tension between heteronomy and autonomy also imbues the relationship between the body and the technology. As noted already, the recording of movement for motion capture requires an extensive amount of repetition. In 'training for', such repetition is presented as a demand that the body will have to meet by acquiring strength and stamina. In instances of 'training with', on the other hand, the technical characteristics of the technology are open for negotiation. For example, Whatley discusses the way the dancers in Gibson's project approached the technologically imposed necessity to repeat their movement as a way to reengage each time with different aspects of the SRT imagery. More radically, the relationship may be reversed, and the specificities of a pedagogy may be positioned as challenges that need to be matched by the technology. For example, in the SRT project, the principles of the pedagogy were treated as a way to

> test the limits and expansion possibilities of motion capture technology, because SRT, […], prioritises stillness, floor-based movement and action generated through image, all of which are not easily 'visible' to the sensors of the motion capture camera system.
>
> (Whatley 2015b: 93)

'Training with', in other words, prioritises the needs of the pedagogy and is independent of economic pressures. 'Training for', however, emphasises the demands that the technology will make of the performer, foregrounding a set of physical skills the performer will need to have in order to match the efficiency of the technology. In significant ways, 'training with' is free of the exigencies that underpin 'training for', a privilege that can all too easily be taken for granted.

Yet, this relation also has a reverse side. The independence that 'training with' enjoys is made possible by institutional and/or governmental structures and support. As such, instances of 'training with' develop within projects that are justified in terms of a digital turn in education, and tertiary education in particular. Often, the inclusion of motion capture in these projects is positioned within a rhetoric of 'technological enhancement' and 'learner's autonomy'. For example, the WhoLo-DancE project aimed to 'support autonomous learning' (Cisneros et al. 2019: 55). Similarly, Mann assumed that 'the motion captured etudes will […] enhance learning by enabling students to work individually, in great detail and at their own pace' (Mann [Chapman] 2018: np). As I argued, these aims might well engender new ways in which training is practised and conceptualised.

What I wish to point out here, though, is that these projects are also tied to a wider agenda and rhetoric. To begin with, the funding of these projects is premised on the adoption of a language that makes specific assumptions about the possible effects of the technology. According to the researchers of the WhoLoDancE project:

The educational objective of the WhoLoDancE project, as listed on the project website, is to 'disrupt the conventional mode of communication in teaching' through the use of technology. It is intended that this disruption could enhance the learning experience of the student, encouraging autonomy through reflection.

(Cisneros et al. 2019: 57)

However, as education scholars point out, the promises inherent in expressions of 'enhancement' and 'assistance' are both difficult to prove and replete with assumptions. Neil Selwyn identifies two key problems with the language of digital education, which particularly resonate with the description of the WhoLoDancE cited above:

First is the increased use of active, deterministic descriptions of the core relationships between technology and education – based predominantly around a privileging of 'learning' and the 'learner'. [...] Second is a heightened language of effect – often in evocative terms of 'impact' or 'transformation'. Here it is presumed that technology will lead to significant changes in educational arrangements and outcomes.

(2016: 439)

According to Selwyn, in addition to suggesting a range of benefits that are debatable, this language also masks 'the complex and compounded inequalities of the digital age' as well as corporate interests underpinning the development and administration of these systems (2016: 440). Echoing Selwyn, Caroline Wake makes a similar observation with regards to the considerable infrastructure and technical knowledge that is needed in supporting these technologies within performing arts education (2018: 61).

Moreover, scholars argue that the inclusion of technology in educational contexts and the development of so-called learning technologies is part of a wider neoliberalisation of education. Reviewing the economics of such a move, Feenberg argues that 'the promise of technology is the transformation of education into a decreasing cost item, like CDs or pencils. Initial investment in courses may be high, but the nth copy will be nearly free. Economies of scale will save mass education from bankruptcy' (2017: 365). According to Feenberg, then, the technologisation of education follows the logic that underpinned the technologisation of labour. Other scholars point out that understandings of autonomous or independent learning also align with a wider ideology of autonomy and self-reliance expected by subjects in neoliberal societies. Patricia Mccafferty identifies a 'cultural shift' in education that aims 'towards the creation [...] of a society of global entrepreneurial citizens' (2010: 546). Similarly, Loveless and Williamson note that, educational technology not only addresses learners as 'active, autonomous and self-responsible'; it also promotes such characteristics 'through new technological languages of schooling' (2013: 14). The technologisation of education, in other words, is part and parcel of a wider ideology guided not only by the financial gains of automatisation, but also by the creation of the neoliberal subject.

It could be objected that the practitioners and researchers involved in the projects reviewed here do not adhere to such ideologies. It could be further argued that, unlike the uniformity caused by mass-scale educational technologies, these projects enliven the learning process by constituting new relationships and interactions between trainers and trainees, trainees and pedagogy. If anything, the projects reviewed here demonstrate an acute sensitivity of the way the technology is bound to complement face-to-face teaching. However, the considerable funding and infrastructure upon which such projects rely inadvertently lead to an adoption of a language of 'educational technology'. This exposes the training to a set of assumptions that circulate outside the training space yet affect the way instances of 'training with' are presented both within and beyond the training studio.

Questions regarding the autonomy of training are, therefore, relative. By being self-funded and offered by private companies or individuals, 'training for' enjoys a degree of institutional independence, which is, however, compromised by its positioning as a nursery for the mocap industry. 'Training with', on the other hand, carves a space outside the applications of mocap in mass entertainment, and prioritises artistic and pedagogic experimentation. Such experimentation, however, is expected to operate as a form of 'enhanced learning', implicitly accepting the assumptions that underpin digital education (Figure 6.8). The question that emerges is whether the gestalt switch that instances of 'training with' can arguably effect on a somatic and individual level becomes undermined by the adherence of these projects to the values of educational technology. To put it otherwise, does a gestalt switch on an embodied and individual level becomes compromised, if it is not followed by an analogous switch in the institutional context?

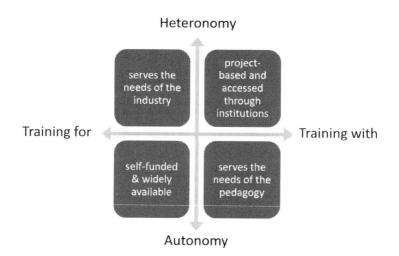

FIGURE 6.8 Heteronomy – Autonomy Axis

Conclusion

As this chapter demonstrated, motion capture has significantly influenced the performer training field, both in giving rise to new training products as well as in offering new possibilities for experiencing and working with established pedagogies. The key point made in this chapter is that instances of performer training practice involving motion capture need to be appropriately differentiated in order to bring into relief the way they meet and depart across a series of nodal points. Towards this end, the chapter proposed a mapping of performer training practices utilising motion capture in terms of 'for' and 'with'. As noted, these categories cannot account for every instance of training nor can they encapsulate all aspects of each project. For example, Thompson's project also involved the use of mocap technology in live performance and, as such, the training included both the use of Marceau's footage for training students in mime as well as the development of their ability to work with motion capture in synchronous environments. The example of Thompson's project demonstrates the propensity of practice to transcend artificial classifications.[10] For this reason, 'training for' and 'training with' are proposed as attitudes towards, rather than categories of, training. Their value lies not in offering neat classifications. Rather they enable a series of juxtapositions that sets in motion a dialectical relationship between training (bodies, pedagogies, learning contexts) and technology (artefacts, discourses, systems of production) in terms of questions of presence and absence, applicable to both the technology and the trainer; tradition and innovation; heteronomy and autonomy.

In the light of the very different assumptions and cultural matrices that underpin 'training for' and 'training with' respectively, it could be argued that the relation between motion capture and performer training confirms a social constructivist thesis. As I explained in the Introduction of this book, a constructivist view of technology asserts that despite its determinations, technology is also significantly shaped by social context. Indeed, as this chapter demonstrated, motion capture can serve the perpetuation of the hegemonic interests that underpin 'virtual labour', but also engender experimentation with novel modes of knowledge transmission. For example, the separation between movement data and image can both form the basis of exploitative contractual agreements as well as free training material from the tyranny of body ideals. In other words, a comparative analysis of performer training practice in terms of 'for' and 'with' foregrounded the way the same technology can be employed differently, serve a diverse set of aims, and become accommodated within different professional and institutional frameworks.

The interplay between presence and absence that underpins different instances of motion capture training also lends valence to Heidegger's thesis that the essence of technology is not identical with the presence or use of technological instruments. Instances of 'training for', specifically, exemplify a situation where the 'technology' in question cannot be limited to the technological artefact. In these instances, the propensities of the technology determine to a considerable extent the social formations and pedagogical processes that underpin training, even when the technological apparatus is not physically present in the studio. It could be further argued that the multiple effects of motion capture, produced regardless of the immediacy of the artefact, illustrate the prescience of Heidegger's account that argued that technology is an encompassing approach to the world. Indeed, the process of capturing, circulating and manipulating data that characterises motion capture can be seen as a paradigmatic exemplification of resources – in this case the performer's/trainee's/trainer's data – becoming 'stored up', 'transformed', 'distributed' and 'switched about' (Heidegger 1977).

As we saw, this very process has been interpreted in radically different ways. According to scholars who write in relation to instances that have been grouped here in terms of 'training with', various combinations between bodies and data have a generative potential, as they crystallise and reveal the poetics of a particular discipline. Moreover, these crystallisations emerge within a process that prioritises the development of the trainee's embodiment and offers the space for rehearsing a 'me-not-me' identity that has an ethical dimension. In this manner, instances of 'training with' are positioned as processes that transcend Enframing and create spaces where our relationship to machines and digital 'others' can become reconfigured. On the other hand, other accounts contextualise the technology within a history and ideology of efficiency. As I argued, instances of 'training for' align with such evaluations both in the way they prioritise technical accuracy as well as in terms of the arrangements they accept with regards to the performer's position in the mocap industry. Whereas Kozel 'emerged from the studio with new ideas regarding my own body, the materiality of digital data, and a shifted ontology by which I mean a shifted sense of what constitutes a being' (2007: 231), Salazar Sutil, Stahl, and Evans respectively alert us to a historical, yet persevering, operation of the technology to engender a subjectivity that is ideologically and somatically driven by efficiency.

A further comparison between 'training for' and 'training with' also reveals that even in instances where the technology is employed in novel ways, the reliance of training on institutional support necessitates a compliance with the agenda of educational technology. Although the use of technology in education may well serve pedagogical ends, it can also smuggle in a set of assumptions about what the technology can and is expected to achieve and how learners are understood and addressed. If instances of 'training for' are shaped by the needs of the industry, instances of 'training with' are argued and financed within a wider framework of digital education. In this case the use of motion capture enables the 'unlocking', 'transformation', 'storing up' and 'distribution' of training itself across a range of media and platforms. Whether saving power also lies in this process, remains to be seen.

Notes

1 Motion capture is also referred to as Performance Capture (PeCap). This latter term emphasises the 'total recording of a performance without cuts using a Motion Capture system' (Delbridge 2015: xi). I will use the term motion capture or mocap throughout the chapter, as this is the term most commonly encountered in both the industry and scholarship.

2 There are resonances between Stiegler's notion of the *pharmakon* and the interplay between danger and saving power suggested by Heidegger. Although Stiegler has engaged thoroughly with Heidegger's thought, he borrows the idea of the *pharmakon* from Plato, whereas Heidegger's source for the interconnections between danger and saving power is a poem by romantic poet Friedrich Hölderlin.

3 This might well change in the near future. Different companies have invested in building body suits that do not require the camera arrays and, as such, provide a portable and more affordable technology of motion capture. However, the cost is still considerable, and the quality of the data is poorer.

4 For a discussion of the interplay between practices of incorporation and inscription practices in digital technology see Timothy Lenoir (2002).

5 Similarly, Delbridge describes a step-by-step process to ease the performer into the mocap environment (2015: 65–73).

6 As Perry notes, each 'Hitting the brief' workshop is distinct and features a 'different thematic or character focus as well as specific performance/movement elements' for example, 'reptilian characters/movement, primates, tribal/ensemble performance' (Perry email communication with author 2020).

7 Nonetheless, as Burston suggests (2005), predicted employment in the film industry for actors was still significantly lower with the bigger inflection noted in animators and media workers.

8 The tools created for the project as well as the function of the various avatars can be seen on the project's website: www.wholodance.eu/Videos/ [accessed 17 April 2020].

9 An image of a dancer working with the HoloLens mask can be seen on the cover.

10 Another example of experimenting with the use of motion capture in live performance is Andy Lavender's project 'Motion capture for live performance: Mask and Avatar' (https://warwick.ac.uk/fac/arts/theatre_s/staff/prof_andy_lavender/ [accessed 6 April 2020]). Matthew Delbridge's work with motion capture (2015) also aims to serve the preparation of performers to work in the mocap industry as well as live performance.

References

ACCAD OSU (Advanced Computing Center for the Arts and Design Ohio State University). 2016. 'Technology for Mime Training and Devising of "There is No Silence"', *Theatre Dance and Performance Training Blog*, http://theatredanceperformancetraining.org/2016/01/technology-for-mime-training-and-devising-of-there-is-no-silence/#more-500 [accessed 16 November 2019].

Allain, P. 2019. 'Physical Actor Training 2.0: new digital horizons', *Theatre Dance and Performance Training Journal*, Special Issue Digital Training, 10 (2), pp. 169–86. doi.org/10.1080/19443927.2019.1609074.

Allison, T. 2011. 'More than a Man in a Monkey Suit: Andy Serkis, Motion Capture, and Digital Realism', *Quarterly Review of Film and Video*, 28 (4), pp. 325–41. doi: 10.1080/10509208.2010.500947.

Ayers, D. 2014. 'The Multilocal Self: Performance Capture, Remote Surgery, and Persistent Materiality', *Animation: An Interdisciplinary Journal*, 9 (2), pp. 212–27. doi.org/10.1177/1746847714527193.

Bestor, N. 2016. 'The Technologically Determined Decade: Robert Zemeckis, Andy Serkis, and the Promotion of Performance Capture', *Animation: An Interdisciplinary Journal*, 11 (2), pp. 169–88. doi: 10.1177/1746847716643928.

Burston, J. 2005. 'Synthespians among us: rethinking the actor in media work and media theory'. In: *Media and Cultural Theory*, edited by James Curran and David Morley. London: Routledge, pp. 250–62.

Cisneros, R. E., Stamp, K., Whatley, S. and Wood, K. 2019. 'WhoLoDancE: digital tools and the dance learning environment', *Research in Dance Education*, 20 (1), pp. 54–72. doi: 10.1080/14647893.2019.1566305.

Delbridge, M. 2015. *Motion Capture in Performance: An Introduction*. Hampshire: Palgrave, Pivot.

Dreyfus, H. 2002. 'Heidegger on gaining a free relation to technology'. In: *Heidegger Reexamined: Art, poetry, and technology*, edited by Hubert Dreyfus and Mark Wrathall. London: Routledge, pp. 163–74.

Evans, M. 2019. *Performance, Movement and the Body*. Hampshire: Palgrave Macmillan.

Evans. M. 2009. *Movement Training for the Modern Actor*. London: Routledge.

Feenberg, A. 2017. 'The Online Education Controversy and the Future of the University', *Foundations of Science*, 22 (2), pp. 363–71. doi.org/10.1007/s10699-015-9444-9.

Feenberg, A. 2015. 'Making the Gestalt Switch'. In: *Postphenomenological Investigations*, edited by Robert Rosenberger and Peter-Paul Verbeek. Lanham: Lexington Books, pp. 229–36.

Franke, A. 2014. 'A Critique of Animation'. *e-flux*, 59, pp. 000–000.

Freedman, Y. 2012. 'Is It Real … or Is It Motion Capture?: The Battle to Redefine Animation in the Age of Digital Performance', *The Velvet Light Trap*, 69 (2), pp. 38–49.

Heidegger, M. 1977. 'The Question Concerning Technology'. In: *The Question Concerning Technology and Other Essays*, translated by William Lovitt. New York: Harper, pp. 3–35.

Hollis-Leick, O. 2019. Email communication with author, April 2019.

Hutchison, S. and Vincs, K. 2013. 'Dancing in Suits: A performer's perspective on the collaborative exchange between self, body, motion, capture, animation, audience'. In: *Proceedings of the 19th International Symposium of Electronic Arts*, edited by K. Cleland, L. Fisher and R. Harley. Sydney, pp. 1–4.

Jennings-Grant, A. 2018. Movement Training for Motion Capture Performance Part 1–3, *Theatre Dance and Performance Training Blog*, http://theatredanceperformancetraining.org/?s=motion+capture&submit=Search) [accessed 19 November 2019].

Karreman, L. 2017. *The Motion Capture Imaginary: Digital Renderings of Dance Knowledge*. PhD Thesis, Ghent University.

Karreman, L. 2015. 'Worlds of MoCap'. *Performance Research*, 20 (6), pp. 35–42. doi: 10.1080/13528165.2015.1111049.

Kozel, S. 2007. *Closer: Performance, Technologies, Phenomenology*. Cambridge, Massachusetts: MIT.

Kozel, S. 2005. 'Revealing Practices', *Performance Research*, 10 (4), pp. 33–44. doi.org/10.1080/13528165.2005.10871449.

Lenoir, T. 2002. 'Makeover: Writing the Body into the Posthuman Technoscape Part Two: Corporeal Axiomatics', *Configurations*, 10, pp. 373–85.

Loveless, A. and Williamson, B. 2013. *Learning Identities in a Digital Age*. Oxon: Routledge.

Mann [Chapman], T. 2020. Email communication with author, April 2020.

Mann [Chapman], T. 2018. *Meyerhold's Biomechanics and Motion Capture*, Leaflet for A UCLan CELT Funded Research Project into movement training for actors, University of Central Lancashire.

Mccafferty, P. 2010. 'Forging a "neoliberal pedagogy": The "enterprising education" agenda in schools', *Critical Social Policy*, 30 (4), pp. 541–63. doi.org/10.1177/02610183 10376802.

Mihailova, M. 2013. 'The Mastery Machine: Digital Animation and Fantasies of Control', *Animation: An Interdisciplinary Journal*, 8 (2), pp. 131–48. doi: 10.1177/17468477134 85833.

Ng, J. 2012. 'Seeing Movement: On Motion Capture Animation and James Cameron's *Avatar*', *Animation: An Interdisciplinary Journal*, 7 (3), pp. 273–86. doi.org/10.1177/17468477 12456262.

Perry, S. 2020. Email communication with author, April 2020.

Perry, S. 2018. Phone interview with author, June 2018.

Pizzo, A. 2016. 'John Dower, Il lavoro con la motion capture: il regista e l'attore Intervista di Antonio Pizzo', translated by Antonio Pizzo, *Acting Archives*, 11 (May), pp. 70–81.

Salazar Sutil, N. 2015. 'Intelligence behind Movement: Laboratories of Biomechanics and the Making of Movement Utopia'. In: *Digital Movement: Essays in Motion Technology and Performance*, edited by Sita Popat and Nicolas Salazar Sutil. Hampshire: Palgrave Macmillan, pp. 35–52.

Selwyn, N. 2016. 'Minding our language: why education and technology is full of bullshit ... and what might be done about it', *Learning, Media and Technology*, 41 (3), pp. 437–43. doi: 10.1080/17439884.2015.1012523.

Stahl, M. 2011. 'The Synthespian's Animated Prehistory: *The Monkees*, *The Archies*, Don Kirshner, and the politics of "Virtual Labour"', *Television and New Media*, 12 (1), pp. 1–22. doi.org/10.1177/1527476409357641.

Thompson, J. 2015. Skype Interview with author, October 2015.

Thomson, I. 2009. 'Understanding Technology Ontotheologically, or: the Danger and the Promise of Heidegger, an American Perspective'. In: *New Waves in Philosophy of Technology*, edited by Jan Kyrre, Berg Olsen, Evan Selinger and Soren Riis. Hampshire: Palgrave McMillan, pp. 146–66.

Thomson, I. 2005. *Heidegger on Ontotheology*. New York: Cambridge University Press.

Tunstall, D. 2012. 'Capturing the Moment: the use of motion capture in actor training', Report on a Palatine Development Award, *The Higher Education Academy*.

Wake, C. 2018. 'Two decades of digital pedagogies in the performing arts: a comparative survey of theatre, performance, and dance', *International Journal of Performance Arts and Digital Media*, 14 (1), pp. 52–69. doi: 10.1080/14794713.2018.1464097.

Whatley, S. 2015a. 'Motion Capture and the Dancer'. In: *Attending to Movement*, edited by Sarah Whatley, Natalie Garrett Brown and Kirsty Alexander. Axminster: Triarchy Press, pp. 193–204.

Whatley, S. 2015b. 'Materiality, Immateriality and the Dancing Body: The Challenge of the Inter in the Preservation of Intangible Cultural Heritage'. In: *The Performing Subject in the Space of Technology*, edited by Matthew Causey, Emma Meehan and Neill O'Dwyer. New York: Palgrave, pp. 82–98.

Wood, K., Cisneros, E. R. and Whatley, S. 2017. 'Motion Capturing Emotions', *De Gruyter Open*, 1, pp. 504–13. doi.org/10.1515/culture-2017-0047.

CONCLUSION

Tools for preparation

The preceding chapters discussed different encounters between performer training and technology across past and present practices. The aim was not to offer an exhaustive mapping of the various applications of technology in the field of performer training nor to deliver a recipe of how technology ought to be used. Rather, the focus has been on the relationships, the series of 'and's', between various manifestations of technology and the histories, practices and discourses of performer training. Following Dewey's conviction that 'the goal of inquiry is not epistemic certainty' but rather the creation of 'ongoing interactions with novel situations by means of constantly refashioned artefactual tools' (Hickman 1992: xii), this study concludes with a presentation of a series of analytical tools that were trialled and developed in the preceding discussions. The aspiration is that these tools will prove robust and relevant enough to be taken forward, on the one hand, in the 'novel situations' which will surely emerge out of the ongoing interactions between performer training and technology; and on the other, in established discourse and practice, by de-familiarising aspects of performer training that have been taken for granted and rendering them 'novel'. These tools are:

An attitude of technology spotting, an ability to identify technology when we see it. A chief task of this book has been to bring attention to performer training practices that have been filed away as anti-, non- or pre-technological, and foreground not only that technology, in different guises, has been ostensibly present in training studios and laboratories, but also that performer training practice has been meaningfully engaged with it. In Chapter 2, I demonstrated that a conceptualisation of good acting as well as a rationale for actor training was connected to the intense technologisation of other crafts as well as the increasing capacities of machines during the late eighteenth century. Similarly, in Chapter 3 I discussed the performer training practice of the Open Theatre, which did not involve a technology as such, but was, nonetheless, guided by the group's intense preoccupation with the dominance of technological rationality in the United States after WWII.

An attitude of technology spotting also foregrounds one of the key methodological issues this study had to address. If, as philosophical understandings of technology stipulate, technology constitutes tool-led interventions in our environment, then it is bound to be present in one form or another in our dealings with the world. How then do we select what to study? This book chose a two-pronged approach, focusing, on the one hand, on specific artefacts and the way they are used, and, on the other, on processes of instrumentalisation, that is, the way in which a resource turns into a tool. As I discussed in Chapter 4, this approach is especially pertinent to the study of performer training, because performer training both features the use of tools for pedagogical purposes and is also characterised by an innate process of instrumentalisation, whereby the trainee turns into an instrument of expression. With regards to the first, the book prioritised artefacts, such as handheld objects, electric light circuits and digital devices, that figure prominently in performer training practice but have not been discussed as forms of technology. It also dealt with a 'background technology'. In Chapter 5, I examined the mobile phone as a device that becomes the focal point of the trainees' attention and looked at the function of the studio space as an organising force of the social and cognitive co-ordinates of learning.

Performer training practice features many more technological entities than the ones examined here, whether these are at the centre of the learning or in the background. One of the aspirations of this book is that it will instigate further interest in the technologies entities employed in performer training practice – cameras, balls, studio floors, ballet shoes, to name just a few; the way they operate in the learning process; and the insights they reveal about specific pedagogies, as well as the relationship between the users, the world of training and beyond. Indeed, if performer training has developed an awareness of its histories, language, politics, and ideologies, then it is reasonable to expect that it also needs to become alert to the technologies that populate physical and/or virtual learning spaces.

An attitude of technology spotting also troubled a crude periodisation between a technological and a pre-technological phase. Although digital technologies now increasingly penetrate the lifeworld as well as contemporary performer training practice, there is no single moment that can be marked out as a kind of beginning of the inclusion of technology in training. If anything, one of the aims of this book has been to extend the chronological remit of the investigation beyond the current (post-digital) moment and demonstrate that the influence and/or use of technology is not a recent phenomenon. Chapter 2 brought attention to the intense technologisation that underpinned articulations of the acting process during the eighteenth century, as well as the use of lights in Stanislavsky's work during the first half of the twentieth century. An area that would merit further attention is the use of technologies in preparatory practices that took place before the Enlightenment and/or in non-Western theatre contexts, as well as a comparative analysis between earlier applications of technology and current ones.

Finally, technology spotting may be useful not only for revealing new aspects of past and present practices. As technological artefacts become naturalised and absorbed within our lifeworld – mobile phones in our hands, cameras opposite our faces, sensing equipment in public and living spaces, medical implants inside our body – the ability to remain cognisant of their presence and function is all the more important. This is not to suggest that technology spotting should be prioritised over other forms of engagement with the lifeworld. It is rather proposed here, at least in relationship to performer training, as an invitation to meet the withdrawal of technology with an enveloping awareness of the different levels and kinds of mediation that structure processes of aesthetic formation and skill acquisition. What might we see (hear, feel, sense) then once we spot technology?

A polyfocal vision. As I argued throughout this book, the kind of seeing advocated here entails a process of multifaceted identification that recognises technology in the surrounding environment, embodied practices, intersubjective realm and institutional spaces. Such polyfocal vision also includes the ability to spot the artefact when it is present, as well as to appreciate the artefact's impact when it is absent. To state the obvious, artefacts are made. And they are made to function according to pre-planned co-ordinates dictated by prior design, the user's skills and social context. A technological artefact, therefore, is always haunted by multiple histories; the history of its production, previous use, the aims it was expected to serve. This baggage becomes particularly heavy when the artefact is an object that has penetrated daily and domestic life. As we saw in Chapter 3, even though no television set was physically present in the training studio of the Open Theatre, television, during the 1960s, had a formative function in how information circulated, meaning was made and identity was formed. Although very different from the television, the phone exerts a similar influence today. As I argued in Chapter 5, regardless of whether the device is present or not, what also needs to be taken into account is how it has shaped the 'already there', that is the cognitive, embodied and social attitudes that structure and give meaning to a pedagogy. Motion capture is also very different from the mobile phone and the television, but, as I concluded in Chapter 6, an analysis needs to be mindful of the wider agendas that make its use in training contexts possible in the first place. My proposition, therefore, is that we need to train a vision that can see the artefact itself and how it may operate within the training space, but also the baggage it brings with it. Although an examination may prioritise a specific focus over others, how wide or narrow we cast the net of the analysis will have ramifications on the insights produced.

An ability to appreciate nuance and complexity. As I discussed in the Introduction as well as in Chapter 3, accounts of technology within the performer training field often tend to be polarised between technophilic and technophobic attitudes. Sometimes, this polarisation is present in the positions voiced by practitioners and may well underpin personal dispositions towards technology. I also demonstrated, however, that such polarisation is also the result of historiographical bias that has projected a set of oppositions between bodies and machines, presence and technology, onto instances of practice that are far more nuanced. Relationships with technology are complex and *need* to be complex because technology is not only something we use, but also something we grapple with. Scholarly accounts as well as pedagogical praxes might therefore have to occupy contradictory or paradoxical positions. As Chapter 2 showed, references to the machine in Stanislavsky's work are underpinned by stark contradictions. On the one hand, the machine denotes a profound automatisation of technique which enables the sleek function of the performer's bodymind. On the other hand, it is associated with mindless repetition of a set of skills or habits. More widely, the enduring tendency to refer to and/or approach the actor's bodymind as an instrument is bound to invoke the spectre of efficient technologisation on the one hand as well as the freedom of creative expression on the other. As I argued in Chapter 3 with reference to the career choices of members of the Open Theatre, and in Chapter 4 with reference to the career paths that are available to performers today, these two positions are not mutually exclusive. They overlap, inform and undermine one another. Attention to nuance and complexity therefore may enable a pedagogy to foreground the ethics involved in different positions towards technology and enable students to navigate the unavoidable slippage between expressive and professional instrumentalisation.

An analytical framework that includes both material and organic resources. One of the preoccupations of this book has been to explore the way in which performer training deals with matter, and to develop an analytical framework that can be applied whether the matter in question is a set of artefacts or the trainee's very organism. This is not to erase the differences between the two but to point out that precisely because performer training practice approaches both types of resource as possible instruments, the same attitude may prevail. In Chapter 2, for example, we encountered an approach towards matter, manifesting in the eighteenth, nineteenth and early twentieth centuries, that sought to control it and bend it to artistic will. In Chapter 4, on the other hand, we encountered an approach towards matter, evident from the mid-twentieth century onwards, that makes space for and listens to matter's behaviour. As we saw in Chapter 4, different twentieth-century pedagogies manifest a significant appreciation for the affordances and behaviours of specific objects and approach them as a source of knowledge.

The interrelationship between organic and material resources also points towards the wider question of mastery. As we saw in Chapter 2, the need for a systematic education for the actor emerges during the Enlightenment period in line with advancements in technology and technique. Against the standardisation that machines make possible in various forms of human activity, the actor is also expected to feature the same kind of exactness and reliability. This understanding continues into the nineteenth century and underpins the call for the systematisation and institutionalisation of actor training programmes. In this configuration, training is presented as a necessary mechanism that will cultivate the actor's 'instrumentalism'; that is, the actor's ability to execute a series of physical and vocal tasks in a precise and fixed fashion, and in this way rid the stage of mistakes and infelicities. As I argued, in this configuration, training was expected to enable the actor to demonstrate the kind of efficiency expected of technology, and, indeed, prove that human beings could be as trustworthy as machines. What is more, whereas theatre accounts foreground the volatility of the human organism, the question of whether machines are in practice as reliable as they are deemed to be in theory is absent. The idea of the actor's instrument continues into the twentieth century and underpins the development of the first concrete system for training actors. In Stanislavsky's System we find an acceptance of the common assumption that an actor has to develop a range of expressive resources to a high standard, so she can navigate the vagaries of inspiration, as well as an appreciation that acting needs to be more than the exact repetition of a role.

As discussed in Chapter 3, in the 1960s, technical mastery becomes contested and performer training becomes tasked with resolving the conundrum of enabling the actor to develop expressive proficiency, which, however, could be qualitatively differentiated from 'mere' technical accomplishment. The way 1960s avant-garde theatre practice squared this circle was by explicitly identifying actor training as a means of preparation of a new sensibility. Training, and the many practices that comprised it, set out to enable collectives and individuals to experiment with sensory, psychological and ideological modalities that transcended, or outright challenged, established ways of being, behaving and acting in the United States in the 1960s. The expectation was that the new sensibility, expressed through an appropriate medium, would enrich and enlarge the experiential gamut of the spectators.

In contemporary configurations, the use of motion capture technology in the game and film industry has brought renewed emphasis on the development of precision, exactness and repeatability. Against a panoptic and tireless technological system, the performer is expected to achieve a level of physical efficiency that resonates with the understanding of good acting put forward by Dennis Diderot and Gordon Craig over a century earlier. As we saw in Chapter 6, the actor's employment in the mocap industry is premised on one's ability for precise repetition, even though the technology is allowed to fail – as it often does, when for example the system cannot calibrate the performer's data according to the co-ordinates of the chosen graphic visualisations. Nonetheless, in the same chapter we also encountered instances of the use of motion capture systems in performer training and/or experimental performance practice that are premised on a responsive attitude. In this configuration, fallibility, understood both in terms of a human mistake as well as a technological glitch, is not only allowed but exploited as a possible source of spontaneity and creativity.

As the performer's expression incorporates additional media and tools, presence, what makes the performer watchable and worth the audience's attention, is no longer premised on the tight control of her expressive media, whether these are parts of her own organism or parts of the technological infrastructure. Rather what is now valued is an ability to make space and work with the prior admission that technology, like humans, is prone to unexpected behaviours. Technological efficiency, therefore, becomes again redeemed by a 'sensible' attitude. The added twist, of course, is that this time such attitude develops through relations with tools, machines and networks. We see therefore that although technologies, as well as aesthetic and cultural contexts, change, the question of mastery persists. In other words, what remains constant amidst the historical and pedagogical variations is that an encounter between humans and machines is bound to position the accomplishment of the former in terms of the capacities of the latter. And such positioning has not only aesthetic but also ethical and political repercussions. As discussed in Chapters 3 and 6, approaches to mastery are not only paradigmatic of one's engagement with tools, they exemplify a distinct approach to the world, equated by Heidegger with technology and techne respectively.

Finally, an ability to extend our definition of instrument to include both animate and inanimate tools becomes all the more important in light of recent calls to performing artists to develop a brand out of a self and in view of the expectation that training curricula should facilitate the development of both expressive and entrepreneurial skills. Against the pragmatic tone of these calls, Chapter 4 sought to demonstrate that self-branding needs to be seen as part of a longer history of instrumentalisation that started with the exploitation of natural resources and culminates in practices of self-exploitation. An understanding of performer training through the philosophy of technology may alert us to the philosophical affinities that creative instrumentalisation shares with professional instrumentalisation, as well as to the fundamentally different ethics that underpin these positions.

A propensity to tinker. The book brought attention to the way specific artefacts became appropriated within learning contexts and the way performer training offers opportunities to explore novel interactions, often beyond quotidian use. Chapter 4 examined the use of a range of tools, which, in some instances, became modified to suit learning purposes, and/or were employed in ways other than the established ones. Future explorations may also focus on the way readily available technologies can offer possibilities for learning outside or beyond prescribed modes. This may not only foster an 'inquerential' attitude towards technology. When the tools in question are digital devices, an approach that offers different interpretations of and/ or purposes for the tool's function, can also upset existing cultures of use. In Chapter 5, I offered an exercise I devised in my own teaching practice as an example of the way the sedimented function of text messaging may open up new ways of engaging with the surrounding environment, offer new hermeneutic strategies for capturing the trainees' process, and finally renew notions of attention. The invitation this book extends to those involved in performer training and wish to use technology is to tinker away and consider how technology might be used in different, novel or unexpected ways.

It is hoped that the five tools listed above, as well as the discussions in the preceding chapters, may prove relevant not only to scholarship on performer training, but also in its actual practice. As performer training is responding to the technologisation of the performing arts industry as well as to institutional preferences towards blended or online modes of learning, the tools presented here might be useful in enabling pedagogues and trainees to navigate a series of questions, concerning the selection and inclusion of ready-made technologies in the learning process; the expectations and assumptions underlining specific artefacts; as well as the additional, non-conventional ways in which artefacts can be used. As such, these tools may contribute towards fostering and/or sharpening experimentation with various technologies that is already happening at a local level but also enable performer trainers to (re)consider the established pedagogies they have been working with.

It is hoped that this study might also be relevant to the creation of practices that combine artistic and embodied knowledges with wider political questions. At the moment this might be an emergent trend. However, if a current emphasis on preparation as a strategy for dealing with different problems is anything to go by, it can be assumed that the ability to enlist somatic disciplines, nurture latent possibilities for perception and sociality, and develop new ones, will matter all the more. To the vocabularies and encounters that seek to draw on in-depth embodied knowing towards responding to environmental and political crises, this book aims to contribute two key ideas: one is that embodied practice and technology are bound in a reciprocal relationship. Embodied practice often takes its cues and/or is facilitated by technology, whilst technology, in order to be used and function properly, relies on some form of embodiment relationship. The second interrelated point is that positioning embodied practice outside the technological sphere would not only be erroneous. It would be missing the opportunity to mobilise somatic intelligence towards opening up new ways of approaching and using technology. In other words, the promise of training to serve as a place of artistic, social and possibly political regeneration, can only be fulfilled when its profound interrelationship with technology is acknowledged and explored.

As such, this book also aspires to serve as a kind of introduction of the performer training field to scholarship on technology. In his conclusion to *Technology and the Lifeworld*, Ihde identifies the actions required for dwelling in the world harmoniously: 'it remains the task of the inhabitants [of the lifeworld] to cultivate the right weight and lightness of movement to maintain a balance within that world. We have not yet done that, but it may be still be possible to learn the movements' (1990: 224). Ihde's expression may be seen as paradigmatic of the lyrical tone that is often encountered in the final sections of scholarly analyses. Yet, the sentence is also revealing of the embodied interactions between inhabitants and lifeworld, and, most crucially, of the processual and 'trainable' dimension of such interactions. This book took Ihde's references to learning movements and negotiating gravity at face value: learning movements and working with weight is what practitioners of performer training arguably do and understand best.

The task that emerges from this study is to occupy a position that recognises the relevance that performer training knowledge may hold for the current moment whilst acknowledging the contradictions and challenges inherent in its practice. The book endeavoured to strike a balance between a position that advocates the promise of training, and technology, to refashion selfhood, and an alertness to the insidious ways in which training, and technology, may serve hegemonic interests. Training is not the 'real' thing. It is an opportunity for exercising a response, so that when the 'real' thing happens – a performance, a rehearsal, or indeed a revolution – one is prepared. By the same token, however, training is real, as it effects a change in the here and now, and it can structure what in the end will be revealed as real and, most importantly, as possible. This book attempted to cut a window between the disenchanted world in which training takes place and (towards) a world full-of-wonder that training can arguably constitute. It is hoped that future analyses, practices and embodied knowledges will take this project further.

References

Hickman, A. L. 1992. *John Dewey's Pragmatic Technology*. Bloomington and Indianapolis: Indiana University Press.

Ihde, D. 1990. *Technology and the Lifeworld: From Garden to Earth*. Bloomington and Indianapolis: Indiana University Press.

INDEX

Aagaard, J. 123–4, 131
absence *171*, 177; of category of
  technological mediation 96; interplay
  with presence 171, 177; of involvement
  38; of mediating effect of alphabet 103;
  of methodical work and commitment
  76; of specific devices 85; of
  technological artefact 21; of technology
  and trainer 150, 171–2
ACCAD (Advanced Computing Centre for
  the Arts and Design) 164
actor training 8, 80; avant-garde, promise
  of 84; dominant approach in United
  States 75; early twentieth-century 60;
  establishment of 23; ethics of 100;
  history, twentieth-century 53;
  institutionalised 171; means of preparing
  new sensibility 186; modern 53; need for
  35; panel on 8; pedagogy 23; Physical,
  Introduction to 16; politics of 3;
  publication on 75; rationale for 182;
  Reader, Routledge 35; Russian lineages
  of 35; turning point in 1960s 86n5; in
  United States, historical examination of
  86n5; viewed as perpetual apprenticeship
  125
actor training course/programme
  institutionalisation of 185; participation
  in 31; Stanislavsky's 36
actor training developments 31; during
  1960s 60; in avant-garde circles 62
actor training practice 23; established 76;
  nineteenth- and early twentieth-century

36; systematisation of 33; twentieth-
  century 45
actor/performer as instrument 21–2, 30, 35,
  54, 76, 93; bodymind as 185
adagios 164, *165*, 172
aesthetic inner (subtle) body-mind 100–1
aesthetic sensibility 72–5, 78
Alexander Technique 75, 92
Alfreds, M. 4, 18, 95, 107–8, 111
Allain, P. 1, 8–9, 16, 171
alterity: pedagogical function of 108;
  relational framework 138; relationship
  105–9, 111, 115, 123–4, 141
anti-technological 21; development of
  psychophysical resources 85; performer
  training practices 182
appropriation 81; of digital technologies 17;
  humans approach nature with inclination
  towards 70–1; of material objects 91; of
  online platforms 17; pedagogical 120; of
  performer training practices 10;
  pharmakon suggests possibility of 126;
  process of 112; tactic of Open Theatre
  82; toolbox evokes sense of 90
Aronson, A. 63, 65–7, 77
attention 129; ability to master 132; alterity
  relationship 105, 123; audience 186; as
  by-product of selection and exclusion
  130; effects of tools and platforms on 16;
  in Embodiment Relationship regulate/
  command 53; mobile phone 124; in
  motion capture focused on movement
  165; Stanislavsky's work on 34

attention, concentrated 69, 129; inability for 131; preference for 121, 132, 138

attention, deep 134; essential for coping with complex phenomena 133; expected in training situation 136; favoured by Stiegler 128; normative cognitive quality expected 132; sense of organisation and immersion underpins 135

attention, directed/directing: away from face-to-face interactions 124; to different parts of physiology and environment 57n25; modes of 130

attention, heightened 121, 131; preference for 138, 142; valorised by psychophysical paradigm 135

attention, hyper 133–4; characterised by switching focus rapidly between tasks 132; multitude of stimuli inherent in 135

automata 106; distinction between actors and 53; eighteenth-century 36, 43, 52, 57n20; increased sophistication of 93; invention of 54; performing/ performance of 23, 33–4, 44; replacement of humans with 45; replica of Queen Marie Antoinette 56n15; toured in European metropoles 56n16

automaton(s) 39, 43; actor as 43–4, 57n20; people becoming 80; Players 53; Tympanon Player 56n15; Vaucanson's 44

autonomous: force of technology 12–13; of human experience, worldly sensibility 25; human subject dethroned by posthuman 14; learners 175; learning, support by WhoLoDancE project 174; learning, understanding of 175; will, distributed cognition replaces 14

autonomy 25, 175; ability/need for self-determination and 84; diminution of power to claim 162; and heteronomy 150, 171, 173–4, *176*, 177; learner's 174; performer training acquires 10; of training 176

avant-garde 64, 1960s scene 63; actor training 84; artistic practice 71; artists 65, 68; circles 23, 62, 86n6; guru 67; performances 61, 85; practices 65, 86n6; project 75–6; sensibility 65

avant-garde experimentation 65; in performer training 55

avant-garde practitioners 65, 68, 78; American 75; resisting technologisation 93

avant-garde theatre 61–2, 75, 1960s 62–4, 84, 151, 186; ability to effect change 76; American 61; captured rapidly shifting consciousness of new age 66; groups 75; practitioners 65–6; scholarship on 61; training 76; view of television 82

avatars *165*, 179n10; figurative or qualitative 166; function of 179n8; seen on screen of mask 167; viewed by dancers 169

Barba, E. 63
Barker, C. 8, 10
Baugh, C. 23, 31, 33
Beck, J. 65, 75–6, 84
Benedetti, J. 63
Berry, M.D. 6, 13, 19, 121–2, 124, 141
Bigsby, C.W.E. 61, 63–5, 75
Bishop, C. 67, 143n9
Blumenthal, E. 67, 77, 80, 83–4, 86n8
Brey, P. 92, 94, 98–101
Brook, P. 18, 63, 67, 93
Bodroghkozy, A. 81–2

Camilleri, F. 1, 18–19, 90, 143n4
Cage, J. 64–5, 135
Camp, P. 32–3
Campbell, C.T. 134–5
Casey, T. 45
Chaikin, J. 20, 61–2, 67, 73, 77–8, 80–1, 83–4, 86n7
circles of attention 36, 51, 53, 57n25, 110, 130, 142
codified: forms 163; movement language 167
cognition distributed 14; enactive, theoretical framework of 130; new modes emerging from digital technologies 126
computer-generated imagery (CGI) 149
Coquelin, C. 30–1, 46–9
counter-cultural: clichés repeated by performers 76; critique 68; ends, technological artefact harness for 82; youth movement in United States 63
Craig, E.G. 31–2, 34, 44–51, 54, 57n19, 57n22, 186
Crary, J. 3, 6, 122, 125, 128–9, 132–4, 143n5
creative industries 10, 25n3, 94; actor professionalisation within 85; hard realities of 112; marketisation of self evident in 115; professional instrumentalisation expected in 24; recent developments 22; technologies of self-exploitation within 114
Crossley, M. 1, 17–18

Cunningham, M. 141

dance ballet 166; of the cellophane 110; company bgroup 127; contemporary 164, 166; Flamenco 166; Greek Folk 163, 166; images of 169; measured 47–8; notators 17; and Performance Training Journal, Theatre 16, 95, 143n1; practitioners 149; screen 127; Theatre, Judson 64; training 9, 135; WhoLoDancE 166–7, 169, 171, 174–5, 179n8
dance form 169; aesthetics of particular 170
dancers 11, 40; avatars 166–7, 169; confronted with self 169; crossover 9; existing within two realities 170; famous 57n19; Flamenco *168*; in Gibson's project 174; modern 9; movement, rendition of 166; state of polyattentiveness 141; working with HoLoLens mask *168*, 179n9
Dewey, J. 91–3, 96–7, 101, 111, 116n2, 116n3, 116n4, 182
De Preester, H. 99–100, 116n6
De Preester, H. and Tsakiris, M. 100
Diderot, D. 23, 31–40, 42–50, 52, 54, 55n6, 56n7, 56n8, 56n10, 56n13, 57n19, 57n20, 60, 76, 80, 186
digital 13; age 175; area of study 13–14; artefacts 2, 16, 121; creation 150; Creativity 143n1; data 154, 178; Department for 25n3; environment 154; equipment 18; humanities 11; identity/self 169; media 14, 115; medium 141; 'others', relationship to 178; performance 32; postdigital moment 183; practices 9; product, composite 150; resources 16; surveillance 122; Theatre 16; tools 167; training 7, 16–17, 115, 143n1
digital education 176, 178; language of 175; turn in 174
digital culture 7, 13, 17; attention as key theme in relation to 121, 142; changes effected by diffusion of 15; contemporary practice in relation to 24; differing approaches to 14; place of training within 16; social and political crises 132
digital devices 115, 183; closing temporal gap between experiencing and writing 140; cultures of use 187; diffusion of 14; experimentation with 1; mobile phone most common 147; use in relation to training practice 121

digital technologies 1, 18, 122; adverse effect on attentive capacities assumed 132; appropriation for training 17; causing epigenetic change 15–16; development for learning of dance 166; difference from non-digital technologies 115; effects of 24; engender modes of attention 126; examined through postphenomenology 94, 116; fragmentation and dispersion of attention caused by 131; harnessed for training purposes 16; inclusion in training 115; incorporation and inscription practices in 179n4; influence performer penetration in daily life 3, 14, 183; training practices 21; influence on regimes predating 32; issues in working with 2; use in performer training 116; use as means to address emerging needs 15
distraction 129, 132, 134; actors required to avoid external 130; ascribed to internal psychological shortcomings 131; differentiation of attention from 129, 131; expensive 155; of focusing on external physical attributes 164–5; instances of 142; as mode of attention 133; as pathology 133; phone use as source of 128; polyattentiveness not threatened by 135; state to be remedied by education in breathing 131; subjectivity prone to 143; technology positioned as source of 155, 162; through use of darting light 110
Dorrestijn, S. 12–13

economy of looks 105, 165
ecstatic surface (sensorimotor) body 100
educational technology 131, 175–6; agenda of 178
electric light 109; circuits 183; propensity to illuminate part of space 110, 130; replacing gas 55n1
embodiment 108; agentic power of 91; aspect of, evaluating 104; attention constitutes process of 125; developed through training 101; dialogue with forms of 139; education in 4; emphasis in performer training studio 95; of form-based methods, canonical 172; by master teacher 164; mediatropic 122, 139; mocap creating sense of double 170; mocap enables better understanding of 168; mode of mobile phone 122; new modes emerging from digital technologies 126; new state of, tool

contributes to 102; novel opportunities for, training with mocap offers 170; practices 5, 90; processes of, cultivation of new practices relies on 126; relationship 98–100; sedimented 138; seen as form of mediation 94; sites of novel experiences of 14; state of, possible to cultivate 143; subsuming, under technology 93; of tools 99; understood as processual and emergent 101

embodiment, performer's/user's: alignment with intentionality of technological equipment 160; stick as instrument to reveal aspects of 104; Zarrilli's fourfold model of 100

embodiment relationship 98, 188; closed circuit between user and artefact 104; development between trainee and technology 172; effects of texting on 139; foundational for trainee 105; in mocap environments 158; multilocal 158; in performer training involving artefacts 138; in play between user and motion-capture suit 147; possible when artefact and user are in contact/interaction 101; required in mocap 158; successful 114; tool as hallmark of 99; use of sticks 116n6, 158; between trainee and artefact 102, 111; We-Tool-World formulation 100

embodiment, trainee's 7; changes in 6; clues emanating from 140; of combat and otherwordly creatures 173; development of 178; material tools constitutive of 111; of particular regime 164; of specific regime/exercise 105; of suggested movement-qualities 109

embody/embodying: creatures, participants expected to 158; dancing body, avatars appear 166; parts of a machine, actor's attempts to 79; intra-organic tools, trainee learns to 105; kinetic relations 139; movement of certain material 110; object's behaviour 108

emotion: actor's training based on 78; appropriate, actor's selection of/control over 46; enacted, audience process of experiencing 40; evoked in spectator 40; exhibit rapid succession of 37; importance in acting 36; ousted by Diderot's acting technique 45; portrayed, actors feeling 44; portrayed, actors should not feel 38

emotional: attitude 50; desires 71; dimension of movement 166; display 82; experience 44, 77; expression 46, 130; intensity 161; life, rich 95; outbursts 37; registers, narrow 77; response of audience 40; with role 36; sensibility 50; traits or dispositions 96; world of the play 46

emotional involvement/engagement 46; aroused in spectators 48; in dramatically charged moments 38; during performance 37; putting an end to 40

Encyclopaedia (*Encyclopédie, ou dictonnaire raisonné des arts et des métiers*) 31–3, 36–40, 42–4, 54, 56n8, 56n10, 56n13

Enframing 70–2, 85, 178

Enlightenment period 12, 45, 50, 183, 185

etudes 164; Meyerhold's 95, 164; motion captured 174

Evans, M. 1–2, 6–7, 14, 19, 90–1, 104–5, 139–40, 149–50, 157, 160–3, 165, 178

Feel/Hear/See/Do 135–6, 141; exercise exploits/disrupts sedimented embodiment of phone use 138; minimal temporal lag 140; trainees working outside 137

Feenberg, A. 12, 69–70, 72–4, 86n3, 86n4, 94, 112, 151–3, 175

fictive: actor training course, Stanislavsky's 36; body (aesthetic outer) 101; diary, Stanislavsky's 52

film 19, 26n3; action, aesthetic of 160; detail available in 154; difference from stage 67; editing 67; exercises 143n11; material 160; and performing arts industry 15; production 153; scene or movement 160; set, infrastructure found on 156; show reel, personal 162; subject matter 158; technological powers of 19; use of mocap in 149–50

film industry 153, 186; predicted employment in 179n7

filmic: cameras, intentionality of 157; montage 82; profilmic realities 154

Fogerty, E. 31, 34, 47–9, 51, 55n2

Franko, M. 44, 57n20

Fuller, B. 67–8

Furse, A. 104–5

Garrick, David 32, 37, 53, 55n3

gender: motion capture denuded of 165; neutral graphics 165; performativity 10

gestalt 99, 103–4; underpinning hermeneutic relationship 105

gestalt switch 25, 151, 170; compromised 176; at intersubjective and somatic level 153; understanding of 152–3

Gibson, R. 166, 170, 172, 174
Gilman, R. 75–6
Goodden, A. 38
Goodman, P. 75–6
Greco, E. 17; movement language 17
Grotowski, J. 63, 67–8, 75–6, 97, 101
Gunkel, J.D. and Taylor, A.P. 7, 115

Hansen, M. 4, 25n1
Hayles, K. 14–15, 130, 132–4, 143n7
Heidegger, M. 4–5, 22, 54–5, 61–2, 68–72,
    76–7, 83, 85, 89, 91, 93, 105, 107, 112,
    114, 123, 151–2, 170, 177–8, 179n2,
    187
hermeneutic relationship 102–3; accessible
    from outside 104; becomes (re)mediated
    141; operates on premise of gestalt 103,
    105; origins in development of writing
    102; underpins trainee/trainer
    interactions 111
Heron of Alexandria 43; see also automata
heteronomy and autonomy 150, 171,
    173–4, 176, 177
Hickman, L. 91, 93–4, 96–7, 116n2,
    116n3, 116n4, 182
homo cellularis 122, 128
Hulton, D. 61, 64, 66, 77, 82

I-Technology-World: hermeneutic
    category 102; relationships 93–4, 98, 111
Ihde, D. 5, 11–13, 22, 60, 70, 89–98, 100,
    102–7, 110–12, 114–15, 116n2, 121,
    123–4, 138, 141, 157, 161, 188; see also
    I-Technology-World
immunity 143; polyattentiveness considered
    as 135; practice of 142
Innes, C. 49, 63, 65–7
innovations: on actor's technique 21; of
    Chaikin and Open Theatre 84; Irving's
    lighting 49–50; Open Theatre, television
    as source of 21; technological 43; in
    theatre lighting 32; theatrical, television
    as resource for 24; tradition and 150,
    171–2, 173, 177; Vaucanson's chief 44
innovative: directions in pedagogy/artefact
    use 112; modes for knowledge
    production and transmission 173;
    practice in content creation/pedagogical
    appropriation 120; training approach,
    Open Theatre's 68
instrument 11, 48, 114; actor's body
    compared to 30, 33–4, 76; cut across
    traditional boundary lines 96; definition
    extended 187; distinction between
    different types 97; embodied processes

constituting 89; humans represented as
    79; material and organic resources as
    possible 185; mechanical 79; player of
    44; related to crafts, development of 43;
    relationship of user with 114; reveals
    aspects of user's embodiment 104;
    scientific 114; technological 70;
    technological, use of 7, 70, 177; theatre
    23, 31; training turns trainees into 6; use
    of 103; see also actor/performer as
    instrument
instrument of expression: actor as 30;
    creative explorations made possible by
    115; development of 7, 85; key aspect
    mastered 53; preparation renders trainee
    into 7, 183; resources turned into 76; self
    becomes 93
instrument, actor's/performer's 21–3, 30–1,
    35–6, 45–6, 48, 50, 53, 60, 89, 91, 114,
    186; development of 22, 54
instruments, musical 30, 56n16, 114;
    relation of musicians with 100
instrumentalisation: of actor's
    psycholphysical resources 85, 91; of
    actor's resources 83; combined with
    technical mastery 80; creative and
    professional, philosophical affinities
    shared by 187; effected within performer
    training practice 93; expressive,
    engendered through performer training
    practice 24; layers of 115; Marcuse's
    view of 71, 76–7; positive attitude
    towards 93; professional, expected in
    creative industries 24; self-branding 114,
    187; of the self serves creative expression
    112; slippage between expressive and
    professional 185; technocratic 76;
    technological 74, 84; transcended by
    aesthetic sensibility 78
instrumentalisation, processes of 7, 21, 183;
    considered from pedagogical perspective
    91; development of resources aimed to
    expose 85; performer's 20
instrumentality 7, 23, 90, 92; soft version of
    112; transformed 72
interaction 140; classroom-based 16;
    embodied 91, 188; emergence of new
    forms of 112; face-to-face 17, 124, 168;
    fluid 152; human–technology 13, 15;
    mediated and unmediated 124; novel
    forms of 108; novel, opportunities to
    explore 187; ongoing, with novel
    situations 182; in pedagogical context
    104; reciprocal 72; remote, amongst
    educators and participants 26n4; social,

lack of 40; taking place across different time zones 26n4; with technologies 4, 125, 132; with world, attention constituted through 125
interaction between: actor and audience 40; artefact and user 101; bodyminds and machines 2; humans and technologies 106; performer training and technology 1, 182; stick and trainee 104; trainee and trainer 111, 138, 173, 176; user, artefact and world 89
intermedial performance 1, 9; creation of, skills specific to 15; development of skills for 17; recent interest in 32; requirements of 15
intermedial: *Actor Prepares* 15; performer 2; practices 9; work premised on symbiosis 15; work, proliferation of 19
intermediary space offered by 'training for' 159
Irving, Henry 25n2, 31–2, 34, 46–50, 54

James, W. 129–31
Joselit, D. 66, 81–2
June Paik: 'prepared' television sets 65, 81; work with television and video circuits 64

Karreman, L. 157, 166, 168–9
Kendal, M. 31, 47, 55n2
Klich, R. 1, 17–18
Kozel, S. 2, 4, 14–15, 136, 141, 149, 152, 169–70, 178

Laban Movement Analysis 155
Lecoq, J. 108–9, 110–11
Lemmens, P. 3, 115, 123, 126
liberate(d): actors, from profilmic realities 154; consciousness 77; by technology 166
liberation: *Essay on* 73, 86n3; training for 75
light 52, 97; beams of 110; changes in 137; darting 57n24; emitted and recorded 147; flickering 130; important resource in actor's craft 51; neon 66; serves as visual manifestation of actor's concentration 52; show 57n25, 111; sources 68; susceptibility to 140; technician 110; tool for actor 110; use of 68; use in Stanislavsky's work 54, 57n25, 109–10, 183; *see also* electric light
lighting, theatre 33; Argand lamps 55n1; cues 57n24; designer 9; developments in 32; effects, without 67–8; equipment 51;

gas 25n2, 55n1; innovations in 32, 49; involvement of Irving with 32, 50; spot 109; Stanislavsky's experimentation with 54; states 32, 51–2, 109; technology 25n2, 109
Living Theatre 63, 65–7, 75–6
Loukes, R. 5, 99–102, 135, 140

machines 3; actor's attempt to embody parts of 79; actors become 40; automation as defining characteristic of 43; automaton Players as 53; creative artists auxiliary and subordinate to 154; depicted in *Encyclopaedia* 42; encounters between humans and 187; enter public sphere 34; hallmarks differentiating humans from 53; human beings trustworthy as 185–6; human partnership with 14; increased sophistication of 93; interactions with bodyminds 2; oppositions between bodies and 184; positive references to 53; relationship reconfigured 178; scenic effect as result of well-designed 42; sensible attitude develops through relation to 186; social environment operates through/as 35; standardisation made possible by 185; theatre 41; used in production process 39; *see also* automata, automatons
Machines (exercise) 78–80
Machines de Théatre 41, 42
machines, capabilities of 44; increasing 182
machines, performance of: advancements in 23; development in/appreciation of 31; enhanced 33
Mann (Chapman), T. 111, 164–5, 168, 172, 174
Marceau, Marcel 164, *165*, 167, 172, 177
Marcuse, H. 4, 55, 61–2, 68–78, 83, 85, 86n1, 86n3, 86n4, 86n7, 93, 123
Marey, E.-J. 147, 161
Massive Open Online Courses (MOOCs) 16, 26n4
mastery 6–7, 15, 92, 111, 185; of both organic and inorganic material 23; desire to gain 49; geared towards 35; of materials and technique 72; move away from 152; technical 46, 54, 62–3, 76, 80, 83–4, 186–7
material tools: constitutive of somatic and intersubjective experience 121; constitutive of trainee's embodiment 111; differ from psychophysical tools 102; for performer training purposes 142; role in trainee actor's toolbox 91

media 4, 178; additional, incorporated by performer's expression 186; commodities, marketized 126; and communication studies 11; complex, military industrial 160; contemporary 123; designer 17; devices 122; digital 14, 115; experienced in negative ways 83; exposed actors as all-too-human 83; external 81; motion capture in comparison with other 173; multi 66; new 14–15; opposition to 67; products, homogeneity of 134; recorded 19, 67, 80; and Sports, Department for Digital, Culture 25n3; technologies, attention appropriated by 133; work in 8; workers, employment of 179n7; *see also* social media

Mauss, M. 94–5; techniques of the body 95

Media-America 82

mediate/mediating: action, nature and culture 85; activities 96–7; effect of alphabet 103; through electronic interface 17; experiences of the world 94; of feedback loop by messaging service 136; forms of performance 18; images 82; language, technologically 102; mobile 127; performance event, mobile phones used in 120; social 131–2; technology 106; world, means of 85

mediated interactions 124; between trainee and trainer's recording 173

mediated manner: of communication 82; of manifesting 158; of reading pedagogy, technologically 172

mediation awareness of level and kind of 184; effects of different kinds of 95; embodiment as form of 94; of the stick 101; technological 96, 98, 124

mediatisation/mediatised 8; images 79; roles 79

mediatrope, mobile-specific 122

mediatropic body 132, 138; embodiment 122, 139

Merlin, B. 57n25, 95, 107, 111, 124, 130

Method Acting 75, 77, 84, 103, 130

methodology 7, 20; of learning 18; of onto-epistemic mimesis 45

Meyerhold's Biomechanics 93, 104, 163; etudes 95, 164; exercises 103, 116n8; Motion Capture recording of *148*; projects 171; sticks used in 93, 111–12, 116n7, 116n8, 116n9; teacher 107, 111; training material 166

mobile phone 106, 121, 141, 147, 184; application for teaching choreography 17; and digital creativity 143n1; embodiment relationship 158; focal point of trainees' attention 183; functionalities of 140; function requires several modes of attention 142; harnessing for pedagogical ends 24; inclusion in exercises 138; literary practices involving 135; as means for creativity 136; negative impact of 123; shapes regimes of attention 124, 128; subscriptions 143n2; training activity incorporated function of 139; world modified/caught up by 127

mobile phone use: daily, gestures/risks associated with 126; in development of novel pedagogical practices 128; as pedagogical compendium 127; in performer training 24, 120–1, 123, 125, 128, 135

mobile phone users: constitutive of 122; trainee competencies as 139

mocap (motion capture) 24, 147, 149, 177, 178n1; application in mass entertainment 176; blind to issues of representation 166; camera system 161, 174; consists of two main components for performer's work 154; dialectic levels 154; differs from mobile phone and television 184; documentation, means of 164; early experiments with 161; effected changes in film production 154; experience with 155; footage, working with 165; gestalt switch in 152; introductory workshops 155; multiple effects of 178; omniscient frame 148; pedagogically sound medium 166; performance 150, 155, 159, 162; popularisation 153; presents motion without image 168; production, creatives involved in 172; projects with 152; renders performer invisible 163; skills 163; summit 162, 172; working in 151–2, 155

mocap artist(s) 158; accomplished 157; collective of 159; creative and embodied capital of 163; experienced 156

mocap data 156; less fixed 173; visualisations watched by trainee 167

mocap environment(s) 170; easing performer into 179n5; embodiment relation in 158; performer in 161; professional 160

mocap industry 150, 153; actor's employment in 186; distinction between acting and technology 155; opening new employment opportunities 163; performer's position in 178; professional

conditions encountered in 159;
professionalisation tailored to needs of 21
mocap industry technology 25, 149, 160–1,
174, 186; affordable 179n3; use in live
performance 177
mocap industry, training for 171, 176;
introduces participants to 157; preparing
performer for working in 149; preparing
performers to work with 21; tailored to
needs of 149
mocap material: key to student learning
164; significance of 172; trainee
engagement with 164
mocap of movement: allows students to
study own 167; brings attention to
essence of 165; compartmentalisation
162; without image 154, 157; objective
analysis 164; recording 174
mocap training 150, 156; aims to cultivate
seamless embodied trainee-technology
relation 158; content of 158;
development of 17; gave rise to new
forms 147; involves proprioceptive and
kinaesthetic education common in tool-
use 157; key providers 153; posthuman
subjectivity 163; prioritises certain
kinetic registers 160; propositional
typology of 149; training for 149, 153;
training with 149, 163, 170
mocap recording(s) 148; of biomechanics
148; employment for knowledge
production and transmission 171;
enhance trainee interpretative abilities
168; of movement 174; of movement
without image 154, 157; produces
distance for trainee 169; reel, production
of 162; use in teaching context 173
mocap systems 161, 169; consists of several
parts 158; intentionality of 157;
precursor of 161–2; use in performer
training 186
Mocap Troupe opportunity to audition for
159
mocap use: enables distribution of training
178; in film and video games industry
150; in live performance 179n10; in
Skinner Releasing Technique 166; in
training contexts 150–1
Mocap Vaults 153, 155, 156; curriculum
158, 162; introductory workshop 160;
production of show reel 162
mocap visualisations: enable learning beyond
the studio 171; experiences of working
with 169–70; watched by trainee 167
movement language: codified 167; created

through Laban Movement Analysis
155–6; Greco's 17
movement training for actors 14, 104, 153,
161; contingent, by default 139;
historio-graphical overview of 161;
knowledge produced through 140;
UK-based company specialising in 153
multilocal: embodiment 158; self 154
Murray, S. 2–3, 5–7, 112
musical composition 133; instruments 30,
56n16, 100, 114; way of speaking verse
32; world 114
musicians 40; actor-musician 8; experience
world as series of possibilities for sonic
exploration 114–15; relationship with
their instrument 100
Muybridge, E. 147

non-mediated: activities 96; contact with
floor 95; experiences of the world 94

onto-epistemic mimesis 52; automata
engendered 43; methodology of 45;
preparation of performers to work in
179n10
Open Theatre 20–1, 24, 61–4, 66–8, 71,
77–85, 86n8, 112, 115, 153, 182,
184–5
organic tools: contemporary references to
93; intra- and extra-organic 94, 96–7,
105, 111; development of 24, 121; made
out of trainee's bodymind 90; skills turn
into intra-organic 105; trainee learns to
embody intra- 105

Palmer, S. 23, 25n2, 50, 55n1, 56n11
paradox 81, 114, 185; actor's 36, 42, 53;
attention-as-problem 129; nineteenth
century 132; in performer training
context 155
Paradox of Acting 23, 31–4, 36–40, 42,
44–8, 54, 55n3, 55n6, 56n7, 56n8,
57n19, 57n20, 60; The First Interlocutor
36–8, 40, 46, 55n5; The Second
Interlocutor 36, 46
Pasolli, R. 79, 81–3
Perfect People exercise 78–81
Performance Group 63, 66–8, 75
performer trainers 35, 113, 140, 188;
awareness of change in artistic practice
16; bestow attention and value on
materiality of objects 112; refer to tools
and toolkits 90; regard everything as
tool/technology 97; use of sticks as
teachers or partners 93

performer training practice(s) 2, 25, 93, 101; alterity relationships 106; appropriation for development of environmental awareness 10; comparative analysis of 177; configuration of attention in 128, 138; development of 20; different approaches to 150; existing assumptions 121; guided by interrelated considerations 164; instrumentalisation engendered through 24; instrumentality, soft version of 112; instruments employed in 7; involving technology 20; for new generation of students 16; of Open Theatre 182; remediating 17; renewed interest in 63–4; resources, material and organic 185; sensitivity towards effects of mediation 95; tensions in 127; using motion capture 151, 177

performer training practice(s), aspects of 170; defining 7; key 150

performer training practice, technology in 1, 20, 149, 183; influence of 21–2

performer training practice tools 91, 121; mobile phones as 120, 125, 135; relation between users and 98; use of and making of 90, 96–7

performer-/actor-as-instrument trope 7, 23–4, 54

performing arts: antagonistic position in relation to technology 19; education, supporting technologies within 175; hybridisation of genres 9; industry, technologisation of 15, 187; learning environments, use of digital resources in 16; never entirely free of technology 19; post-human pedagogy specific to 18

performing arts training: de-coupled from 10; marked by wave of entrepreneurialism 113; and practice 18

Perry, S. 155–6, *159*, 179n6

pharmakon 24, 126–7, 179n2

Pitches, J. 1–2, 16–17, 35, 53, 93, 103–5, 116n7

polyattentiveness 135, 141–2

post-digital 183; world 13

post-human/posthuman 14; entanglements of flesh and machine 19; pedagogy 18; potential for rethinking how learning takes place 18; representations in synthespians 163; subjectivity 14, 163

postphenomenology 22, 24, 85, 89–92, 94, 96, 111, 114–15, 116n2, 123

pre-technological 183; human cultures 13; performer training practices 182

presence 25; achieved by mechanisation of technique 53; electric 19; of human avatar 166; notions prioritised 85; opposition to technology 184; in pedagogy, of reference points for actor's process 104; of phone in studio 127

Presence of the Actor 80–1

presence of technological artefacts 21, 34; within psychophysical practices 19

presence of technology 150; ability to recognise 89; ability to remain cognisant of 184; in academic institutions 149; at beginning of training 155; in contemporary societies, intensifying 3; digital 21; in performer training 2; use of technological instruments 177; telepresence 17

presence-absence *171*; dialectical relationship of training and technology 177; interplay or tension of 171, 177; of technology and trainer 171–2

presence, actor's/performer's 15, 18, 61, 67–8, 77, 80, 186; avant-garde emphasis on 62; emphasis placed by theatre practitioners 66; theatre language focuses on 21

psychophysical: activity, unmediated 155; disposition 92; orientation 86n5; paradigm 18, 130, 135, 139, 142; postpsychophysical 18; practices 18–19, 92; presence, development of 80; resources 24, 85, 91, 97–8; tools 102; training 99, 130, 135, 143

psychophysicality 1, 19; dominant discourse of 18

recessive (visceral) body 100

recognition(s): accorded to events in the environment 135; a-subjective 161; of bodies, social and political 150; Open Theatre group's first 83; as technical process of identification 161; of theatre as civic institution 36; trainee undergoes series of 95

Reilly, K. 2, 43–4, 56n15

remedial: potential of digital technology 126; technology as way of capturing 126

(re)mediated hermeneutic relation 141

Renaud, L.T. 2, 8

Riskin, J. 43–4

Roach, J. 34–8, 52–3, 55, 55n3, 55n4, 55n6, 56n8

Rosenberger, R. 101, 123–4, 136–7

Salazar Sutil, N. 147, 161, 178
Schechner, R. 63–4, 66, 75–6
Scott, J. and Barton, B. 1–2, 9, 15, 17
selfhood construction and control of,
    movement as technique for 161;
    critical redefinition of 4;
    polyattentiveness acknowledges other
    claims to 135; profound changes in 6;
    refashion 188
sensibility 4, 37; acting derives from 36;
    aesthetic 72–5, 78; attained 74; attuned
    74; avant-garde 65; benefits of acting
    without 40; dimension for creating 74;
    disposition which accompanies organic
    weakness 55n5; emotional 50;
    importance for actor's artistic process and
    performance 46; importance of
    technique over 37; new 4, 74–5, 186;
    not antithesis of reason 46; recast as
    technical accomplishment 47; refutation
    of 37, 40, 45; value system based on 170;
    worldly 4, 25n1
sensitivity 92, 95, 142, 176
Serkis, A. 154, 157–8
settings, formal 136; industry 160;
    institutional 143, 153, 164; of lighting
    cues 57n24; performer training 153;
    professional, position of trainee/
    performer in 112; professional,
    technologisation of 15; social,
    cultural and political 98; socio-cultural
    150; static, constraints of 154; Western
    20
Shapes in Motion 153, 155; introductory
    workshop 158, *159*, 162; workshop
    participants 159
Skinner Releasing Technique (SRT) 166,
    170, 172, 174
social media 116n12; accounts 122;
    platform 17
Spatz, B. 2–3, 10, 95
Stahl, M. 162–3, 178
standing reserve 70, 114, 170
Stanislavsky System 35, 86n5, 86n6, 95,
    107, 130, 186; derivatives of 75
Stanislavsky Toolkit, Complete 57n25, 95
Stanislavsky, K. 23, 30–6, 49–55, 57n19,
    57n22, 57n23, 57n24, 57n25, 107,
    109–11, 129–31, 156, 183, 185
Stiegler, B. 3, 24, 125–8, 131–4, 143n7,
    179n2
synthespians 149; displace/alienate creative
    and technical cultural workers 162;
    representation of posthuman 163;
    training turns performers into 162

T'ai Chi Ch'uan 75
techne 11, 23, 60–2, 72–4, 83, 112, 151,
    187
technological 18, 70, 152; actions/activity
    30, 57n23; apparatus 150, 162, 178;
    approach to nature 70; assemblage 158;
    assemblage, complex 150; capacity to
    produce 74; change 129; change of
    eighteenth century 12; devices 9, 13, 15,
    18, 21, 30, 53, 66, 81, 141; dominance
    24; domination 61, 72; efficiency 186;
    Enframing 85; environment 3, 18;
    equipment 7, 49, 157, 160; excitement
    19; feat of theatrical lights 34;
    fetishisation 93; glitch 186; influences
    extending beyond stage design and props
    33; ingenuity, pedagogical application of
    52; innovation 43; instrumentalisation
    74, 84; instruments 7, 70, 177;
    intentionality 106; intervention 91;
    languages of schooling 175; making 72;
    mediation 96, 98, 124; optionalisation 5;
    pedagogical processes 91; performer
    training 6, 53; possibilities of the
    medium 82; powers of film 19; practices
    connected to the body 32; process of
    training 24, 33; rationality 20–1, 24, 61,
    65, 69, 71–2, 74, 77, 80, 93, 115, 183;
    reality 71; resources, synthesis between
    organic and 36; sentiment in self-use 92;
    side of scientific practice 11;
    sophistication 44; sphere 188; system
    154, 158, 186; use of eyeglasses 94; way
    of being in the world 61
technological advancement/improvement
    19, 43, 53, 111; enhancement 174;
    implementation of 25n2
technological artefacts 12, 20, 70, 102, 177;
    appropriation for pedagogical purposes
    24; designed to function in the
    background 121; development during
    eighteenth century 54; human
    intentionality mediated by 106; means of
    socialising knowledge/activating
    memory 126; naturalised and absorbed
    within lifeworld 184; offer access to/
    reading of world aspects 106; penetration
    of 13; performer training not featuring
    21; possible source of knowledge 110;
    professional identity dispersed across 163;
    provide standard of performance 110;
    relationship of user to 98; sequence
    with scientific theory 70; significance
    linked to intentional pedagogical
    outcomes 123

technological artefacts, harnessed for/use of 112; artistic-pedagogical ends 128; counter-cultural ends 82; existing 1; as way of knowing the human organism 44

technological artefacts, presence or absence of 21, 34; in psychophysical practices 19

technological development 12, 36, 43, 66; impact of 55n6

technological entities 183; employed as tools for learning 110; mimicking behaviour of 52

technological infrastructure 186; of performance 2; provided by institutions 16; for training in re-perceiving 153

technologies, acculturation of specific 13

Technology and the Lifeworld 188

television 20, 68, 106, 184; capturing the small screen 83; Chaikin's stance towards 86n7; culture shared by baby boomers 81; defined American culture in 1950s and 1960s 62, 66; demonised 'other' by avant-garde theatre 82; experienced in negative ways by Open Theatre 83; exposed actors as all-too-human 83; footage of assassination scenes 67, 82; function in Open Theatre work 80; fundamental difference from stage 67; guerrilla groups 65; ideology of technological rationality 24; opposition to 80; prepared, of Nam June Paik 64–5, 81; primary source of innovations for Open Theatre 21; sanitised images circulated in 79; series 8; social function of 81; technological power of 19; theatre unable to compete with seductions of 67; way of achieving social adherence 81

Thompson, J. 152, 164–5, 167–8, 170, 172–3, 177

Thomson, I. 3, 151–2

tools 4, 25, 92, 96, 109, 182; additional, performer expression incorporating 186; analytical 23, 25, 182; animate and inanimate 187; annotation 172; in common 95; contemporary references to 93; created for project 179n8; designed for expression 100; digital 167; embodiment of 99, 101, 158; engagement with 187; of expression 24; fostering experimentation with technologies 188; handheld 90, 115; inclusive attitude towards 95; instruction 165; involvement in human activity 94; not limited to material objects 95–6; as partners or teachers 106; in performer training practice 91; psychophysical 102;

resources referred to as 96; tangible 95; for teaching, online platforms as 17; technology 15, 22; trade 38; ways they extend the body 99; *see also* material tools, organic tools

tools, relationship with 22, 115, 186; embodied/embodiment relation with 101, 158; trainee's 22, 24, 105; user's 98

tools, use/used for 32, 39, 97–8, 113, 187; aimed at developing generic skills 106; pedagogical purposes 183; in training 7, 16, 89–90, 111

Tortsov 31, 53, 109–10, 130

tradition 25; of acting 154; of acting and performance, break denied 155; of Acting, Science and the Stanislavsky 35; Anglophone 31; classical 89–90; and innovation 150, 171–2, *173*, 177; of pragmatism 92

traditional: boundary lines, cut across 96; dance training 9; Marxist thought 70; and non-productive definition of education 134; view of source of knowledge residing with teacher 172

trainers 104, 137–8, 143, 177; actor 153; allow space for actors' sensitisation to objects 107; become attuned to trainees 105; digital devices owned by 147; explore development of mechanised technique 54–5; hermeneutic act of looking-sensing 141; influenced in relating to world by mobile phones 121, 126; invested in the process 105; involvement 135; job, key component of 172; in Lecoq method 108; look at clues specific to skills and competencies 105; mocap owned by neither trainees nor 147; movement 140; notion of expressivity 30; overview of exercise, suspension of 141; pick up clues from trainee's embodiment 140; presence-absence of 150, 171–2; read bodies of trainees 168; role 16; watching visualisations of mocap 167; work of 156

trainers–trainees interactions: between 111, 138; with 176; face-to-face encounters 171, 173; unable to see each other 141

training for 25, 150, 159–60, 178; ability to express new forms, importance of 75; actors 9; attitude towards training 177; degree of institutional independence 176; familiarising trainee with requirements of technology 172; institutes split between performer and technology 155; introduces physical skills required by technological apparatus 162, 174; introductory workshops 171; liberation 75; mastery of technical skill 76; motion capture 17, 149, 153–4, 156, 158, 163, 166, 171, 174; new form of training 172; self-funded 164, 173; syllabus draws on visual codes of popular culture 173; use of phone in 120; *see also* movement training for actors

training for and training with, dialectic between 25, 150, 153, 170–4, 177–8

training studios 16, 75, 95, 127, 137, 176, 182, 184

training with 25, 150, 153, *171*, 173–4, *176*, 177; motion capture 149, 163, 170; technology 171–2

training with, instances of 164, 166; develop within projects 174; technology complements teaching 172; within/ beyond training studio 176

Tunstall, D. 149–50, 166–9

tweaking 105, 112

Übermarionette 31, 34, 48–9, 57n21

UCLAN *148*

unmediated activities 97; interactions 124; manner of manifesting 158; psychophysical activity 155; *see also* non-mediated

Vartanian, A. 42

Vaucanson, J. 43–4, 56n17

video 26n3; art 66; circuits 64; editing techniques 67; extract from students' work 108; footage of assassination 82; of Lecoq working with cellophane 108–9; material 93; recordings of Marceau 165; YouTube 155

video games 19, 26n3, 133, 149–50, 155; aesthetic of 160; production 156; subject matter 158

visual codes 154, 160, 162, 166, 173

Wake, C. 1, 16, 18, 175

Watson, I. 6, 10

We-Tool-World formulation 100

Whatley, S. 4, 149, 166, 170, 174

WhoLoDancE 166–7, 169, 171, 174–5, 179n8

Wilson, T. 104, 106–7, 116n8

Wrathall, M. 3–5, 112

yoga 34, 57n23, 75

Zanotti, M. 17, 120, 127–8

Zarrilli, P. 2, 5, 8, 93, 99–102, 116n5, 125, 130–1, 143n6

Zazzali, P. 86n5, 113, 130–2